POETRY IN THE BRITISH ISLES

Poetry in the British Isles

NON-METROPOLITAN PERSPECTIVES

Edited by

Hans-Werner Ludwig *and* Lothar Fietz

CARDIFF
UNIVERSITY OF WALES PRESS
1995

© The contributors, 1995

British Library Cataloguing in Publication Data

A catalogue record for this book is available from the British Library.

ISBN 0-7083-1266-7

Typeset by Action Typesetting Limited, Gloucester
Printed in Great Britain by Dinefwr Press, Llandybïe, Dyfed

The main focus of this volume is the poetry written in the indigenous territorial languages of the British Isles during the second half of the twentieth century. But the book is a discussion rather than a survey. It is concerned with poetry's relation to place, and its role in the self-definition of communities as the monolithic ideologies of the nation-states fragment into a mosaic of peoples, languages, cultures and between-cultures.

After a polemical introduction which leaves us in no doubt that questions of place and region, centre and periphery, are urgent and political as well as literary, the book divides into three sections.

The first establishes a historical perspective, from the English nationalism of the Elizabethan period, through the ambiguities and contradictions of Romanticism and the metropolitan concept of culture advocated by Matthew Arnold, to the debates of our own century; Pound on provincialism – Tomlinson versus Larkin, Seamus Heaney and the Field Day pamphlets.

The central section of the book not only displays the rich variety of contemporary poetry being written in Ireland, Scotland, Wales and non-metropolitan England, but gives a sense of the issues and internal tensions within those communities which poetry addresses. A final section consists of case studies in which particular authors and texts that relate to the overall theme are considered in greater detail.

Contents

Acknowledgements

The editors and publishers wish to thank all the poets who have allowed their work to be reproduced in this book. For permission to reproduce complete poems the publishers wish to thank the following: Gwasg Gomer for permission to use Waldo Williams's 'Mewn Dau Gae' (from *Dail Pren*, 1956); Tony Conran for his translation of 'Mewn Dau Gae' – 'In Two Fields'; and George Mackay Brown for his 'Water'.

The Contributors

DAVID ANNWN is Head of English Degrees at Wakefield District College, Yorkshire. He is author of *Inhabited Voices: The Poetry of Seamus Heaney, Geoffrey Hill and G. M. Brown* (1984) and many essays on contemporary poetry. His recent publications include *The Spirit/That Kiss*, a selection of his own poems 1973–93, and *A Breton Herbal*, translations of Eugene Guillevic.

GARETH ALBAN DAVIES is Emeritus Professor of Spanish in the University of Leeds, Yorkshire. He has also published extensively in the Welsh language, and in English on Welsh letters and affairs. His Welsh contributions include three volumes of verse, a volume of translations from Spanish poetry, and essays on Gide and Lorca for a collection entitled *Y Llenor yn Ewrop* (1976). He has also published an American and an Australian diary, as well as a book entitled *Tan Tro Nesaf* (1976), an account of life in the Welsh colony in Patagonia. He is currently editor of a Welsh-language series published by Yr Academi Gymreig (and University of Wales Press) of translations from other languages – German, Latin and Greek, French, Chinese, Scottish Gaelic, etc.

LOTHAR FIETZ is Professor of English Literature at the University of Tübingen. His publications are mainly concerned with structural and functional aspects of the English and American novel and drama (Swift, Dickens, Wilde, Lawrence, Huxley, Durrell, Hemingway; Shakespeare, Fulke Greville, Tourneur, Sheridan, Pinter, Shaffer). His interest in literary theory documents itself in two books, *Funktionaler Strukturalismus* (1976) and *Strukturalismus* (1982; 2nd edn. 1992). His last book, entitled

Fragmentarisches Existieren: Wandlungen des Mythos von der verlorenen Ganzheit, came out in the spring of 1994.

ROBERT GARRATT is Professor and Chairman of the English Department at the University of Puget Sound, Tacoma, Washington. He is the author of *Modern Irish Poetry: Tradition and Continuity from Yeats to Heaney* (1989) and co-editor of *The Poem: an Anthology* (1990). He has written a number of articles on Irish literature and contemporary poetry. Currently, he is at work on a history of Irish poetry. He was visiting Professor of English at the University of Tübingen in 1988–9 and again in 1995.

RAYMOND HARGREAVES has been teaching German language and literature at Leeds University since 1958. His publications include: 'Brecht's Courage' in *Stand* (1965); 'Die Novelle in den *Wahlverwandtschaften*' in *MLR* (1967); 'Nietzsche and Pascal' in *JES* (1978); 'Mörike's Cousin, and An Affinity with Thomas Mann' in *For Lionel Thomas. A Collection of Essays* (1980); 'Images of War in German Poetry, 1937–1941' in *JES* (1986); 'Nietzsche and Sterne' in *Anglo-German Studies*, The Leeds Philosophical and Literary Society (1991). He is co-translator, with Roger White, of Wittgenstein's *Philosophische Bemerkungen* (1975).

CHRISTOPHER HARVIE is Professor of British and Irish Studies at the University of Tübingen. Born in Scotland in 1944, and educated at the High School and University of Edinburgh, he taught for eleven years at the Open University. He is the author of, among other books, *The Lights of Liberalism* (1976), *No Gods and Precious Few Heroes, Scotland since 1914* (1981, 3rd edn. 1993) and most recently *The Rise of Regional Europe* and a history of North Sea Oil: *Fool's Gold* (1995).

JEREMY HOOKER is a poet and critic. His books of poems include his selected poems, *A View from the Source* (1982), and *Their Silence a Language* (1993), a collaboration with the sculptor Lee Grandjean. He has published two books of essays on modern literature, *Poetry of Place* (1982) and *The Presence of the Past* (1987), and monographs on David Jones and John Cowper

Powys. He directs the MA in Creative Writing course at Bath College of Higher Education.

URSULA KIMPEL has taught English Literature at the Department of English, University of Tübingen. She has published on Scottish poetry and has made a name for herself as a translator of English, Scottish and Irish poetry. She is working on a dissertation on Goethe's concept of 'Weltliteratur' and the ensuing debate in nineteenth-century Britain.

RAINER LENGELER is Professor of English at the Rheinische Friedrich-Wilhelms-Universität, Bonn. He has published widely on modern British and Irish authors, and is the editor of *Die englische Literatur der Gegenwart: 1971–1975* (1977). Recent publications include *Shakespeares Sonette in deutscher Übersetzung: Stefan George und Paul Celan* (1989) and *Literaturgeschichte in Nöten. Überlegungen zu einer Geschichte der englischen Literatur des 20. Jahrhunderts* (forthcoming).

HANS-WERNER LUDWIG is Professor of English at the University of Tübingen. He has published widely on the history of English poetry (English and Scottish popular ballads, the sonnet), and on Victorian and twentieth-century Engish poetry (Hopkins, Pound, Eliot, Auden, Larkin, Hill, Heaney) as well as in the field of media studies. His books include *Barbarous in Beauty: Studien zum Vers in Gerard Manley Hopkins' Sonetten* (1972), *Arbeitsbuch Lyrikanalyse* (1979) and *Made in Britain: Studien zur Literaturproduktion im britischen Fernsehen* (with E. Schenkel and B. Zimmermann) (1992). He is currently working on a study of William Blake.

SABINA SHARKEY is a Lecturer and Course Director for British Cultural Studies at the Centre for British and Comparative Cultural Studies, University of Warwick. She has published on gender and colonialism and on Irish Studies and is currently writing a book on gender and colonial representation in Ireland.

K. E. SMITH is Senior Lecturer in Literature at the University of Bradford. He has published work on the later eighteenth century, on dialect writing and on modern poetry. At present he is working on a study of the early Blake.

M. WYNN THOMAS is Professor of English, University of Wales, Swansea and was recently Visiting Professor at Harvard University. His books include editions of works by Emyr Humphreys and Morgan Llwyd as well as critical studies of both writers. He is also the author of *The Lunar Light of Whitman's Poetry* and *Internal Difference: literature in twentieth-century Wales*. He recently edited *The Page's Drift*, a collection of essays to mark R. S. Thomas's eightieth birthday.

NED THOMAS is the author of books on George Orwell, Derek Walcott and Waldo Williams. His *The Welsh Extremist – a Culture in Crisis* (1971) interpreted modern Welsh literature and society to an English-reading audience. A former lecturer in English literature at the Universities of Salamanca, Moscow and Aberystwyth, and founder-editor of the magazine *Planet*, he is at present Director of University of Wales Press and of the Mercator Project on European Minority Languages.

DERICK THOMSON was Professor of Celtic at the University of Glasgow from 1963 to 1991. He has published widely on Scottish Gaelic topics, for example *An Introduction to Gaelic Poetry* (1974, 1990), *The Companion to Gaelic Scotland* (1983, 1993) and *European Poetry in Gaelic Translation* (1990). He edits the quarterly *Gairm*, and has published much poetry, including his collected poems, *Creachadh na Clàrsaich/ Plundering the Harp* (1982).

ROBIN YOUNG teaches British and European literatures at the University of Wales, Aberystwyth. He is the author of a study of Ibsen, *Time's Disinherited Children* (1989), and is at present working on a bilingual edition of an Ibsen play. He reviews regularly for Anglo-Welsh periodicals and is also a translator of modern Scandinavian poetry.

'My country will not yield you any sanctuary': A polemic by way of preface

CHRISTOPHER HARVIE

1

A. I meet you in an evil time.
B.   The evil bells
    Put out of our heads, I think, the thought of everything else.
A. The jaded calendar revolves,
    Its nuts need oil, carbon chokes the valves,
    The excess sugar of a diabetic culture
    Rotting the nerve of life and literature;
    Therefore when we bring out the old tinsel and frills
    To announce that Christ is born among the barbarous hills
    I turn to you whom a morose routine
    Saves from the mad vertigo of being what has been.
B. Analogue of me, you are wrong to turn to me,
    My country will not yield you any sanctuary,
    There is no pinpoint in any of the ordnance maps
    To save you when your towns and town-bred thoughts
        collapse,
    It is better to die in situ as I shall,
    One place is as bad as another. Go back where your
        instincts call
    And listen to the crying of the town-cats and the taxis again,
    Or wind your gramophone and eavesdrop on great men ...

I start with the best of the thirties poets, not just because MacNeice's irony, skill, idealism and decent observation in indecent times are needed. The 'Britain' in which the Ulster classicist lived – though a BBC man he was never a narrow metropolitan – is again in crisis. Will it survive this time? 'The music of things happening' is occurring on the margins, those places where MacNeice himself said that we might 'see the end of our own actions'. The sounds are not always pleasant: the falsity as well as the imaginative thrill of MacPherson's *Ossian* is there, but the society of the poem is political *and* fricative in Scotland, Wales and Ireland, and parts of non-metropolitan England, while London literary culture seems to have atrophied. Not simply into cliquery – what's new about that? – but into a domination of imaginative literature by Carlyle's auld enemies, mechanism and the cash nexus.

For a political writer and historian, the chance that my colleagues have given me is a dangerous temptation to be vatic. A powerful poetic is erupting along the length of what we call – for want of a better term (a significant point in itself) the 'Celtic Fringe': moreover, certain of its recurrent themes echo the fundamental critiques made of the industrial age at its outset. As the central state and its scientific materialist foe both falter, *Ossian's* contemporaries speak again. Adam Ferguson's concept of the corruption of the *polis* through wealth, Adam Smith's rhetoric and morality of 'sympathy' come back into play.

But hold on. MacNeice's line in the same poem, 'An Eclogue for Christmas':

> Let us lie once more, say 'What we think, we can'
> The old idealist lie.

is salutary. These days one has to be alert, because imaginative literature – poetry in particular – has also been inveigled into political *management*. The euphoric, democratic optimism which swept across Europe with the collapse of the Warsaw Pact pitted intellectuals – poets, musicians, historians – against a Stalinist bureaucracy, stumbling from the non-place of utopia to the non-place of dystopia. 'Havel to the Castle!' Havel is now locked in the Hradcany; banker Klaus has the key, and Charter 77's ideal of a civic, democratic Czechoslovakia has vanished. The rough beasts of plutocracy and populism have not taken long to tame the poets; red banners still possess the streets, but they advertise Coca-Cola and Marlboro.

Was the intellectual interregnum fortuitous? Had a general 'privatization' of social life, west and east, caused canny professionals – bureaucrats, technologists and party organizers, representatives of an internationalized post-print-capitalism – to keep their heads down until the idealism had spent itself? Were we seeing the writer as stooge? The writer as entrepreneur/

proletarian in the soft technology of the information industries? With this in mind, there could be a dismayingly economic explanation of provincial energy. 'Outside London' is cheap, in these non-literate days. Faber, once MacNeice's publisher and under Eliot the centre of poetry in English, still sustains London's literary establishment, surviving on the royalty cheques it gets from Sir Andrew Lloyd Webber and *Cats*. The cost of metropolitan living has driven the great tradition defensive. Anthony Thwaite and Andrew Motion's obsequies on Philip Larkin, once cited as the welfare state's Matthew Arnold, showed – at great length – a character as politically embarrassing as Yeats and Pound, but without any of their daemonic energy. In the resulting – and commercially calculated – *brouhaha*, Larkin's poetry was scarcely discussed. A drift of biographies, piling up in former corridors of power, reflected a metropolitan élite drowsily but profitably talking to itself, its hefty volumes resting, perhaps even read, on the coffee-tables of the south-east. The ultimate in this necrophilia, the Trollope cult, led John Major to give President Clinton a first edition of *The Way We Live Now* (1878). Did this unwittingly endorse the other Trollope – the Irish politician and polemicist brilliantly reconstructed by Owen Dudley Edwards – anathematizing a state far gone in criminality and incompetence?

2

'The centre cannot hold' and so on? Quoting great literature out of context is part of the old, dangerous – and genuinely 'British' – habit of transposing difficult scientific discourse into vivid metaphor. So MacDiarmid's 'It is our turn now. The call is to the Celt' is already suspect, and dealings with poetry by a political writer carry added risks.

Get things in proportion. In the bleary days of Christmas 1992 it was possible to go into a store in Aberystwyth and find *not a single book*, not even a Jeffrey Archer or a Jackie Collins. Prytherch's grandchildren moved in malls of CDs, videos and video games. The monarchy was toppling, the government execrated; a tanker loaded with oil smashed into the Shetlands. The fug of television- and alcohol-induced satiety was momentarily cracked by visions of old women starving into skeletons and younger women haggard after rape, a modern town freezing and leaching flame; Serbian irregulars shooting a Bosnian minister; those irregulars under the command of a psychologist who writes stories for children. Switch to another channel, or to the video, and the catatonia of the festive season continued on course. Did poetry – regional or otherwise – matter in the least?

MacNeice's balefulness was reassuring, even if all too relevant. It had all happened before:

> . . . when we bring out the old tinsel and frills
> To announce that Christ is born among the barbarous hills

But 'My country will not yield you any sanctuary' – that sounded even more desperate in 1992. In our evil times is the poetry of place – poetry about place or the poetry of definable political regions, or the poetry of the minority languages of 'these islands' – only the mutterings of a remnant of Matthew Arnold's remnant? Or, worse still, has the academic status of many, perhaps most, of its makers evolved a small but perfectly formed, portable subject, processed for the student consumer; like the campus novels of Malcolm Bradbury and David Lodge, which resemble nothing so much as the teaching units of the Open University, ingeniously packaging theory, primary and secondary sources, and summer school sex?

But on the periphery the politics of poetry is not just important, but *defining*. MacNeice was aware, when he went to the Hebrides with Hector MacIver in 1935, that, besides the commercial vanities, the ganglions of fascism and approaching war reached out to the lochs and turf-stacks. No doubt that he would have foreseen the caverns under the Argyllshire hills, with enough nuclear bombs to wipe out life on earth, the caesium-polluted heather, the civil war dragging on for a quarter of a century in his own Ulster. This sort of menace concentrates the mind, makes it seek an adequate language. On 12 December 1992, 25,000 – not all of them Scots – marched through Edinburgh at the time of the European Summit, demanding self-government. They were addressed by various Scottish opposition MPs, who scarcely promoted the idea of a parliament by going for one another, and by the novelist William McIlvanney and the poet and folklorist Hamish Henderson. The 25,000 sang Henderson's 'Freedom Come All Ye'. Not only did the arts unite where conventional politics threatened to tear apart, they showed again the resilience they had given Scotland in the dog days after the referendum of 1 March 1979:

> Now come all ye at hame wi freedom
> Never heed what the corbies craw o' doom
> In ma hoose a' the bairns o' Adam
> Will find breid, barley-bree an' pentit room.

If I suggest Scotland as an exemplar (I can think of analogous developments in Wales and Ireland) it is because of the complexity as well as the immediacy of Henderson's song – one of four possible Scottish national anthems, each dragging political meaning in its wake. The 'Freedom Come All Ye' is egalitarian, historical, international, civic; its republican radicalism may be exiled from metropolitan discourse, yet the sheer difficulty of its task forces self-definition. And thus survival, because politics need the right words. There is no acceptable name for the archipelago on which Scotland, Wales, Ireland and England find themselves, and the use of 'Britain' – even by the Conservative government – seems radically to have diminished. Ironically, this indicates the continuing power of a discourse which is literate and civic. The separate nationalities, the minority languages, even the regional element in England, have persisted, against a government whose dogmatic centralization never quite got the measure of the arts, and which now – with the devolution of the Scottish and Welsh Arts Councils and higher education – seems to have given up the fight.

3

But MacNeice's question still stands. Is the regional culture scene a refuge? A second home for a superficially cosmopolitan metropolis, which deals in the currency of international English as part of the cash nexus, not out of intellectual and moral compulsion? This may have been the case in T. S. Eliot's day, but surely no longer. In Britain the regional is conscious, controversial and unpredictable, aware that its lyricism may get stuck on the emotional level, lacking the verifications needed for rational politics. That way lie unacceptable associates, manifest in the continuing torment of Northern Ireland: a 'tribalism' of the

structurally unemployed and depoliticized, in which women hold
the society together while their men drink and boast and fight,
and the only common language is, bizarrely but inevitably, the
self-pity of Country and Western.

But this survival of the lyric, at whatever debased level, can
also be a challenge, with different modulations as one moves
round the fringe. Wales is, in one way, the most fractured, with
culture following the fissures of Denis Balsom's 'Three Wales
Model'. Is 'British Wales' the Kingsley Amis country, of 'Main
Square, Aberdarcy':

> The journal of some bunch of architects
> Named this the worst town centre they could find.
> But how disparage what so well reflects
> Permanent qualities of heart and mind?

in which the metropolitan Grand Cham showed he was once
subtler and more understanding? Is it that debatable post-
industrial 'Welsh Wales' whose need for constant definition
creates a painfully literate politics of environment and history,
projected in baroque English: from Dylan Thomas and Gwyn
Thomas to Raymond Williams and Gwyn Alf Williams? Is it Y
Fro Gymraeg and the Revd R. S. Thomas, armed not in the old
way, denouncing Dafydd Elis Thomas for going soft on the
language, and the need to defend its last fortress? Or Elis
Thomas, with a Ph.D. in Welsh poetry, going to the House of
Lords, manoeuvring Wales as a European region – the relation-
ship out of which this book has emerged? The only helpful
answer – one which applies to Scotland and to Ireland – is the
pluralistic one. One cannot see the periphery, or even the indi-
vidual nationalities, whole: one can try to see a constant dialogue
of communities with their individual members and with one
another. Language and lyric must simultaneously give voice to
the community and make it communicate.

The poetry of the Welsh Eisteddfod with its formal rules codi-
fied in the Middle Ages is still a living tradition. Has it more
Hans Sachses than Beckmessers? We have to take this, and the
Scottish Mod on trust, when we cannot speak the languages, but
the capacity of major poets such as Waldo Williams and Sorley
Maclean to innovate within these traditions, and the technical
virtuosity of English-language poets on the edge of this culture –

Manley Hopkins, MacNeice himself – suggest the quality of its resources. The bilingualism of certain key interpreters – Iain Crichton Smith, Emyr Humphreys, Declan Kiberd – indicates, moreover, a balancing move from the communal and formal to the personal and experimental: a stance which can be risky and disturbing, but also enormously enriching.

4

> Between my finger and my thumb
> The squat pen rests.
> I'll dig with it.

Seamus Heaney's determination is typical of the 'sympathy' of the periphery, in being both conservative and radical. It reminds us that this particular archaeology is taking place within a land-scape, historically, socially, ethnically, linguistically determined. The practitioners do not just have to be poets, but teachers, critics, historians, linguists. Tom Leonard's explorations of urban, industrial west Scotland present parallels to Heaney on several levels – besides his poetry, his biography of James Thomson and his remarkable anthology *Radical Renfrew* (1990). This makes us remember how the regional poetics, and their various registers, from the 'local verse' which still lubricates cele-bration and mourning to the public competitions and the statesman stuff of the leading performers, occupy a complex, only partially documented history.

The Communist George Thompson, teaching in the west of Ireland in the 1930s, found the 'poet' still an established part of the local community, the work song or waulking song or 'Come all ye' inseparable from daily life. The recently published essays of Hamish Henderson, *Alias MacAlias* (1992), show how deeply rooted the political poetry of post-war Scotland has been in the contentious business – almost unfathomable in Germany for obvious reasons – of the recovery of the folk tradition. Most recently an animated debate about the origins of the Celticism of the eighteenth century has stimulated interest in the legacy of Adam Smith: the theorist of 'sympathy' in his *Theory of the Moral Sentiments* (1759). The restatement of Smith's influence as rhetorician and moralist on Ossian MacPherson and Burns, posits an intuitive community held in creative tension – partly by literature – with the mechanistic universe of free exchange. A timely point, when the nonsense currently being uttered in Smith's name looks like rivalling the mayhem caused by Marxist dogmatism.

5

The paradox of the regional lyric is its intellectual and emotional *centrality*. Its range of concerns cannot simply be rendered as the self-satisfactions of individualism or nationalism. It goes out from an essentially political community concerned about its definition, where its boundaries actually are, while the 'national' presupposes that people think in a particular way because they are who they are. The regional is concerned about the civic, and the civic about universals: what people believe and how they act, and where this intersects with communal identity and environment. It stems from the symbiotic relationship between 'Britain', its *polises*, and their linguistic and cultural traditions. It is also a part of that relationship.

Earlier, all this tended simply to be filed under 'Celtic nationalism'. This is slapdash. The poetry of Yeats and indeed of MacDiarmid shows a concentration on the civic theme of good government which is the reverse of the volkish or the vatic. Yeats's much-misinterpreted 'Easter 1916' is essentially about the difference between the public life and the 'daemonic images' of nationalism. The social – fricative, lively, open – confronts the state, the 'multiple man' of Hobbes, 'greatest among all of the beasts for pride'. The civic tradition's ideal of the corporate and collaborative nature of the *polis*, crushed by British state violence, becomes the symbolic but lifeless totem of Irish nationalism: 'the stone's in the midst of all'. Civic politics are difficult, disillusioning, taxing, leading to the curses of 'September 1913' and to MacDiarmid's 'To Circumjack Cencrastus'. Yet they are, in poetry as well as public life, essential. The older MacDiarmid and Yeats were, *qua nationalists*, much simpler and less interesting figures.

Patrick Geddes, sociologist, home-ruler, prophet of civics, believed his Dublin town plan, if executed, would have obviated Easter 1916. An Enlightenment fantasy? But he was the man who christened the Scottish Renaissance and encouraged MacDiarmid. The difference between centre and periphery is less about *ethnies* than about the *scale* of action. The English tradition of political sovereignty, from Bentham and the Fabians out of Hobbes, presupposes great power status and a central national myth, broadcast by the Oxbridge clerisy, and filtering its way down the delectable layers of class. The Anglican rector who recruits Matthew Price for Cambridge in Raymond Williams's *Border Country* (1961) sees himself as an alien in the Welsh world of eisteddfod and chapel. Price's – and Williams's – later resolution to 'measure the distance' implied a corresponding distancing from the generalized account of the human emotions given, say, by Larkin. English magisterialism is perhaps deceptive, given the intellectual complexity of English poets – Barnes or Tennyson, Hardy or Bunting – who have used, or lived close to, a vernacular. But it is a tone that lasts.

I have argued elsewhere that this Anglo-Saxon attitude has much to do with the distinctive role of the Lake District in the early days of print capitalism. Wordsworth, Coleridge, Thomas Arnold and later Matthew Arnold, English clerisy with fingers burned by European utopias, did not constitute the region as *polis* but *appropriated* it as emblem of national qualities. A frequent phenomenon in later nineteenth-century nationalism – Karelianism in Finland, 'the West' in Ireland – this 'composed' socio-cultural relationships, in Lukács's term, into a conservative *Gemeinschaft*. The English version and its anthromorphic projections – from Wordsworth to Beatrix Potter – went on to inform the reform of the public schools and the moulding of character, the foundation of the National Trust and the conserving of heritage. Its values spread out to colour, subtly and persuasively, the other containers of the English culture establishment, from the Bloomsbury Group to the Laura Ashley chintz.

The historic centrality of this combination of mythic commonwealth and hard-edged commerce, and the ease with which it was able to co-opt potentially subversive performers from the other national traditions – Scott and Carlyle preceding Matthew Arnold's deft annexation of Celtic literature in 1867 – is one way of accounting for the unselfconsciousness, until quite recently, of the peripheral cultures. Even in the 1920s, when the centre was buckled by the impact of the First World War, MacDiarmid and the other provincials were *politically* disadvantaged by the departure of Ireland and with it a political prospect of home rule. In time, they were marginalized by other metropolitan, synoptic figures – themselves provincial in origin – Eliot and Auden, who re-emphasized the emblematic idea. Auden did this in his combination of industrial romanticism with a Calvinism transposed into literary catechism, Eliot in an attempt to get back to the Anglican imperialism of the King James Bible and a worked-out programme, in *Notes Towards a Definition of Culture* (1948), for keeping the regions usefully but firmly in their places.

It would have been distressing to Eliot that the Scottish tradition began to revive, largely under Communist tutelage, just when he had allocated it this secure, unsubversive role. The ballads were pre-national; to be found in a variety of cultural settings, from the Shetlands to India. Yet their renewal in the late 1940s by Hamish Henderson and others, was also cosmopolitan, stemming from the civic movement of the Enlightenment, transmitted across the Atlantic, and returning via Roosevelt's New Deal, and folklorists such as Alan Lomax. The Scots and Irish project to record and recover folk-song was in fact to be of crucial importance in bringing Calum MacLean (brother of Sorley) and Henderson in contact with a wealth of song assumed to have been crushed out of the folk-memory by the assault of Calvinism and industrialization.

This recovery had metropolitan roots, as it was part of that quixotic but nonetheless thorough defence of British culture undertaken by the intellectuals of the Communist Party of Great Britain – from Arnold Kettle to Raymond Williams. The upshot of this, modulating through the New Left to an alignment with political nationalism, was to give both an internationalism and a civic identity to poetry on the periphery, and its links with the other arts, which has acted as a significant leaven over the last forty years. Poetry in Scotland has been popular, broadcast by writers-in-residence, sharing a frontier with folk-song and rock; it has been cosmopolitan in content and organization – in the stimulus that it has given to translators such as Robert Garioch and Edwin Morgan. At the same time, the setting up of the Poetry Library in Edinburgh in the early 1980s linked the function of poetry closely to the preservation of the *polis*.

This social preoccupation, not unique to Scotland, has interwoven with individual achievements, notably the remarkable didactic career of Philip Hobsbaum in helping to animate, between the 1950s and the 1980s, first an Ulster and then a Glasgow literary revival. The social voice of poetry may, of course, be lively within the peripheral – and Jewish – traditions, because of the habit of song, in kirk, chapel and synagogue, as well as in the bothies and tinkers' camps. This also fuses with the persistence of religious forms of argumentation, deductive 'common-sense' philosophy, and the classical tradition. In Scotland the psalms and the discourse of Bible criticism – and Freudian and Jungian psychoanalysis – were alike politically significant in the 1920s. Significantly, the major therapies which followed the collapse in Scottish self-esteem after the failed referendum of 1 March 1979 were literary: the foundation of the magazine *Cencrastus*, the Poetry Library, Cairns Craig's project of a four-volume *Literary History of Scotland* (1988–90). And the text of the revival that followed was taken from a novelist who is also playwright, illustrator, poet and 'theoretical historian': Alasdair Gray's 'Work as if you were living in the early days of a better nation.'

6

In a famous aside the Cambridge critic F. W. Bateson, with Compton MacKenzie in mind, talked of the accent of the *métèque* as marking the voice of imaginative writing marginal to the central English tradition. Recently, in a bold interpretive venture, the Scots poet and literary critic Robert Crawford has attempted to invert the traditional historiography of poetry in English and in *The Devolution of English Literature* (1992) has argued that the discipline itself is substantially Scots-created and provincial in character, not in a restrictive sense but in considering itself a part of an international literature. Edwin Morgan entitled his translations of Mayakovsky into Lallans 'Wi' the haill voice', a pugnacious lyricism which drew both on the variety of the poetics within his own country, and the resources of an international identity. This is something which is not confined to Scotland, or the Celtic periphery, but has issued in the concerns and robust epic techniques of a poetic international, from Morgan and Heaney to Derek Walcott and Les Murray.

'I knew a very wise man so much of Sir Christopher's senti-
ment', wrote Andrew Fletcher of Saltoun, defender of Scotland's
parliament against the Act of Union of 1707, 'that he believed
that if a man were permitted to make all the ballads, he need not
care who should make the laws of a nation.' As the heavy
weaponry of print-capitalism runs into greater and greater
trouble, with the accountants reigning where Eliot once sat,
Fletcher's appeal still seems to function, creating a social rhetoric
more persuasive and resonant than London's polite, whispered
monologues.

Notes

A more heavily documented version of my approach can be found in
'British Perspectives on European Regionalism' in L. Fietz, P. Hoffmann
and   H.-W.   Ludwig   (eds.),   *Regionalität,   Nationalität   und
Internationalität in der Zeitgenössischen Lyrik* (Tübingen, Attempto-
Verlag, 1992) 66–82. This drew heavily on the approach of J. G. A.
Pocock in *The Machiavellian Moment* (Princeton University Press,
1975), in conjunction with Benedict Anderson, *Imagined Communities*
(London, Verso, 1983) and Tom Nairn's fierce and frequently hilarious
The Enchanted Glass: Britain and its Monarchy (London, Radius,
1988).

In terms of the various traditions, I have to admit to a bias towards
Scottish-originated interpretations, modified I hope by the contents of
this volume. Much of these have been derived from Cairns Craig,
general editor, *The History of Scottish Literature* (4 vols., Aberdeen,
Aberdeen University Press, 1988–1990) supplemented by Robert
Crawford, *Devolving English Literature* (Oxford, Clarendon, 1992),
supplemented by William Donaldson, *Popular Literature in Victorian
Scotland: Language, Fiction and the Press* (Aberdeen, Aberdeen
University Press, 1986) and Hamish Henderson's collected essays *Alias
MacAlias* (Edinburgh, Polygon, 1992).

I
CENTRE AND PERIPHERY IN
HISTORICAL PERSPECTIVE

1

Topos/Locus/Place:
The rhetoric, poetics and politics of place,
1500–1800

LOTHAR FIETZ

When Geoffrey Grigson edited *The Faber Book of Poems and Places* in 1980[1] and when Jeremy Hooker entitled his collection of essays and reviews *Poetry of Place*,[2] a household word such as 'place' endowed with many shades of meaning began to develop into a critical concept within the framework of a new aesthetics of regionality taking its place beside the aesthetics of universality at the opposite end. Though the struggle between universality on the one hand, and individuality, on the other, has a long past,[3] the idea of place, uniqueness and regional identity or autonomy attained a new relevance in a specific historical and political situation, when the idea of 'devolution' began to take on shape on a theoretical level and subsequently failed in practical politics.

Though the classificatory literal use of 'place' in the context of poetics is a fairly recent development, the figurative use of the Greek and Latin words 'topos' and 'locus' has played a central role in rhetorical theory since antiquity. Figuratively speaking, 'topoi' are points of reference or aspects which have to be observed in the development of an argument. Matthieu de Vendôme[4] named seven such 'places' upon which a logical or plausible argument rests 'quis, quid, ubi, quibus auxiliis, cur, quomodo, quando', and Thomas Wilson in his *Arte of Rhetorique* (1560) rendered these categories in an easy couplet:

> Who, what, and where, by what helpe, and by whose:
> Why, how, and when, do many thynges disclose.[5]

This basic network of 'places' or 'points of reference' comprising the ideas of subject, object, place, means, cause, mode, and time was extended to include subcategories such as species, genus, property (= proprium), definition, etc. The strict observance of this set of fixed points of reference was meant to endow an argument with a systematic structure. Another meaning of 'topos' in rhetoric takes on shape when we consider the mnemonic function attributed to 'places' such as the manor, the temple, the cathedral, the theatre, and the landscape. Bearing this *pentad* of 'places' in mind, each of which could be associated with a prearranged set of ideas, the rhetor, by falling back on this well ordered topography of the mind, could re-evoke the various ideas associated with a specific visual 'point of reference' and thus rely on the functioning of memory by association.

The function assigned to the category of 'place' in rhetoric aims at a well-structured, i.e. systematical and logical, argument, designed either to persuade or convince the audience. There is, however, but one step from structuring to stereotyping, and thus in modern literary criticism[6] the meaning of 'topos' begins to overlap with the ideas of 'cliché', 'stereotype', and 'commonplace' (= *koinos topos, locus communis, Gemeinplatz*) implying both invariability *and* continuity plus triteness and banality.

For the Renaissance the philosophical idea of 'place' was closely connected with the idea of a universe the diversity of which was ordered and structured by the unifying principles of hierarchy and correspondence. There is no need to reproduce the well-known metaphysical and political commonplaces of the time in detail.[7] Suffice it to quote the relevant passage from Shakespeare's *Troilus and Cressida* where Ulysses, the mouthpiece of orthodoxy, develops the semantic context of the word 'place':

> The heavens themselves, the planets, and this centre
> Observe degree, priority, and place,
> Insisture, course, proportion, season, form
> Office, and custom, in all line of order.[8]

'Place' in this context is a special image for the idea of 'degree' or 'rank' within a hierarchical order, major aspects of which are interpreted by concepts such as priority, insisture, course and proportion implying rank, stability, direction and the balanced relation of parts to the whole. By means of concepts like season, office, custom and nature, the body politic and tradition are related to the same model of interpretation in which the basic category of 'place' is one of the key concepts.

It is to be expected that the poetry of the Renaissance will reflect this philosophy of hierarchy and correspondence and that geographical places will be assigned a hierarchical place in the overall order of places and will be shown to correspond with other places of the same hierarchical rank.

The absolute opposite to historical and geographical places subject to hierarchical placement is the 'not-place' referred to as *u-topia* which – due to the fact that in English *u-topia* is a homophone of *eu-topia* – is understood to be a 'good' and 'ideal' place in comparison with the real places of this world. There are latent mythico-utopian undertones in the idyll and the pastoral springing from the traditional country–town dichotomy and culminating in Rousseau's Romantic criticism of the history of civilization as a process of alienation leading away from, or even destroying, nature.

Literature or poetry understood to be a criticism of life never has been nor ever will be neutrally and disinterestedly descriptive. The attitudes towards 'places' have changed: the shift from the 'encomia' of the metropolis to the Romantic praise of nature and the countryside to contemporary regionalism has always reflected partiality and interest in specific historical situations. The question arises whether these shifts and valuations taking place within the extra-poetical context of politics and reflecting a regrouping of the value system can be dealt with from a disinterested scholarly point of view. 'Poetry of Place' implies 'Politics of Place' and politics can only be judged from an ethical basis. Thus the question of a poetics of place must – via an analysis of the 'Politics of Place' – lead on to the ethical premises of both politics and poetry. This means, in a more concrete way: does the obvious shift from the centre to the periphery – one remains aware of the orthodox implications of 'centre' and 'periphery' –, from the metropolis to the regions, imply an ethical category such as liberation? It is easy enough to come to terms with the problem of decentralization and regionalism on a political level, but what are the criteria justly, i.e. ethically *soundly*, to evaluate devolution, secession, regionalism, as facets of the process of democratization? Where do we get hold of the ethical implications of a process which, since the Renaissance, has led away from thinking in terms of a universe towards the idea of a pluralistic universe and further on towards a decentralized multiverse of persons and places?

In the middle of this process only tentative answers can be given concerning the shifts in the political and aesthetical value system. Jeremy Hooker highlights some of them when he objects to the 'images of a false unity imposed throughout Britain by a national or Anglo-American "centre" '. 'Cultural uniformity' and a 'centralized consciousness'

> are the principal causes of dull or conventional vision as far as the actual and potential life of particular places and the problematic reality of modern Britain are concerned. The same image-making processes are responsible for the valuation of places for their local colour, as picturesque deviations from the centralized norm or picturesque contributions to a generalized variety. In both cases, what is at issue is the truth of images to reality – which I take to be a writer's first concern.[9]

In Hooker's argument political and aesthetical issues are causally related: if we take 'aesthetics' in its etymological meaning as a branch of philosophy concerned with the study of objects perceptible to, and affecting, the senses, centralism is made responsible for the blunting of the senses, as it has kept on producing schematized views both of the centre and the periphery, which in a process of habitualization have been internalized and automatized to a degree that they have become void of mimetic truthfulness. The *new* aesthetics of place going hand in hand with a revaluation of the regions hitherto treated as, and considered to be, peripheral has a long way to go to overcome conventional aesthetics and art: automatizations and habitualizations characteristic of the traditional view of places, will have to be replaced by a new way of looking at places, which means that through critical 'defamiliarization' the senses must be sharpened again both for the stereotypes as stereotypes and for the places in their own right, including both centre and periphery. Thus the central issue of the new poetics of place is

> seeing places with understanding and sympathy and, therefore, with insight into the cultural, social, and linguistic factors that make them specifically human, as well as with feeling for their physical and atmospheric qualities.[10]

Looked at through the critical programme of the contemporary poetics of place the poetic stereotypes deriving from the ideas of universalism and centralism in past ages become transparent as such. This chapter will attempt to trace major aspects of the changing relationship between the politics and the poetry of place from the Renaissance to the Romantic periods.

Patriotism and nationalism have always been most powerful agents in producing a 'centralized consciousness' and a sense of hierarchy concerning countries and nations. When Samuel Daniel in his sequence of love sonnets made the lover compare Delia, his 'ioyfull North', to 'Albion, glory of the North' he drew on the conventionalized rhetoric of patriotic poetry:

> Florish faire *Albion*, glory of the North,
> *Neptunes* darling helde betweene his armes:
> Deuided from the world as better worth,
> Kept for himselfe, defended from all harmes.[11]

Shakespeare in *Richard II* (1595), indebted to Daniel's *The First Fowre Bookes of the ciuile warres* (1595), made use of a similar, though more exquisite, rhetoric Daniel had used in *Delia*. England for him is a

> . . . fortress built by Nature for herself.
> Against infection and the hand of war,
> This happy breed of men, this little world,
> This precious stone set in the silver sea,
> Which serves it in the office of a wall,
> Or as a moat defensive to a house,
> Against the envy of less happier lands;
> This blessed plot, this earth, this realm, this England,
> This nurse, this teeming womb of royal kings.[12]

Shakespeare's encomium of England adds biblical images to Daniel's rhetoric: England, 'this other Eden, demi-paradise' is seen as a place of delight and bliss, besides – according to Daniel – being independent of, protected from, and better than, the rest of the world. England, 'this little world' or microcosm also reflects the divine order of the macrocosm.

The rhetoric of this patriotic eulogy of England is neither new nor unique: the French poet Du Bartas had used similar rhetoric in his *Création du Monde*,[13] part of which was translated into English by John Eliot in *Ortho-Epia Gallica* or *Eliot's Fruits from the French*, in 1593:

> O fruitfull France! most happie Land, happie and happie and happie thrice!

O pearle of rich *European* bounds! O earthly Paradise!

. . .

Bastillyons fower borne in thy bounds: two Seas and mountaines
    double.[14]

'Paradise protected' is a current rhetorical topos which was used
again by Joshua Sylvester when he translated Du Bartas' eulogy
of France into a eulogy of England in 1605:

> All-haile (deere ALBION) *Europes* Pearle of price,
> The Worlds rich Garden, Earths rare Paradice:
>
> . . .
>
> *Fenc'd from the World* (as better-worth then That)
> With triple Wall (of Water, Wood, and Brasse)
> Which neuer Stranger yet had power to passe.[15]

These contexts could be supplemented by texts from other plays
by Shakespeare, and passages selected by the Elizabethans from
classical authors such as Virgil, Caesar, Plutarch, or by texts from
G. Peele's *Edward I* and *Arraignment of Paris* or Daniel's *Ciuile
Warres*[16] in order to demonstrate the productivity and stereotyp-
ical nature of the encomiastic rhetoric of patriotism and
nationalism. Daniel's England 'Deuided from the world as better
worth' is identical with Sylvester's England '*Fenc'd from the
World* (as better-worth then That)'. This is, as it were, the lowest
common thematic denominator of all the texts analysed so far,
the reductionist quality of which manifests itself both on the
thematic and rhetorical level.

The assumption of a hierarchical order among states is in
keeping with the basic Elizabethan assumptions concerning the
order of the whole universe, the unifying principle of which was
thought to be a hierarchical structure informing each link of the
'vast chain of being'.[17] The universalization of, and attribution of
an ontological status to, the idea of hierarchy in the Tudor myth
helped to stabilize the system and the newly attained self-esteem
resting on a feeling of superiority. In keeping with the current
assumptions of his age Edmund Spenser subjected even the geo-
graphy of places and rivers to that universal system of hierarchy
and degree, thus creating the illusion of unity in diversity pervad-
ing all layers of reality: on the occasion of the 'marriage of the
Thames and the Medway' the personifications of the rivers of
England meet in the Hall of Proteus, who in Greek mythology

tended the seals of Poseidon. Arion, who is said to be the inventor of the dithyramb and who, having been thrown overboard by pirates, was saved by a dolphin charmed by his music, plays on the harp. The natural and geographical order of rivers and places is dissolved and transformed by a technique of allegorical personification and anthropomorphization into a world strongly resembling the court and fitting the universalized pattern of hierarchy and degree:

> So went he [Arion] playing on the watery plaine
> Soone after whom the louely Bridegroome came,
> The noble Thamis, with all his goodly traine,
> But him before there went, as best became,
> His auncient parents, namely th'auncient Thame.
> But much more aged was his wife then he,
> The Ouze, whom men do Isis rightly name;
> Full weake and crooked creature seemed shee,
> And almost blind through eld, that scarce her way could see.
> . . .
> And round about him [Thames] many a pretty Page
> Attended duely, ready to obay;
> All little Riuers, which owe vassalage
> To him, as to their Lord, and tribute pay:
> The chaulky Kenet, and the Thetis gray,
> The morish Cole, and the soft sliding Breane,
> The wanton Lee, that oft doth loose his way,
> And the still Darent, in whose waters cleane
> Ten thousand fishes play, and decke his pleasant streame.[18]

In this allegorization of landscape the stereotypes engendered by the feudal system begin to merge with pastoral conventions. Personification and anthropomorphization, here used to create the illusion that the universe, in spite of its diversity and multiplicity, is a continuum and a unity held together by 'degree', would from a nineteenth-century point of view be dismissed as 'pathetic fallacy' blurring the borderlines between the heterogeneous *and* autonomous areas in a pluralistic universe. The subjection of heterogeneity and autonomy to unifying principles or processes is a highly political procedure aiming at the stabilization of political hierarchy in the name of a divine order.

The poeticity of the Elizabethan poetry of place was rooted in the principle of unity, continuum, degree, and correspondence. Thus London, by which the Thames is 'beautified', is compared to the 'diadem embattled wide with hundred turrets',[19] which Old Cybele, the mother of all living things, wore when she went to Jove's palace. By way of association Spenser establishes a unifying relation, or a continuum between the Phrygian deity and the Phrygian town of Troy, on the one hand, and London as 'Troynovant',[20] on the other. By establishing a poetical correspondence between myth and history, i.e. mythical and historical persons and places, the illusion of sameness and continuity is produced; and closely connected with this basic strategy, the river Thames is associated with Cybele, Rhea and Demeter, and the place called London endowed with ennobling mythical qualities.

Spenser's mythology is neither new nor original but a variation on the correspondence established between Troy and London which can be found long before Spenser's *Fairie Queene* or *Prothalamion*, e.g. in William Dunbar's encomium (1465–1530) *To the City of London*:

> London, thou art of townes A *per se*.
>   Soveraign of cities, semeliest in sight,
> Of high renoun, riches, and royalytie;
>   Of lordis, barons, and many goodly knyght;
>   Of most delectable lusty ladies bright;
> Of famous prelatis in habitis clericall;
>   Of merchauntis full of substaunce and myght:
> London, thou art the flour of Cities all.
>
> Gladdith anon, thou lusty Troy Novaunt,
>   Citie that some tyme cleped was New Troy,
> In all the erth, imperiall as thou stant,
>   Pryncesse of townes, of pleasure, and of joy,
>   A richer restith under no Christen roy;
> For manly power, with craftis naturall,
>   Fourmeth none fairer sith the flode of Noy:
> London, thou art the flour of Cities all.[21]

The encomiastic topos of London as the New Troy was kept alive at least to the beginning of the eighteenth century. Shortly after the Great Fire of 1666, John Crouch in *Londinenses Lacrimae* deplored the destruction of '*Britain's envy'd Troy*',[22] but he deliberately refrained from pushing the parallel between London and

Troy too far. As a Royalist, he rejected the Trojan-Horse thesis, i.e. treason as the possible cause of the incendiary, but rather considered 'Sin' to be 'the Common Cause'.

When William Fenne re-established a positive correspondence between London and Troy in *Londinium: or, The Renowned City of London* (1669) and praised London as 'the great Emporeum of the world' he was first and foremost engaged in producing a counterpart to Juvenal's third Satire on Rome.[23]

The Transylvanian speaker of Fenne's poem falls back into the encomiastic vein of the *laus-urbis* poetry of the Tudor Age:

> Fair *Troynovant!* the glory of this Isle!
> All things being rich, and nothing-mean, or vile.[24]

Under the restored monarchy, which Dryden continued to celebrate, the Troy Myth was thoroughly revived. Taking the mythological allusions Spenser had elaborated on for granted, London in an anonymous poem entitled *Troia Rediviva, or, The Glories of London*, the capital as the seat of royalty was glorified as the reincarnation of Troy.[25]

While the poetry of place of the 1670s was reviving the conventions and topoi of the earlier encomiastic poetry of the metropolis, occasional new tones became audible. Henry Vaughan (1594–1666), who had strong affiliations to Breconshire, saw the metropolis in a different light. In his *Rhapsody . . . written upon a new meeting with some of his friends at the Globe Tavern* he neither taps the mythical nor the heroical tradition but by focusing on the corruption and sinfulness of London rather draws on the mood of Juvenal's satires:

> Should we go now a-wand'ring, we should meet
> With catchpoles, whores, and carts in ev'ry street:
> Now when each narrow lane, each nook and cave,
> Signposts, and shop doors, pimp for ev'ry knave,
> When riotous sinful plush, and tell-tale spurs
> Walk Fleet Street, and the Strand, when the soft stirs
> Of Bawdy, ruffled silk turn night to day;
> And the loud whip, and couch scolds all the way;
> When lusts of all sorts, and each itchy blood
> From the Tower Wharf to Cymbeline, and Lud,
> Hunts for a mate, and tired footman reels
> 'Twixt chairmen, torches, and the hackney wheels.[26]

The visual and sensual richness and realism of the picture here drawn of London has nothing to do with the erudite mythologizing of the encomia. The picture conveys the impression of experience instead of learning. The basic attitude resembles that of Juvenal's Umbricius. The allergic reaction to the monstrous city is even greater and more explicit in Abraham Cowley's *Of Solitude*:

> . . . methinks I see
> This monster, London, laugh at me,
> I should at thee too, foolish City,
> If I were fit to laugh at misery,
> But thy estate I pity.

> Let but thy wicked men from out thee go,
> And all the fools that crowd thee so,
> Even thou who dost thy millions boast,
> A village less than Islington will grow,
> A solitude almost.[27]

Though Cowley's poem lacks the visual imagination, concreteness of observation and 'local colour' of Vaughan's poem they share the spirit of rejection towards the metropolis. The apparent actual experience of the moral corruption of London merges with the disgust prefigured in Juvenal's satire on Rome. Thus poems such as these have to be considered both from a point of view of intertextual relatedness and of mimetic and realistic fidelity.[28]

Swift's *Description of the Morning* (1709) evokes and mocks the pastoral mode[29] and his *Description of a City Shower* (1710) shows even greater complexity: 'Careful observation'[30] of the symptoms foreshadowing the shower merges with allusions to the 'country shower' in Virgil's *Georgica*.[31] An ironical inversion of the panegyrical pastoral mode makes itself felt, leading up to the last part of the poem (ll. 53–63). There is a reference to Troy again, but it is no longer meant to evoke a correspondence between the virtues of Troy and Troynovant but is clearly indicative of unheroic banality, of life in modern London: during the shower the beau seeks shelter in a sedan chair covered with leather, and he is frightened by the rain pelting down on the roof:

> Box'd in a Chair the Beau impatient sits,
> While Spouts run clatt'ring o'er the Roof by Fits;
> And ever and anon with frightful Din

The Leather sounds, he trembles from within.
So when Troy Chairmen bore the Wooden Steed,
Pregnant with *Greeks*, impatient to be freed,
(Those Bully *Greeks*, who, as the Moderns do,
Instead of paying Chair-men, run them thro')
Laoco'n struck the Outside with his Spear,
And each imprison'd Hero quak'd for Fear.[32]

Correspondence has given way to comparison and the heroic virtues predominant in the encomiastic mode have petered out into the unheroic trembling of the Beau. The idea of decline, underlying Swift's concept of history, overshadows the final part of the poem. London cannot begin to compare with Troy due to Swift's conviction that history is a process of decline. And that is why London appears to him as the cesspool of the modern world:

Now from all Parts the swelling Kennels flow,
And bear their Trophies with them as they go:
Filth of all Hues and Odours seem to tell
What street they sail'd from, by their Sight and Smell.
They, as each Torrent drives, with rapid Force
From *Smithfield*, or St. Pulchre's shape their Course,
And in huge Confluent join at *Snow-Hill* Ridge,
Fall from the *Conduit* prone to *Holborn-Bridge*.
Sweepings from Butchers Stalls, Dung, Guts, and Blood,
Drown'd Puppies, stinking Sprats, all drench'd in Mud,
Dead Cats and Turnip-Tops come tumbling down the Flood.[33]

The *City Shower* culminates in an orgy of mud marking the distance between the Troynovant eulogies and the actual experiences of the metropolis towards the beginning of the eighteenth century. The disgust with, and the disillusionment about, the centre does not automatically imply greater attention for the 'periphery'. The eighteenth century's interest in individual places beyond the city is *cum grano salis* hampered by a predilection for generic phenomena:

The business of a poet . . . is to examine, not the individual, but the species; to remark general properties and large appearances. He does not number the streaks of the tulip, or describe the different shades in the verdure of the forest . . . he must disregard present laws and opinions, and rise to general and transcendental truths, which will always be the same . . . He must write as the interpreter of nature, and the legislator of mankind, and consider himself as presiding over the thoughts, and manners of future generations; as a being superior to time and place.[34]

It goes without saying that the poetry of the eighteenth century cannot be reduced to an 'aesthetics of the generic' but it is as evident that the climate of opinion of the so-called Enlightenment period favoured the general ideas of the 'book of nature' rather than the uniqueness of individual places and regions. However popular Macpherson's Ossianic epics may have been and however great the intended contribution to heightening the national self-awareness and self-assurance of the Scots, the attempt to initiate something like a Gaelic revival remained a literary episode in the eighteenth century. The antithesis which the age was more interested in than in the opposition of metropolis versus region derived from the primary understanding and experience of the town as the symbolic place of civilization. Thus the counterpart of the town was not individual regions, but in a more general and abstract way the country signifying nature. Even Romantic poetry of place, however vivid the local colour of, for instance, the Lakes may be, was still rooted in the more general pre-Romantic dichotomy of nature versus civilization, a dichotomy which was productive all through the eighteenth century.

Though we are still far from perceiving places in their own right, which does not only imply a poetics of individualization but at the same time a deliberate politics of place, there can be no denying the fact that the Romantics had developed an acute sense of place. Wordsworth in his *Prelude* describes his arrival in London: he knew London by hearsay, had 'fond imaginations' which, however, in the end gave way to 'the real scene'. The 'din of towns and cities'[35] which he had escaped on a tour to Tintern Abbey in 1798 assaults and overwhelms him in a traumatic way. The only thing that seems to have continuity in Wordsworth's London is 'the Babel din, the endless stream of men, and moving things'.[36] Everything else appears to be discontinuous and – through the absence of an inner coherence – frightening:

> Here, there, and everywhere a weary throng,
> The comers and the goers face to face,
> Face after face – the string of dazzling wares,
> Shop after shop, with symbols, blazon'd names,

> And all the tradesman's honours overhead;
> Here, fronts of houses, like a title-page
> With letters huge inscribed from top to toe;
> Station'd above the door, like guardian saints,
> There, allegoric shapes, female or male;
> Or physiognomies of real men,
> Land-Warriors, kings, or admirals of the sea,
> Boyle, Shakespear, Newton, or the attractive head
> Of some Scotch doctor, famous in his day.[37]

The hierarchies and correspondences structuring the pictures of the world and of the metropolis in Renaissance poetry have given way to a string of contiguous but unrelated impressions; the Platonic idea of the One and the Many, or of unity in diversity, has given way to discreteness and multiplicity exemplified by London experienced as a multiracial city:

> Now homeward through the thickening hubbub, where
> See – among the distinguishable shapes –
> The Italian, with his frame of images
> Upon his head; with basket at his waist
> The Jew; the stately and slow-moving Turk
> With freight of slippers piled beneath his arm.
> Briefly, we find (if tired of random sights
> And haply to that search our thoughts should turn)
> Among the crowd, conspicuous less or more,
> As we proceed, all specimens of man,
> Through all the colours which the sun bestows,
> And every character of form and face,
> The Swede, the Russian; from the genial South,
> The Frenchman and the Spaniard; from remote
> America, the Hunter-Indian; Moors,
> Malays, Lascars, the Tartar and Chinese,
> And Negro Ladies in white muslin gowns.[38]

The picture of a coherent and meaningful universe, metaphorically structured by the 'chain of being', has been replaced by the picture of a multifarious and incoherent society and disintegrating culture. Salvation and redemption could only be hoped for in a sphere situated 'beyond' modern civilization manifesting itself most acutely in the capital in particular, and in towns in general. For the Romantic mind, the modern 'beyond', logically enough, had its place in nature, from which modern man was thought to have been alienated in the course of civilization. Nature, panthe-istically conceived of as a continuum comprising both human and non-human reality, was endowed with attributes originally bestowed upon saviour figures: it was thought to be capable of redeeming man from the modern disease of alienation from nature. Though nature in the raw, it is true, was thought to be the opposite of urban civilization, there was still a long way to go before the Romantic antithesis of civilization versus nature was complemented by the contemporary antithesis of centre/metropolis versus periphery/region bearing strong cultural and ethnical implications of which the Romantic period was not yet aware.

The process of pluralization and dissociation of a once homo-geneous cultural awareness continued on various levels. The nineteenth century witnessed the emergence both of the 'two nations' and the 'two cultures', and – towards the end of the century, in the Celtic Renaissance – a growing emphasis on ethnico-cultural difference rather than centralist homogeneity. But it also witnessed the reactions to the growing plurality and multiplicity. In the name of 'the best that has been thought and said' the Arnoldians advocated a 'classical' culture, which in their mind was insolubly linked to the idea of 'centre' and 'metropo-lis', from the point of view of which the periphery had to appear as provincial or even parochial.

The nineteenth century marks a complex and many-faceted stage of transition in the history of rivalling ideas and in the developments which, since the Renaissance, have gradually led away from the orthodox metaphysics of a universe to the modern experience of a multiverse of individuals and unique 'places' en-titled to an identity, culture, and literature of their own.

Notes

1   Geoffrey Grigson (ed.), *The Faber Book of Poems and Places* (London, 1980).
2   Jeremy Hooker, *Poetry of Place: Essays and Reviews 1970–1981* (Manchester, 1982).
3   Cf. Note 33.
4   Cf. H. F. Plett, *Einführung in die rhetorische Textanalyse* (Hamburg, 6th edn., 1985).
5   Thomas J. Derrick (ed.), *Arte of Rhetorique* (New York, 1982), 55.

6   Cf. E. R. Curtius, *Europäische Literatur und lateinisches Mittelalter* (Bern/München, 1958; 6th edn. 1967); cf. E. Mertner, 'Topos und Commonplace', in G. Dietrich and F. W. Schulze (ed.), *Strena Anglica*, Festschrift für O. Ritter, (Halle, 1956), 178–224; cf. W. Veit, 'Toposforschung', *DVjs* 37 (1963); 120–63.

7   Cf. E. M. W. Tillyard, *The Elizabethan World Picture* (London, 1943; rpt. 1978).

8   Kenneth Palmer (ed.), *The Arden Edition of Troilus and Cressida*, (London, 1981), I.3, ll. 85–8.

9   Hooker, op. cit. 11.

10 Ibid., 13.

11 Samuel Daniel, *Delia* [1592], in Herbert Grabes (ed.) *Elizabethan Sonnet Sequences* (Tübingen, 1970), 84 (Sonnet No. 44).

12 Peter Ure (ed.), *The Arden Edition of King Richard II* (London, 1978), II.1, ll. 40–51.

13 Cf. Livre II: *La seconde Semaine: Les Colonies*.

14 Cf. *King Richard II*, op.cit., 206.

15 Cf. ibid., 207: *Deuine Weekes and Workes*.

16 Cf. ibid., 50.

17 Cf. A. O. Lovejoy, *The Great Chain of Being* (Cambridge, Mass., 1948).

18 A. C. Hamilton (ed.), Edmund Spenser, *The Fairie Queene* (London, 1977), 512 f.: Book IV, Canto XI, Stanzas 24, 29.

19 Cf. ibid., 27.

20 The parallel drawn between London as Troynovant and Troy rests on a misunderstanding and misspelling of the name of the British tribe of the 'Trinovantes', who settled in Essex near Chelmsford at the time of the Roman invasion. Geoffrey of Monmouth in his *Historia Regum Britanniae* (1130–38) still used the correct spelling (cf. *The History of the Kings of Britain*, translated and introduced by Lewis Thorpe [Harmondsworth], 1966, 81), whereas Renaissance writers and historiographers – carried away by association – propagated the idea that the 'Trinovantes' had been descendants of Trojans and had founded London. Hence the name Troynovant.

21 Grigson, op. cit., 143.

22 For this and the following information I am much indebted to Michael Gassenmeier, *Londondichtung als Politik: Texte und Kontexte der City Poetry von der Restauration bis zum Ende der Walpole-Ära* (Tübingen, 1989), 49.

23 Ibid., 102 f.

24 Ibid., 105.

25 Gassenmeier draws attention to a series of contemporaneous poems celebrating the 'Beauty', the 'Glories', the 'Magnificence', the 'Stateliness', and the 'Charity' of the metropolis. Cf. Gassenmeier,

op.cit., 96 ff., notes 144–8.

26   Grigson, op. cit., 156.

27   Grigson, op. cit., 157.

28   Literary conventions tend to be reactivated in situations when they lend themselves to the presentation of similar experiences of reality. But they can also lead a life of their own, lacking representational function, as period pieces cherished for the sake of their aesthetic value alone.

29   Cf. F. Schirrmacher, 'Arkadische Dämmerung: Jonathan Swift, *A Description of the Morning*', in H.-J. Zimmermann (ed.), *Antike Tradition und Neuere Philologien*, Symposium zu Ehren des 75. Geburtstages von Rudolf Sühnel (Heidelberg, 1984), 71–9.

30   Cf. I. l: 'Careful Observers may fortel the Hour.'

31   I, ll. 431–538; cf. A. Löffler, '*The Rebel Muse*', *Studien zu Swifts Kritischer Dichtung* (Tübingen, 1982), 72.

32   Robert A. Greenberg and William B. Piper (ed.), *The Writings of Jonathan Swift* (New York, 1973), 519f.

33   Ibid., 520.

34   Samuel Johnson, *The History of Rasselas* [1759], Chapter X: 'A Dissertation upon Poetry'.

35   Cf. William Wordsworth, 'Lines Composed a Few Miles Above Tintern Abbey, on Revisiting the Banks of the Wye During a Tour. July 13, 1798'.

36   William Wordsworth, *The Prelude* (1799, 1805, 1850), authoritative text, ed. by Jonathan Wordsworth, M. H. Abrams, Stephen Gill (New York/London, 1978). Book VII: 'Residence in London', ll. 158f.

37   Ibid., ll. 171–83.

38   Ibid., ll. 227–43.

2

At the margins: Outsider-figures in nineteenth-century poetry

ROBIN YOUNG

1

The principles by which the cultural historian selects are by no means obvious. Is cultural history the history of taste? Should it try to reproduce the aesthetic assumptions of the society in which the artwork was produced? Or should it be most concerned with those works of literature, art, music which seem most profoundly to convey the spirit of the age – even if such works remained unpopular with the majority, or even almost unknown, in the artist's lifetime? There are periods of cultural history (not many, admittedly, and most of them thought of as Golden Ages, in which popular taste and high creative endeavour seem at least in part to coincide) in which such questions may appear less than urgent or central. At other times the only way of evoking a true sense of the relationship between an age and its deepest cultural intelligences may be to explore the tensions between established taste (the picture which the controlling forces in society wish to project of themselves) and the isolated truth-tellers – those who contrive to give a truer picture, or keep alive the deepest values of the societies at whose margins they work.

> Indessen dünket mir öfters
> Besser zu schlafen, wie so ohne Genossen zu seyn,
> So zu harren und was zu thun indeß und zu sagen,
> Weiß ich nicht und wozu Dichter in dürftiger Zeit?[1]

> [Meanwhile it seems to me often
> Better to sleep to life than linger thus companionless,
> And what to make of it all and what to say
> I don't know; why be a poet at all in these barren times?]

Hölderlin's question rings as true of British culture in the early 1800s (which had neither the polycentrality of the German-speaking states to exploit nor the cultural capital of the *Goethezeit* to fall back on) as it does of the society in which it was written. Most of the major European Romantic movements had one or more writers so 'companionless', so far outside the mainstream of their 'barren times', that they could only function in some private, alternative world – whether of dreams, drugs, madness or the exploration of some private place or language insulated from the corruptions and commonplaces of the age. It is not that such writers are not 'of' their time – rather that they perceive and react against its characteristics with such intensity that the normal aesthetic categories of their contemporaries do not seem to apply. And it is especially fascinating to consider the cultural history of an age through the refracting lens of such dissident sensibilities. This chapter will focus mainly on three such writers – William Blake, John Clare and William Barnes – and will try to use their work as a means of interpreting the relationship between 'central' social-aesthetic ideals and the implicit criticism of these ideals by figures 'at the margins'. Such refraction involves distortion, of course. But so does every perspective. And it is to be hoped that such an approach will reveal as much about the more 'central' figures of the age as it does about the writers most directly under discussion.

2

At first sight, it is obvious, a truism of literary history, that what we still call the Romantic Age (taken in its widest chronological sense) was a period of enormous broadening of literary consciousness. In poetry, in travel-writing, in the cult of the picturesque, one senses an imperial expansion of the cultural imagination, in terms as much of geographical latitude and longitude as of emotional range and inner space. It would be all too easy to construct a model of literary development in which, from the middle of the eighteenth century onwards, writing in Britain and Europe became dramatically less urbane, less metropolitan, far more inclusive in subject matter (in the cultivation of the Gothic and the exotic, on the one hand, and of the lowly and the rustic on the other) and more adventurous in its imaginative range than the neo-classical vision of their predecessors could have allowed. Yet it would be very misleading to assume that such an amplification of subject-matter, such an apparent recentering of authorial point of view automatically implied a fundamental shift in the centres of cultural power.

It must be emphasized at the outset that, just as cultural hegemony is as much a matter of class as of geography, so the notion of centre and periphery is not only a matter of place but of social perspectives and social values. Few writers in English up to that point had been quite as formed by urban, even metropolitan experience as William Blake, who had spent nearly all his early life within a mile or two of the centres of political power. Yet Blake's vision of Albion is infinitely more exotic, more eccentric than that of Coleridge or William Wordsworth. They evoked images of a universal patriotism which overlooks all faults and equates freedom with unquestioning conformity to national and family stereotypes:

> O dear Britain! O my Mother Isle!
> Needs must thou prove a name most dear and holy
> To me, a son, a brother, and a friend,
> A husband and a father! who revere
> All bonds of natural love, and find them all
> Within the limits of thy rocky shores . . .[2]

> In our halls is hung
> Armoury of the invincible Knights of old:
> We must be free or die, who speak the tongue
> That Shakespeare spake; the faith and morals hold
> Which Milton held. – In everything we are sprung
> Of Earth's first blood, have titles manifold[3]

But Blake was prepared, then and always, to examine the legitimacy of these 'bonds of natural love' (a telling phrase):

> The weeping child could not be heard,
> The weeping parents wept in vain;
> They strip'd him to his little shirt,
> And bound him in an iron chain;

> And burn'd him in a holy place,
> Where many had been burn'd before;
> The weeping parents wept in vain.
> Are such things done on Albion's shore?[4]

Thus the fate of 'A Little Boy Lost', who dares to question the possibility of 'loving one's neighbour as oneself'. Blake's concept of Albion is universal, de-centred, no longer a patriotic cypher but a paradigm of suffering, self-torturing humanity. In the last, chaotic, prophetic books, place-names are jumbled, distances fused in a heroic, doomed attempt to make new sense out of old divisions:

> Scotland pours out his Sons to labour at the Furnaces;
> Wales gives his Daughters to the Looms; England, nursing Mothers
> Gives to the Children of Albion & to the Children of Jerusalem.
> From the blue Mundane Shell even to the Earth of Vegetation,
> Throughout the whole Creation, which groans to be deliver'd,
> Albion groans in the deep slumbers of Death upon his Rock.[5]

Taken on one level these may (except to Blake's most devoted admirers) sound like the dreams of a half-crazed visionary. But they imply, on their own terms, a wholeness of experience radically at odds with the deeply partial conception of Britain current amongst even the more enlightened of Blake's contemporaries.

3

Blake's poetry may seem an eccentric point of departure for this chapter. That is, precisely, its point. By annihilating the concepts of centre and periphery he at least creates the possibility of a new order, rather than reproducing the old one in disguise. Yet it is significant that this was an isolated vision. The *Lyrical Ballads* sold (eventually) in their thousands.[6] Blake remained, an authentic voice of the people, virtually unheard outside literary coteries for nearly a century. In one sense, this may simply reflect the tendency of the Romantic movement as a whole and of its more extreme members (Blake, Hölderlin, Stagnelius, Schack Staffeldt) in particular, to move so far 'ahead of their time' that they suffered a literary fate like that of the brimstone butterfly in Mörike's poem:

> Grausame Frühlingssonne
> Du weckst mich vor der Zeit...
> So muß ich jämmerlich vergehn
> Und wird der Mai mich nimmer sehn
> In meinem gelben Kleid.[7]

[Terrible sun of the spring time
Too early you waken me . . .
So I must die in wretchedness
And May-month will never see
Me bright in my golden dress.]

But the implication of the phenomenon for the relation between poet and audience is worth a moment's reflection, not least because it throws into relief the relative success of such collections as the *Lyrical Ballads*. If ever there were a case of involuntary, half-aware polycentrality, with the author mediating uneasily between reader and subject matter, this collection is it. The Preface to the 1805 edition of the *Ballads* reflects the uncertainty exactly. The very conception of 'the reader' who might 'look coldly' on these representations of 'low and rustic life', even though the poem's language is 'purified indeed from what appear to be its real defects' – all this is a far cry from Burns's poems, say, or the genuine Border Ballads, or (one suspects) the ordinary language of its living subjects. The very limpness of these poems as ballads, or narrative structures of any sort, seems to enact the social unease which lies at their heart. And the non-conversations which so regularly punctuate Wordsworth's poetry at this period (Simon Lee and his benefactor; the unseen interlocutor of 'We are Seven' and 'Anecdote for Fathers'; most of all, the epic non-communication of 'Resolution and Independence') represent a social as well as a personal unease: the agonized, at times almost catatonic uncertainty of a writer suspended between a perceived audience and an obstinately remote subject-matter.

The first publication of the *Lyrical Ballads*, shifted from Cottle's of Bristol to a London publisher just before the first issue of 1798,[8] might serve as a symbol for the uneasy relationship between poet and public – a public so different from the people described in the poems that the whole project might be seen as a venture in imaginative anthropology. Or rather, as several ventures, since both poetry and Preface afford a fascinating glimpse into the assumed psychology and social attitudes of the putative readership as much as of their frequently pre-literate subjects.

The shifts and turns and evasions which this complex relationship implied are subject-matter for a quite different sort of study from the present one. But they do form a fascinating template against which to measure both the monstrously self-sufficient directness of Blake's earlier poetry, and the equally hermetic but very different intensities of John Clare. Of Clare, as of Wordsworth, it could be said that he was a deracinated poet uneasily contemplating his severed social roots. Yet whereas imaginative distance for Wordsworth conferred liberation as well as social exile, for Clare, whose life, whose whole culture was derailed by economic forces over which he had no control, exile entailed only loss. A comparison of the sense of reality to be gained from the two men's poetry illustrates almost to the point of caricature the nature of the cultural disjunction which afflicted English poetry in the period. Whereas Wordsworth tends to interpose himself as medium filtering out reality:

> The old Man still stood talking by my side;
> But now his voice to me was like a stream
> Scarce heard; nor word from word could I divide[9]

Clare is his own interpreter; and his poems take place in a cosmos which has been reduced to absolute locality, of a few miles, a few yards, even (in the sequence of poems on birds' nests, for example) a few inches:

> Aye here it is stuck close beside the bank
> Beneath the bunch of grass that spindles rank
> Its husk seeds tall and high – tis rudely planned
> Of bleached stubbles and the withered fare
> That last years harvest left upon the land
> Lined thinly with the horses sable hair
> – Five eggs pen-scribbled over lilac shells
> Resembling writing scrawls which fancy reads
> As natures poesy and pastoral spells
> They are the yellow hammers . . .[10]

What is happening here is not only or simply a matter of breadth of visual focus. Whereas Wordsworth's poetry interposes between the subject of the poem and the reader-as-subject a whole series of moral assertions and social-imaginative uncertainties, Clare (though he may moralize *post facto*) is nakedly, defencelessly direct. Where Wordsworth disdains specifics, Clare is captivated, even enslaved by them. His horizon bounded by a parish which, as his control over his own destiny dwindles, is growing narrower by the hour, he resorts to the microcosm of natural

observation which increasingly displaces the expected explo-
ration of social and personal relationships. Until, in the poems of
his madness, total isolation, long implied, is at last acknowl-
edged, and he is reduced to the final helpless-defiant 'I am':

> I was a being created in the race
> Of men disdaining bounds of place and time: –
> A spirit that could travel o'er the space
> Of earth and heaven, – like a thought sublime,
> Tracing creation, like my maker, free, –
> A soul unshackled – like eternity,
> Spurning earth's vain and soul debasing thrall
> But now I only know I am, – that's all.[11]

4

Wordsworth and Clare, between them, illustrate some of the
strains inherent in the nature of English culture in the first
decades of the nineteenth century. They might seem to have little
in common, save the common cultural situation to which their
very different *oeuvres* represent such divergent reactions. Yet in
one respect their work does run in parallel. Each sought to create
a poetic language which could unite the provincial – the language
of living men and women – with the language of the literate
reading public in a single discourse. In neither case was the
attempt entirely successful. But in literature, failure can be at
least as revealing (and often as honorable) as success.
Wordsworth's poems hover uneasily (in some poems, inter-
minably) between the *faux-naif* and a peculiar language of
metaphysical self-invocation which is all his own. Clare's
language is more subtle in its fluctuation between verbal regis-
ters, and even more strained:

> . . . while in peace cows eat and chew their cuds
> Moozing cool shelterd neath the skirting woods
> To double uses they the hours convert
> And turn the toils of labour into sport
> Till morns long streaking shadows loose their tails
> And cooling winds swoon into f[l]uttering gales
> And searching sunbeams warm and sultry creep
> Warming the teazing insects from their sleep
> And dreaded gadflyes with their drowsey hum

On the burnt wings of mid-day zephers come
Urging each lown to leave his sports in fear
To stop the gadding cows from sturting bye
Droning unwelcome tidings on his ear
That the sweet peace of rural morns gone bye[12]

As so often in his work, the force of dialect words ('moozing', 'lown', 'gedding', 'sturting') and precision of observation ('morn's long streaking shadows loose their tails'; 'sunbeams warm and sultry creep/Warming the teazing insects from their sleep') is countered and undermined by the conventional literary vocabulary and syntax in which they are set; '... neath the skirting woods/To double uses they the hours convert'. And the way in which the apparent precision of the late-Augustan diction is subverted by the ambiguity of the syntax and the total absence of punctuation only serves to emphasize an impression of disturbance and discontinuity.

In one sense, what these verbal shifts and uncertainties might seem to reflect is not just the fragmentation of Clare's immediate society – the village of Helpstone as its social structure was transformed by enclosure, the commonality of land-users replaced by a growing divergence between landowners and the new proletariat of landless poor[13] – but an uneasiness, far more wide-ranging and just as deep, in society at large. And this uneasiness is also reflected in the implied readerships of Wordsworth and Clare. At least it is unambiguous whom the *Lyrical Ballads* are *for* – they are directed at readers of taste and a modicum of social awareness, and most definitely not at the (often pre-literate) social groupings whose lives they explore.

Clare's poems pose much more complex problems not just of reader-response but (a related yet distinct issue) of reader-*identity*. Even less than the *Ballads* are these poems conventional narratives. Rather they celebrate, in a memorably literal sense, 'moments of vision'; and the point of view of the visionary is that of a consciousness even more isolate than the projected fictive 'I' of Coleridge's poetry. Clare's poems perceive the natural world in almost hallucinatory detail; and as they convey these perceptions they also suggest a sense both of psychic displacement (the 'I' substituted by the natural objects perceived) and of social isolation. 'Where he passes beyond description he becomes insignificant', C. H. Herford wrote of Clare.[14] It is precisely this fatal (and fatalistic) awareness of non-significance which characterizes him both as individual poet and as representative of a culture in crisis.

5

When Clare uses dialect words, they are set in a philological and even a syntactical context which is that of a (sometimes rather dishevelled) version of the standard English of his day. Much the same is true of the work of 'the ploughman poet' Robert Bloomfield and even that of 'the Corn-Law Rhymer', Ebeneezer Elliot. Working in different parts of the country, each sought to represent his individual experience of the periphery to the literary culture of the centre. If Clare has achieved in the late twentieth century a greater measure of recognition from a very different literary culture, whose nature he could not have foreseen, this is as a result of the intense watchfulness of his individual voice, and because he celebrates an isolation which has now grown much more general, not because he was truly representative of a culture wider than himself.

The case of the great Dorset dialect poet William Barnes is not less revealing, but very different. At first sight, his should be a yet more problematic case than that of John Clare. Clare at least can be identified *post facto*, as the authentic (and authentically disregarded) bard of the dispossessed. Barnes's background and his relationship to it are more complex and apparently more contradictory.[15] Born of farming stock, he became successively solicitor's clerk, schoolteacher and country clergyman. Educated (one might think) away from – if not physically out of – his background, he produced a body of poetry in his native tongue which is without equal amongst the dialect literature of nineteenth-century England. Yet Barnes was also, by sympathy and (mainly self-) education, an internationalist, with a knowledge not just of French, German and Italian, but of Welsh, Persian and Urdu as well. There is no doubt that Barnes's experiments with exotic, especially Persian verse-forms had great significance for Thomas Hardy's poetic practice.[16] When G. M. Hopkins experimented with *cynghanedd*, he was following the lead set by William Barnes.[17]

This erudition and breadth of sympathy may seem startling if considered side by side with the relative insularity of many of his English contemporaries. Yet it exhibits a pattern not at all unfamiliar in the European poetry of the day. Scattered through many literatures, one finds instances of 'provincial' intelligences, often country clergymen or schoolmasters, not infrequently expressing themselves in the dialect of their home region, who combined great erudition and intellectual curiosity with an (apparently) almost childlike directness of attachment to place and a corresponding directness of expression. One thinks of J. P. Hebel in Switzerland, Mörike in Swabia, Blicher in Denmark, Aasmund Vinje and Ivar Aasen in Norway. For most of them, physical isolation from the metropolitan currents and fashions of the age was the prerequisite (whether they were happy in that exile or not) for that special, individual de- or re-centering of the subjective universe in the face of advancing urbanism and capitalism which their work evokes.

The role of language in all this is vital. For a poet – for any writer – consciously to write as though he were not at the centre of his world can be a disaster. Yet to use a language already formed by a centralist, canonic past is to begin from a point already shifting under pressure of determinants built in to the past of the language. It is the poet's vocation to renew the words (s)he uses. Even in the words of English Romantics closer to the centres of cultural power (Keats, Shelley) tensions between the literary language(s) of the past (especially, in Keats's case, the Elizabethans) and the poet's need to 'make new' created strains difficult to guard against whilst retaining creative spontaneity. In Clare, as we have seen, the disjunction between the inherited language of the centre and the isolated, observant consciousness of the self at the periphery often gives an impression of disturbance and displacement. In the dialect poems of William Barnes such a feeling is almost entirely absent.

This is not in any ordinary sense a matter of self-confidence; Barnes was outwardly amongst the most retiring of men. Nor was it a matter of conscious radicalism. Whereas Clare was very much aware, in a confused way, of the injustices of the time and of the plight of being without property in an age in which human status was linked more and more closely to ownership, Barnes was in no conventional sense a progressive. On the contrary, he seems to have opposed the Chartists, and to have advocated, if anything, a view of life closer to that of the idealized yeoman farmer whose outlook depends upon the possession of sufficient resources to stand outside the swirling social currents of the day:

> Let other vo'k meäke money vaster
>   In the aïr o' dark-room'd towns,
> I don't dread a peevish mëäster;
>   Though noo man do heed my frowns,
> I be free to goo abrode
> Or teäke ageän my hwomeward road
> To where, vor me, the apple tree
> Do leän down low in Linden Lea.[18]

It is perhaps not irrelevant that it is these lines, in a sanitized, standard English version, which in Vaughan Williams's very beautiful setting have formed many people's introduction to Barnes's work.[19] They have been appropriated, in other words, to the dreams of an urban community which regards the life of the rural poor as an attractive relic, a subject for social nostalgia, rather than the tough world which Barnes knew and Hardy showed it to be. But it is unfair to blame Barnes for this; and in any case his claims on our attention have nothing to do with the ideological correctness (or otherwise) of his position. They depend, rather, on the intensity of his response to life, and on the richness and authenticity of the language in which it is expressed:

> O small-feäc'd flow'r that now dost bloom
> To stud wi' white the shallor Frome,
> An' leäve the clote to spread his flow'r
> On darksome pools o' stwoneless Stour,
> When sof'ly-rizèn aïrs do cool
> The water in the sheenen pool,
> Thy beds o' snow-white buds do gleam
> So feäir upon the sky-blue stream,
> As whitest clouds, a-hangen high
> Avore the blueness o' the sky –[20]

The patterning of light and dark, swift and slow in the opening lines give way to a gathering ecstasy in which the colours burn and dazzle. No nineteenth-century poet, not even Coleridge or Hopkins, could surpass the vividness and directness of Barnes as colourist;[21] and if his vision lacks their metaphysical overtones and reflections, this surely adds to the primal intensities of his surrender to the immanence and immediacy of the visible world. And an essential element of his power is the richness, directness, intensity of his language. In his astonishing cumuli of whiteness, sound modifies colour; the precision and pallor of the standard-English 'white' is enriched by a sound-world of difference. And the dazzling effect of the alternation between blue and white is achieved with such simplicity, so little seeming art, that it is easy to ignore the sophisticated (in ways it needed to be) hypersensitivity to language which made the vision possible.

Barnes's range may seem narrow, his view of the world outside Dorset often sensible and humane, but also hermetic and timid, yet in one way, at least, he had a more powerful and significant voice than Clare. His view of life may be – *is* – more restricted. But few poets of the century did more to 'donner un sens plus pur aux mots de la tribu'.[22] Even if Barnes had not been such an important source for the other, more outwardly daring renewers, Hardy and Hopkins, he would still have been, in an essential sense, one of the central voices of the age.

6

To view the literature of Britain in the earlier nineteenth century through the refractive lenses of these refractory outsider-sensibilities is to become more sharply aware of the extent to which the history of literary values may diverge from that of conventional or accepted taste. At a lower (but perhaps deeper) level than the high metaphysical preoccupations of Wordsworth, Tennyson, Browning and Clough, a poetry was being written which was of value both in itself and as a reflection of life and sensibility outside the traditionally book-consuming classes. In this context, the terms 'central' and 'peripheral', whilst not rendered meaningless, take on an entirely altered meaning which has implications for our interpretation of works in the central canon just as much as for those whom it excludes. In comparing the work of Blake, Clare and Barnes, it is striking how closely the effects of social alienation resemble those of cultural-geographical distance. Imperialism, culturally as economically and militarily, strikes inwards as well as outwards; and it seems only reasonable to align the terms used to describe the effects of cultural centralism with those used to imply social control.

Yet it would be foolish to assume that those outsiders were not just as much affected by the intellectual and social currents of the day as were writers whose work was more congruent with established taste. Certainly, one can see a cultural progression perceptible in the writers discussed, from the globalist, revolutionary ambitions of Blake, through the despairing particularism of Clare to the serene quietism of Barnes, a progression which reflects trends familiar from other British and indeed European writing of the period. (One has only to think of the transition from the insurrectionary work of Grabbe and Büchner to the quietism of Stifter, Mörike and Storm.) In Britain, at least, this shift also reflects the ways in which the expression of authentic feeling was being driven underground by the ruthless pieties of the new commercial-industrial age.

However, it would be profoundly mistaken to reinterpret the progression described in this chapter as a record of failure. Barnes's poetry may have been disregarded, outside Dorset, for most of his lifetime. But Hopkins – another unknown in his own lifetime, but the most forward-looking of Victorian poets – knew him as a 'perfect artist ... of a most spontaneous inspiration'.[23] Blake was to be revalued by Yeats in Ireland and Kassner in Austria – and hailed as one of the most authentic voices of the age.[24] In each case it was precisely the writer's distance from the conventional poetry of his day which was perceived as the touchstone of his powers as a truth-teller.

Perhaps it is not entirely coincidental that the period which saw the 'rediscovery' of these writers' work coincided with the point at which the balances of literary power in Europe were changing dramatically. For the first time since the Renaissance, it was the works of writers in a 'minor' literature (Ibsen, Strindberg, Hamsun) which were recognized as the leaders of literary innovation. And just as these writers 'at the margin' became the central figures of the new age, so *within* the major literatures writers hitherto neglected, at the social or geographical margins (in Ireland, in Wales, amongst the German- and Swedish-speaking minorities in Bohemia and Finland), were about to be recognized as the progenitive influences they have since become. It was a recognition which marks a decisive shift in cultural history, and its implications are as important and relevant today as they were nearly a century ago.

Notes

1   J. C. F. Hölderlin, 'Brod und Wein', vii, in the *Große Stuttgarter Ausgabe* (Stuttgart, 1951), Vol. II, 90–95 [94].

2   S. T. Coleridge, from 'Fears in Solitude', [lines 176–81] in *Poetical Works* (Oxford Standard Authors, 1969), 262.

3   W. Wordsworth, from the sonnet 'It is not to be thought of that the Flood', written 1802, in *Poems* (ed. Hayden), (Penguin English Poets), 1977, Vol. I, 560–1 [561].

4   W. Blake, from 'A Little Boy Lost', in *Complete Writings*, ed. Keynes, 1972, 218–9.

5   W. Blake, *Jerusalem*, Ch. 1, *Complete Writings*, op. cit., 637.

6   On the publishing history of the *Lyrical Ballads*, see Roper's edn., (1968) 265–8.

7   E. Mörike, 'Zitronenfalter im April', in *Sämtliche Werke*, ed. Baumann, Stuttgart, 2nd edn., 1961, Vol. I, 209.

8   See D. F. Foxon, 'The Printing of *Lyrical Ballads*, 1798' in *The Librarian*, ix, (1954) 221–41.

9   'Resolution and Independence', in William Wordsworth, *Poems*, I, op. cit., 551–6 [555].

10 John Clare, 'The Yellowhammer's Nest', in the Oxford Authors edn. of Clare's works, ed. Robinson and Powell, 1984, 230.

11 'Sonnet, "I am" ', *ibid.*, 361–2 [362].

12 'Rural Morning', *ibid.*, 66–70 [70].

13 On the social background of Clare's poetry, see John Barrell, *The Idea of Landscape and the Sense of Place* (Cambridge, 1972), 98–120.

14 In C. H. Herford, *The Age of Wordsworth*, 1899, 186.

15 On the detail of Barnes's life, see T. W. Hearl, *W.B.*, Dorchester, 1966 and A. Chedzoy, *W.B.*, Wimborne, 1985.

16 On Hardy's formal experimentation (though I suspect he undervalues Barnes's influence rather) see D. Taylor, *Hardy's Metres and Victorian Prosody* (Oxford, 1988), especially 172–266.

17 Though Hopkins himself rather disparaged Barnes's use of *cynghanedd* – see his letter to Patmore, 6 October 1886 (*Further Letters of G. M. Hopkins*, ed. C.C. Abbott, Oxford University Press), 2nd edn., 1956, 370–1 [371].

18 'My Orcha'd in Linden Lea', in *The Poems of William Barnes*, ed. Jones, London, 1962, Vol. I, 233–4 [234].

19 'Original words in Dorsetshire [*sic*] dialect are printed below *the standard words* [my italics] in most copies' – M. Kennedy, *The Works of Ralph Vaughan Williams* (Oxford University Press, 1964), 408.

20 'The Water Crowvoot', in *The Poems of William Barnes*, op. cit., I, 297–8 [298].

21 On Barnes's use of colour, see G. Grigson's essay in *Poems and Poets*, 1969, 165–7.

22 Mallarmé's words (from 'Le Tombeau d'Edgar Poe', *Oeuvres Complètes*, Pleiade edn., 1945, 70) are less incongruous in this context than they might appear. There is no inherent contradiction between dialect and stylistic purity; rather the contrary.

23 To Robert Bridges, 1 September 1885, printed in Abbott's edn. of the *Letters to Robert Bridges* (2nd edn., Oxford University Press, 1955), 220–1 [221].

24 See Yeats's work, with E. J. Ellis, on Blake's manuscripts, his introduction to the Muses' Library edition of Blake, Kassner's essay in *Die Mystik, die Künstler und das Leben* (1900) and his remarkable *Novelle* on Blakean themes, 'Die Hochzeit zwischen Himmel und Hölle'.

Further reading

L. Colley, *Britons* (Yale University Press, 1992).

S. Copley and J. White (eds.), *Beyond Romanticism* (London, 1992).

H. T. Dickinson, *British Radicalism and the French Revolution* (Oxford, 1985).

E. J. Hobsbawm, *Industry and Empire* (London, 1969).

W. J. Keith, *The Poetry of Nature* (Toronto, 1980).

J. Lucas, *Romantic to Modern Literature* (Brighton, 1982).

R. Porter and M. Teich (eds.), *Romanticism in National Context* (Cambridge, 1988).

B. Richards, 'The Diction of Victorian Poetry' in *English Poetry of the Victorian Period* (London, 1988).

R. Sales, *English Literature in History: 1780–1830: Pastoral and Politics* (London, 1983).

E. P. Thompson, *The Making of the English Working Class* (London, 1963).

3

Province and metropolis, centre and periphery: Some critical terms re-examined

HANS-WERNER LUDWIG

The current debate about regionalism in contemporary literature centres on a number of critical terms which are inextricably bound up with value judgements. While 'regionalism' today has positive connotations, 'provincialism' is on the whole a term of contempt.[1] The terms 'nation' or 'nationalism' vary considerably with respect to the values attached to them, depending on whether from the secure vantage point of achieved nationhood one praises its achievements or advocates some greater political unit such as a united Europe. The situation is completely different for Third World countries or regions within a nation state which strive for full nation status as a mark of liberation and independence. Central terms such as region, province, and nation carry with them a host of associations, connotations, and ideological presuppositions, which are usually – and sometimes quite intentionally – left unexplained. For, as a leading west German politician has recently said, revolutions are no longer fought by occupying post offices and railway stations but by occupying the central concepts of intellectual history. Not infrequently the meanings of such concepts are quite deliberately, and sometimes unobtrusively, changed. This chapter will examine some of these central concepts in such a way as to show the burden of historical meanings which each carries, and will do this in five stages:

1. Current discussions of provincialism and centralism in culture frequently refer back to the nineteenth-century debate about these concepts, notably to Matthew Arnold. I shall therefore start with an analysis of Arnold's plea for a centralist English culture.

2. Ezra Pound's essays 'Provincialism the Enemy' will serve

to show the continuation of this debate into the first half of the twentieth century, informing much of the politics of modernism.

3.   A further step in the development of the term provincialism may be seen in the debate about the merits and demerits of the 'Movement' poets, notably Philip Larkin, a debate which owes much to Charles Tomlinson's attack in the *Essays in Criticism* of 1957.[2]

4.   The terms 'centre' and 'periphery' have in the mean time been further defined and turned into tools of political science. Here they are used to describe the relationship of developed nations and Third World countries or relationships of domination of various periphery cultures by the core culture within a state.

5.   Finally, this specific use of these terms in the field of political science has also spilled over into the sphere of cultural debates. Examples of this are provided by recent numbers in the Field Day Pamphlet series.[3] Seamus Heaney provides an interesting test case. I want to demonstrate how he has argued within the imperialist and post-colonialist matrix, and also how he has recently attempted to go beyond this frame of reference.

Towards a metropolitan culture: Matthew Arnold

When Matthew Arnold delivered his lecture 'The Influence of Academies on National Spirit and Literature', at Oxford on 4 June 4 1864, and his series of lectures on Celtic literature, also at Oxford on 6 and 7 December 1865, 24 February 1866 and 26 May 1866, he was drawing heavily on his 'French connections'. On his journey to France in 1859 he had been in contact both with Sainte-Beuve and Renan. While he used the former's writings on the French Academy as material for his lecture on academies, it was the latter's *Essais* which together with Henri Martin's *Histoire de France* were the source of most of his ideas about the Celts. As Her Majesty's Inspector of Schools, Arnold had some first-hand experience of the school system in Wales, on which he first reported in 1853. He had, it is true, also visited the 1864 Eisteddfod at Llandudno and the few descriptive paragraphs at the beginning of 'On the Study of Celtic Literature' read as a piece of direct reporting. But taken as a whole, both these essays and the lecture on the academies are an attempt on the part of Arnold to graft, as it were, French ideas onto an

English discourse. These reports, lectures, and essays show Arnold's preoccupation with a centralized culture in Britain which he envisaged as predominantly English and for which he strove to establish a rank similar to that of France or Germany.

Arnold cribbed the basic opposition of provincialism versus urbanity, from Sainte-Beuve, in particular from his piece on the history of the Académie Française in his *Causeries du Lundi* series (19 July 1858). Arnold praises the French Academy for its all-pervading, centralizing influence on the national culture of France:

> Well, then, an institution like the French Academy, – an institution owing its existence to a national bent towards the things of the mind, towards culture, towards clearness, correctness, and propriety in thinking and speaking, and, in its turn, promoting this bent, – sets standards in a number of directions, and creates, in all these directions, a force of educated opinion, checking and rebuking those who fall below these standards, or who set them at nought.[4]

On the other hand he finds such a centre lacking in England, and while he judges the English national mind ('the spirit of our nation') to be bent against such a centre of intellectual activity as the French Academy he nevertheless holds up the French model to his fellow-countrymen as the ideal of centralized standards in culture. Arnold is aware of the fact that 'urbanity' in Sainte-Beuve is first and foremost not an abstract social value but – in this respect very much like the gentleman ideal – a quality of character in human beings denoting moral sense, 'cultured-ness', elegance, cheerfulness, tact, and ease of mind.[5] He presents John Henry Newman as the epitome of this ideal:

> In a production which we have all been reading lately, a production stamped throughout with a literary quality very rare in this country ... – *urbanity*; in this production, the work of a man never to be named by any son of Oxford without sympathy, a man who alone in Oxford of his generation, alone of many generations, conveyed to us in his genius that same charm, that same ineffable sentiment which this exquisite place itself conveys, – I mean Dr Newman, – an expression is frequently used which is more common in theological than in literary language, but which seems to me fitted to be of general service; the *note* of so and so, the note of catholicity, the note of antiquity, the note of sanctity, and so on. Adopting this expressive word, I say that in the bulk of the intellectual work of a nation which has no centre, no intel-

lectual metropolis like an academy, like M. Sante-Beuve's 'sovereign organ of opinion', like M. Renan's 'recognised authority in matters of tone and taste', – there is observable a *note of provinciality*. Now to get rid of provinciality is a certain stage of culture; a stage the positive result of which we must not make of too much importance, but which is, nevertheless, indispensable, for it brings us on to the platform where alone the best and highest intellectual work can be said fairly to begin. Work done after men have reached his platform is *classical*; and that is the only work which, in the long run, can stand. All the *scoriae* in the work of men of great genius who have not lived on this platform are due to their not having lived on it. Genius raises them to it by moments, and the portions of their work which are immortal are done at these moments; but more of it would have been immortal if they had not reached this platform at moments only, if they had had the culture which makes men live there.[6]

This lengthy paragraph is remarkable in many ways. Firstly, Arnold introduces the notion of 'urbanity', only however to use Newman, as indeed Sainte-Beuve and Renan, as authorities to pronounce judgment on the English culture of his day. Secondly, it is important to note that Arnold slips in the term 'intellectual metropolis' and thus shifts the emphasis from '*urbanité*' versus '*provincialité*' to 'metropolis' versus 'province'. Thirdly, Arnold sees provinciality – the causes of which he describes as 'remoteness from a centre of correct information ... want of a centre of correct taste' (245) – as a low stage in the development of a culture which has to be overcome. On the other hand, centralist or metropolitan culture is praised profusely as 'classical'. In describing this classical culture Arnold comes close to the formula which he was to use over and over again to define culture, as the 'pursuit of our total perfection by means of getting to know, on all the matters which most concern us, the best which has been thought and said in the world',[7] as the object and indeed the result of criticism which he defined as 'a disinterested endeavour to learn and propagate the best that is known and thought in the world'.[8]

While central or metropolitan culture is classical, provincialism for Arnold lacks balance, lucidity, graciousness, felicity. It is emotional and appeals to 'blood and senses'.[9] Again, as 'urbanity' was first and foremost a quality of character in a human being and only by transference a characteristic of classical culture, 'provinciality' in Arnold is also applied to characterize deficiencies in human beings, in this case in a whole group, the Puritans or Nonconformists whom Arnold considers to be the very opposite of culture:

> But we have got fixed in our minds that a more full and harmonious development of their humanity is what the Nonconformists most want, that narrowness, onesidedness, and incompleteness is what they most suffer from; in a word, that in what we call *provinciality* they abound, but in what we may call *totality* they fall short.[10]

If the attainment of culture is conceived of as a process, of stages of development towards the one and only aim of a classical culture, as Arnold conceives it, then education is one means of influencing such a development. It is, therefore, not surprising that Arnold, the inspector of schools, should advocate the use of English in Welsh schools as a means of forming one nation out of the various parts of the British Isles:

> There can, I think, be no question but that the acquirement of the English language should be more and more insisted upon by your Lordships in your relations with [the elementary schools of Wales], as the one main object for which your aid is granted. Whatever encouragement individuals may think it desirable to give to the preservation of the Welsh language on grounds of philological or antiquarian interests, it must always be the desire of Government to render its dominions, as far as possible, homogeneous, and to break down barriers to the freest intercourse between the different parts of them. Sooner or later, the difference of language between Wales and England will probably be effaced, as has happened with the difference of language between Cornwall and the rest of England; as is now happening with the difference of language between Brittany and the rest of France; and they are not the true friends of the Welsh people, who, from a romantic interest in their manners and traditions, would impede an event which is socially and politically so desirable for them.[11]

Arnold derived from his French sources – in particular Ernest Renan and Henri Martin[12] – an interest in the characteristics of races, in particular the Saxons and the Celts. This particular brand of intellectual racism which was shared by many during the nineteenth century went together with a related interest in phrenology and perhaps did more to prepare the ground for twentieth-century fascism than we are on the whole aware. Arnold, son of 'the Celt-hating Dr [Thomas] Arnold',[13] who understood his own lecture series as an 'attempt at fusion and conciliation' follows Renan in his praise of the cultural achievements of the Celts and conceives of the English as a happy mixture of Saxon and Celtic ingredients. Although he concedes that both Englishmen and Welshmen will have to transform themselves if they want to compete among the European nations, he nevertheless sees the process of cultural unification of Britain as one in which English culture plays the central role. As expected, the language question is in the forefront of his argument, which follows a pattern of imperialist rhetoric of which, to our own shame and detriment, we have seen too much in the twentieth century.

> *Blanc, rouge, rocher, champ, église, seigneur,* – these words, by which the Gallo-Roman Celt now names white, and red, and rock, and field, and church, and lord, are no part of the speech of his true ancestors, they are words he has learnt; but since he learned them they have had a world-wide success, and we all teach them to our children, and armies speaking them have domineered in every city of that Germany by which the British Celt was broken, and in the train of these armies. Saxon auxiliaries, a humbled contingent, have been fain to follow; – the poor Welshman still says, in the genuine tongue of his ancestors, *gwyn, goch, craig, maes, llan, arglwydd*; but his land is a province, and his history petty, and his Saxon subduers scout his speech as an obstacle to civilisation; and the echo of all its kindred in other lands is growing every day fainter and more feeble; gone in Cornwall, going in Brittany and the Scotch Highlands, going, too, in Ireland; – and there, above all, the badge of the beaten race, the property of the vanquished.[14]

As we have seen, Arnold conceives of the propagation of culture as a national task:

> Again and again I have insisted how those are the happy moments of humanity, how those are the marking epochs of a people's life, how those are the flowering times of literature and art and all the creative power of genius, when there is a *national* glow of life and thought, when the whole of society is in the fullest measure permeated by thought, sensible to beauty, intelligent and alive.[15]

It is easy to see why for Arnold, in propagating 'the fusion of all the inhabitants of these islands into one homogeneous, English-speaking whole, the breaking down of barriers between us, the swallowing up of separate provincial nationalities' as a 'natural

course of things', as a 'necessity of what is called modern civili-
sation', the suppression of the Welsh language is an aim of the
first importance in educational politics:

> The sooner the Welsh language disappears as an instrument of the
> practical, political, social life of Wales, the better; the better for
> England, the better for Wales itself.[16]

On the other hand it is equally clear that the language question
has always lain at the heart of any campaign for an independent
Wales. Thus one of the slogans of the 1960s was: 'a nation
without a language is a nation without a heart' ('*cenedl heb iaith
cenedl heb galon*'). Or, as Seamus Deane put it with regard to the
similar problems of Irish writers: 'A place deprived of its speech
is rendered deaf to its traditions.'[17]

'Provincialism, the enemy': Ezra Pound and modernist metropolitan culture

When Ezra Pound came down hard on provincialism in a series
of four contributions to *The New Age* in 1917[18] this was a
continuation of Arnold's argument for a centralized culture. It
was, however, set out with the aggressiveness and one-sidedness
typical of Pound. He saw in provincialism a special combination
of ignorance, lust after uniformity and the will to impose one's
limited view of things on others:

> Provincialism consists in: . . . An ignorance of the manners, customs
> and nature of people living outside one's own village, parish, or
> nation.
> . . .
> Provincialism is more than an ignorance, it is ignorance plus a lust
> after uniformity. It is a latent malevolence, often an active malevo-
> lence.[19]

He saw the spirit of provincialism embodied in Napoleon, 'a
belated condottiere' coming from 'a barbarous island' and
exhibiting 'an idiotic form of ambition which had been civilised
out of his more intelligent, more urban contemporaries'.[20] Above
all he found it in the Prussian nation state ('Deutschland über
alles'), the Junker, and the 'Germano-American "university"
ideal' which he criticized for producing nothing but specialist
scholarship, 'unconnected with life', and therefore not

knowledge of a general and useful kind. In Pound's eyes this is a system which enslaves rather than liberates:

> It is evil because it holds up an ideal of 'scholarship', not an ideal of humanity. It says in effect: you are to acquire knowledge in order that knowledge may be acquired.
> . . .
> The system has fought tooth and nail against the humanist belief that a man acquires knowledge in order that he may be a more complete man, a finer individual, a fuller, more able, more interesting companion for other men.
>
> Knowledge as the adornment of the mind, the enrichment of the personality, has been cried down in every educational establishment where the Germano-American 'university' ideal has reached. The student as the bondslave of his subject, the gelded ant, the compiler of data, has been preached as a *summum bonum*.
>
> This is the bone of the mastodon, this is the symptom of the disease; it is all one with the idea that the man is the slave of the State, the 'unit', the piece of the machine.
>
> Where the other phase of the idea, the slave of the State (i.e. of the emperor) idea has worked on the masses, the idea of the scholar as the slave of learning has worked on the 'intellectual'. It still works on him.[21]

And he adds his own creed, his plea for 'civilisation' which for him is inevitably bound up with the metropolis, ideally the axis Paris–London collapsed into one point or at least connected by the Channel tunnel and a fast train service:

> Fundamentally, I do not care 'politically', I care for civilisation, and I do not care who collects the taxes, or who polices the thoroughfares. Humanity is a collection of individuals, not a *whole* divided into segments or units. The only things that matter are the things which make individual life more interesting.
>
> Ultimately, all these things proceed from a metropolis. Peace, our ideas of justice, of liberty, of as much of these as are feasible, the immaterial, as well as material things, proceed from a metropolis. Athens, Rome, the Cities of the Italian Renaissance, London, Paris, make and have made us our lives.[22]

Pound concludes his argument with a vicious attack on what he sees as a separatist movement in Ulster – in fact a tendency among English liberals and socialists to get rid of Ulster:

> Among the present sub-sectional criers within your Islands I hear no

voice raised on behalf of civilisation. I hear many howling for a literal and meticulous application of political doctrine; for a doctrinaire application, for a carrying *ad absurdum* of a doctrine that is good enough as a general principle. Neither from South Ireland nor from Ulster has anyone spoken on behalf of civilisation, or spoken with any concern for humanity as a whole. And because of this the 'outer world' not only has no sympathy, but is bored, definitely bored sick with the whole Irish business, and in particular with the Ulster dog-in-the-manger. No man with any care for civilisation as a whole can care a damn who taxes a few hucksters in Belfast, or what rhetorical cry about local rights they lift up as a defence against taxes. As for religion, that is a hoax, and a circulation of education would end it. But a nation which protects its bigotry by the propagation of ignorance must pay the cost in one way or another. Provincialism is the enemy.[23]

Cairns Craig has analysed T. S. Eliot's and Edmund Burke's stance as 'writers from the peripheries who offer the core culture an image of itself which, in its flattery, will act as a mask for the writer's own uneasiness about his acceptability within it'.[24] Or, in Tom Paulin's analysis of T. S. Eliot's relationship to English culture, this attitude is proof of the 'outsider's empathy with the heart of a culture'.[25] Pound's élitist, and in its consequences deeply inhumane, argument[26] can also be seen as the ploy of a man from the periphery, from the provincialism of America,[27] striving to set himself up as a magisterial voice in the London of the first and second decades,[28] as some kind of mandarin or pundit in the cultural sphere. It can, therefore, be easily turned against Pound himself. On the other hand, and this is where the importance of Pound's text for the present debate lies, it is basically a magnified and coarsened version of Arnold's argument showing the consequences of tendencies already very much present in Arnold, but perhaps less noticeable under the surface of that more civilized discourse.

The Movement as provincialism: Tomlinson on Larkin and the ensuing debate

The debate about the provinciality of Philip Larkin and the Movement poets is so well known that it need not be retold in detail. It is, however, instructive within the present context because it represents perhaps the first head-on attack on the English core culture itself. Charles Tomlinson's attack on Larkin's 'intense parochialism'[29] was a reaction to the refusal, on the part of Larkin and some other poets who were grouped together as the 'Movement', to place themselves within the mainstream tradition of European culture and acknowledge the achievements of modernism:

> Over forty years ago two Americans and an Irishman attempted to put English poetry back into the mainstream of European culture. The effect of those generations who have succeeded to the heritage of Eliot, Pound, and Yeats has been largely to squander the awareness these three gave us of our place in world literature, and to retreat into a self-congratulatory parochialism.[30]

Indeed, the return of the Movement poets to a 'genuinely English' literary tradition was contemporaneous with, and can perhaps even be seen as a side-effect of, an enormous centralization of British culture in the fifties and sixties.[31] But what Tomlinson objected to was not so much the metropolitan character of much of British culture of that time but the narrowness of vision of these poets. This is the by now famous polemical phrase which has triggered critical reactions from many quarters:

> They seldom for a moment escape beyond the suburban mental ratio which they impose on experience.

'The word suburban', as John Carey has reminded us, 'seems to have stopped meaning suburban in a strictly geographical sense quite early in its history.'[32] If Carey connects the term with demographic developments in the twenties and thirties he is, however, quick to identify its use with an upper-middle-class or intellectualist contempt of a typical set of social values:

> London suburbs of cheap lower-middle class housing spread over much of what had been the Home Counties countryside. This provided a humane solution to the slums and diseases of late Victorian London. The slum dwellers were rehoused in the new suburbs. The typical suburban householder was not a manual worker but a low-paid office worker. The usual generic word for them was 'clerks'. The attitude of the intellectuals and modernist writers of the 20s and 30s towards the 'clerks' and the suburbs was one of

contempt. Eliot's representation of the small house-agent's clerk with one bold stare in the *Waste Land* is typical . . .

The other thing the intellectuals despised the suburbs and clerks for, apart from the fact that they had spoiled the countryside, was that they were philistines. They were only half educated, not having been to public school or universities they were not interested in philosophy or in the fine arts or poetry, or any of the components of the old upper-middle-class culture.[33]

This argument is intended to operate in two ways: on the one hand, it denounces Tomlinson's attack as élitist; on the other, it prepares the way for a revaluation of suburbia and, consequently, the poetry of Philip Larkin:

Is contemporary English poetry suburban poetry? Is Larkin a suburban poet? The answer I think is yes, or largely so, and I should argue not only that it is nothing to be ashamed of, but that the attitude critics like Tomlinson and the Leavises despised as 'suburban' is actually the only sane and honest attitude with which the modern world can be confronted – at any rate by English writers. For one thing, of course, modern man in England is largely suburban man. The great proportion of the public and particularly the reading public lives in suburbs. The limitations that the word suburban is meant to evoke are the real constrictions, the real conditions of life, that the late 20th-century Englishman has to face. A major element in this suburban consciousness is a sense of diminished possibilities; a realisation that life is no longer heroic; an acknowledgment that human existence is both doomed and ultimately futile. That may seem pessimistic, but it is not necessarily so. The task of the poet, in these circumstances, is to evolve, for modern man, an attitude that will allow him to face ultimate futility without ceasing to value life.

There were, of course, other attempts to rescue Larkin's poetry from the charge of provinciality and 'little Englandism' and to assert Larkin's position as realistic and honest, or even as the only one possible.[34] But the drift of Carey's argument serves to obscure the real issue, the charge of 'intellectual laziness of mind adopted as a public attitude and as the framework for an equally provincial verse'.[35] This debate demonstrates also the stability of the dominant meaning of 'provinciality' since Arnold's times as an attitude of mind rather than a geographical or geopolitical term. Seen in its long-term effects this was only the first in a series of attacks on the very heart of English culture, and this alone explains the violent reactions. It angered representatives of the English core culture as much as Stephen Spender did in his address to the Cheltenham Festival of Literature in 1967, when he pronounced that 'the centre of poetic activity in the English language has shifted from London to New York and San Francisco' and then went on to compare the situation of the English writer *vis-à-vis* America with that of the Irish writer *vis-à-vis* England:

> Henry James praised Hawthorne for being a provincial novelist. It is now the turn of English writers to have to consider the problems resulting from what has become the provincial relationship of their island to the central Transatlantic literature in the same language. It is tempting to think of the shift from English to American influence in our century as the swing of the pendulum. But there will be no swing of the pendulum back in our direction. In relation to America, England has become as Ireland was to England. As with Ireland, our danger is of becoming a culture of 'great hatred, little room', acrimoniously clinging to our memories of past greatness climbing down the ladders of the great tradition into exhausted wells.[36]

It is deeply ironic, and no small justification of Tomlinson after almost twenty years, that Hugh Kenner, attentive critic of twentieth-century British culture in all its facets, in a recent book whose very title, *The Sinking Island*, must be anathema to the English literary establishment, should have ruled magisterially: 'Yes, London is no longer the centre of poetry', and that, of all places, he should have come to this conclusion in Charles Tomlinson's garden in rural Gloucestershire.[37]

Centre and periphery: The imperialist matrix

When, in 1972, Alan Brownjohn advocated an attitude of 'healthy and indignant resistance' against the provincialist 'neurosis' wrongly wished upon English poets, he listed some of the stock arguments in this debate only to reject them. The first point to be dismissed was the interrelationship of military, economic and cultural hegemony:

> There is a general, cultural argument which allies supremacy in the arts to military and economic power, and thus establishes the predominance of the United States in poetry as in these other ways. This is a sort of vulgarity which does not require a serious response.[38]

The argument, however, has much wider ramifications than Brownjohn would wish to admit, and it is perhaps no undue digression to review briefly the concepts of centre and periphery as developed in political geography and political science. For while in earlier studies the relationship of core and periphery was used as part of a predominantly geographical model[39] The scope of some of these concepts was greatly extended in the sixties. The emphasis in the centre-periphery model was no longer on spatial relationships but on relationships of values and beliefs and on the power structures through which these are reinforced by the political and cultural élites:

> The central zone is not, *as such*, a spatially located phenomenon. It almost always has a more or less definite location within the bounded territory in which the society lives. Its centrality has, however, nothing to do with geometry and little with geography. The centre, or the central zone, is a phenomenon of the realm of values and beliefs. It is the center of the order of symbols, of values and beliefs, which govern the society . . .
>
> The centre is also a phenomenon of the realm of action. It is a structure of activities, of roles and persons, within the network of institutions. It is in these roles that the values and beliefs which are central are embodied and propounded.[40]

Johan Galtung uses a centre-periphery model arranged in concentric circles – 'a decision making *nucleus*, surrounded by the *center*, which again is surrounded by the *periphery*' (the latter sometimes subdivided further into 'periphery' and 'extreme periphery') and a nine-point scale to calculate relative positions of persons in social systems. Here

> the social center occupies positions that are socially rewarded, and the social periphery positions that are less rewarded and even rejected. In the centre are the topdogs of the society, in the periphery the underdogs.[41]

He later extends all this to cover relationships between nations which, in common parlance, come under the heading of imperialism:

> The world consists of Center and Periphery nations; and each nation, in turn, has its centers and periphery . . . Imperialism will be conceived of as a dominance relation between collectivities, particularly between nations . . .

Imperialism is a relation between a Center and a Periphery nation
so that

(1) there is *harmony of interest* between the *center in the Center*
nation and the *center in the Periphery* nation,

(2) there is more *disharmony of interest* within the Periphery nation
than within the Center nations,

(3) there is *disharmony of interest* between the *periphery in the
Center* nation and the *periphery in the Periphery* nation.[42]

Galtung's attempt to distinguish five separate types of imperial-
ism – economic, political, military, communication, cultural – has
come under critical fire from those who believe that these are
rather facets of one and the same structure of domination. Be
that as it may, what is of interest in this context is precisely the
interconnectedness of political, social and cultural phenomena. It
is clear that in such a relational model individual nations can be
defined in respect to various relationships at the same time.
Taken one step further, the model serves in the analysis of the
internal relationships within a country, as, for example, in
Michael Hechter's *Internal Colonialism: The Celtic Fringe in
British National Development, 1536–1966.*[43] 'Fringe' itself is a
term which presupposes the core–periphery relationship. Again,
it would go far beyond the scope of this chapter to present more
than a summary of the central concepts of Hechter's book and to
point to the two conflicting models which are used to analyse the
relationship of core cultures and minority cultures: on the one
hand, the 'diffusion model of national development', which
posits a general evolutionary process, the levelling of economic
differences through industrialization and acculturation on the
part of the peripheries and therefore, ultimately, the integration
of core and periphery; on the other, 'internal colonialism',
Hechter's own approach, in which the core is seen to dominate
the periphery politically and to exploit it materially so that the
differences betwen core and periphery are not diminished but
heightened by attempts on the part of the periphery to 'reactively
assert its own culture as equal or superior to that of the relatively
advantaged core'.[44] It is, however, clear that relational models of
this kind have explicitly or implicitly become part of the ongoing
debate on regionalism and nationalism.[45]

Colonialism, post-colonialism and beyond:
The example of Seamus Heaney

Terry Eagleton has insisted on the relational character of the concept of nationalism, analogous to that of 'social class', and, therefore, on the real or philosophical difficulties of escaping this matrix in the struggle of a people for self-identity.[46] Seamus Heaney's statements on the politics of Anglo-Irish culture over the years can serve to illustrate the matrix as well as characteristic attempts to overcome it altogether. Heaney's position *vis-à-vis* the centre-periphery model can be traced through five distinct stages which are here grouped in a systematic rather than a chronological way.

First, and this is a rather early phase in Heaney's development, Heaney describes himself as a writer from a cultural periphery who is influenced by the double pull both from the centralist culture and from the regional culture. In this he accepts the imperialist matrix as the inevitable condition of the Anglo-Irish writer.

> To some extent the enmity can be viewed as a struggle between the cults and devotees of a god and a goddess. There is an indigenous territorial numen, a tutelar of the whole island, call her Mother Ireland, Kathleen ni Houlihan, the poor old woman, the Shan Van Vocht, whatever; and her sovereignty has been temporarily usurped or infringed by a new male cult whose founding fathers were Cromwell, William of Orange and Edward Carson, and whose godhead is incarnate in a rex or caesar resident in a palace in London. What we have is the tail-end of a struggle in a province between territorial piety and imperial power.[47]

As regards poetic language, he recognizes a similar predicament to his own in MacDiarmid, whom he sees as labouring under a characteristic form of language consciousness:

> There is an uncertainty about language here, peculiar not just to MacDiarmid, but to others who write generally in English, but particularly out of a *region* where the culture and language are at variance with standard English utterance and attitudes. It can be a problem of style for Americans, West Indians, Indians, Scots and Irish . . .[48]

One typical reaction of the peripheral writer was to take over the value system of the core culture and to play the role assigned to him within that system, – that of the entertainer, who satisfies the core culture's demand for folklore or exoticism. For Heaney this was Dylan Thomas's dilemma:

> It struck me recently just how clear a case of marginalisation Dylan Thomas now appears to be; a case of somebody who accepted the regional forecast even as he seemed to be totally involved with his own weather. His contributions to the BBC . . . are symptomatic of a not irreprehensible collusion with the stereotype of the voluble Taffy. His purely lyric gift was in the keeping of an intelligence insufficiently wary; indeed his was a clear case of a provincial imagination as defined by Patrick Kavanagh: always looking over its shoulder to see if the metropolis was in favour of its subjects and procedures.[49]

A possible antidote against the writer's self-consciousness is, secondly, for the poet to get his bearings, as it were, through myth and language. It is here that Heaney stresses the importance of the poet's rootedness in a particular place and a particular local idiom:

> But I like to remember that Dante was very much a man of a particular place, that his great poem is full of intimate placings and place-names, and that as he moves round the murky circles of hell, often heard rather than seen by his damned friends and enemies, he is recognized by his local speech or so recognizes them.[50]

Similarly:

> [it is this] 'fidelity to the unpromising, unspectacular countryside of Monahan' . . . which makes for Kavanagh's appeal to the majority of Irish people . . . In this case, the local idiom extends beyond the locale itself.[51]

It is precisely through such a faithful adherence to the locale that the work of the regional poet can attain universal significance. Thus Heaney quotes with approval Patrick Kavanagh:

> *Parochialism* is *universal*; it deals with the fundamentals. It is not by the so-called *national* dailies that people who emigrate keep in touch with their roots [but the *local* Irish papers].[52]

Thirdly, Heaney sees as another, and much admired, option for the writer from the periphery Joyce's solution: a self-confident redefinition of the centre–periphery relation:

> For its survival, [talent] has to take thought and be born again, responsible and independent, exposed to the knowledge that while a

literary scene in which the provinces revolve round the centre is demonstrably a Copernican one, the task of talent is to reverse things to a Ptolemaic condition. The writer must re-envisage the region as the original point. [*Stephen Dedalus, Class of Elements, Clongowes Wood College, Sallins, Co. Kildare, Ireland, Europe, The World, The Universe*][53]

Fourthly, Heaney has described a marked shift within the core culture itself which results in a diversified and polycentric cultural scene in England, for which the 'Englands of the mind' of three English poets – Ted Hughes, Geoffrey Hill and Philip Larkin – are symptomatic. The plural form is deeply significant here: 'All three treat England as a region – or rather treat their region as England.[54] Heaney has analysed, as indeed have others, this preoccupation with various 'Englands of the mind' as a crisis of the central English culture:

> I believe they [Hughes, Hill, Larkin] are afflicted with a sense of history that was once the peculiar affliction of the poets of other nations who were not themselves natives of England but who spoke the English language. The poets of the mother culture, I feel, are now possessed of that defensive love of their territory which was once shared only by those poets whom we might call colonial – Yeats, MacDiarmid, Carlos Williams. They are aware of their Englishness as deposits in the descending storeys of the literary and historical past. Their very terrain is becoming consciously precious.[55]

This loss of self-confidence on the part of the representatives of the mother culture has placed them in a position earlier on occupied by the writers from the peripheries:

> I think that sense of an ending has driven all three of these writers into a kind of piety towards their local origins, has made them look in, rather than up, to England. The loss of imperial power, the failure of economic nerve, the diminished influence of Britain inside Europe, all this has led to a new sense of the shires, a new valuing of the native English experience . . .
>
> [Donald Davie's book *The Shires*] is yet another symptom that English poets are being forced to explore not just the matter of England, but what is the matter with England.[56]

The loss of centrality of the former core culture leads Heaney, finally, to assume a reversal of roles between former centre and former peripheries where a cultural rebirth can be achieved only through the powers of the periphery:

Because civilizations are finite, in the life of each of them comes a moment when centres cease to hold. What keeps them at such times from disintegration is not legions but languages. [Greece and Rome are examples.] The job of holding at such times is done by men from the provinces, from the outskirts. Contrary to popular belief, the outskirts are not where the world ends.[57]

How far such a reversal of roles may have gone already can be gauged from Heaney's praise of the achievements of the poet Derek Walcott, a writer from the Caribbean:

There is a magnificence and pride about this art – specifically the art, not specially the politics – that rebukes that old British notion of 'Commonwealth literature': Walcott possesses English more deeply and sonorously than most of the English themselves. I can think of nobody now writing with more imperious linguistic gifts.[58]

It is perhaps safe to assume that Heaney's use of the word 'imperious' is meant as a direct reference to the imperialist matrix, in order to indicate, however, that the roles have changed.

Beyond the centre-periphery model?

The last examples, in particular, show the distance Heaney has travelled. But it is obvious that Heaney is still arguing within the matrix of centre and periphery. The question which arises from all this is: under which conditions may it be possible to move completely beyond this frame of reference? One thing, at least, is clear. A radical change in the political set-up of Europe will be necessary for this to happen. In this respect, then, both the criticism of nationalism and internationalism[59] and the plea for a Europe of the Regions[60] may well point in the right direction.

Notes

1 'The very term "regional novel" is likely to provoke a variety of reactions, ranging from delighted anticipation of pastoral nostalgia to impatience with a presumed lack of centrality. It may, therefore, be useful to begin with a rudimentary distinction between "regional" and "provincial". In current British usage both adjectives denote the non-metropolitan. But whereas "provincial" carries the negative overtones of a culturally impoverished uniformity, "regional" is usually taken as indicating singularity, specific cultural

patterns, distinctive local identity.' (Anthony Mortimer, 'The early regional novel: notes toward a theory', *Anglistentag 1980 Giessen*, ed. Herbert Grabes [Grossen-Linden, Hoffmann, 1981], 211.) 'I am aware that "regional" has changed in recent years from a bad word to a good word, in Canada at any rate...' (Margaret Atwood, Introduction, Margaret Atwood (ed.), *The New Oxford Book of Canadian Verse in English* [Toronto, Oxford University Press, 1982].)

2 Charles Tomlinson, 'The Middlebrow Muse', *Essays in Criticism* 7 (1957), 208–17.

3 Terry Eagleton, *Nationalism: Irony and Commitment*, Field Day Pamphlet No. 13 (Derry, 1988); Fredric Jameson, *Modernism and Imperialism*, Field Day Pamphlet No. 14 (Derry, 1988); Edward W. Said, *Yeats and Decolonization*, Field Day Pamphlet No. 15 (Derry 1988).

4 Matthew Arnold, 'The Literary Influence of Academies' [1864], *Prose Works*, ed. R. H. Super, vol.3 (Ann Arbor, 1962), 241.

5 C. A. Sainte-Beuve, 'Madame de Caylus et de ce qu'on appelle urbanité', *Causeries du Lundi*, III (October 28 1850) (Paris, Garnier, n.d.), 56–77; 'Histoire de l'Académie Française par Pélisson et D'Olivet ...', *Causeries du Lundi*, XIV (19 July 1858) (Paris, Garnier, n.d.), 195–217.

6 'Literary Influence of Academies', op. cit., 244f.

7 Matthew Arnold, *Culture and Anarchy*, Preface [1869], *Prose Works*, ed. R. H. Super, vol.5 (Ann Arbor, 1965), 233.

8 'The Function of Criticism at the Present Time'; cf. *Culture and Anarchy*, 237, also 240, 244f., 249, 252; 'provincialism and loss of totality' (254).

9 'The provincial spirit, again, exaggerates the value of its ideas for want of a high standard at hand by which to try them. Or rather, for want of such a standard, it gives one idea too much prominence at the expense of others; it orders its ideas amiss; it is hurried away by fancies; it likes and dislikes too passionately, too exclusively. Its admiration weeps hysterical tears, and its disapprobation foams at the mouth. So we get the *eruptive* and the *aggressive* manner in literature; the former prevails most in our criticism, the latter in our newspapers. For, not having the lucidity of a large and centrally placed intelligence, the provincial spirit has not its graciousness; it does not persuade, it makes war; it has not urbanity, the tone of the city, of the centre, the tone which always aims at a spiritual and intellectual effect, and not excluding the use of banter, never disjoins banter itself from politeness, from felicity. But the provincial tone is more violent, and seems to aim rather at an effect upon the blood and senses than upon the spirit and intellect; it loves hard-hitting rather than persuading.' Ibid., 249).

10   Matthew Arnold, *Culture and Anarchy*, Preface, op. cit.

11   From Arnold's first report as inspector of schools about the use of English in Wales (1853), *Prose Works*, ed. R. H. Super (Ann Arbor, 1962) vol.3, 500.

12   Ernest Renan, 'La Poésie des races celtiques', *Essais de morale et de critique* (4th edn. Paris, 1889); Henri Martin, *Histoire de France depuis les temps les plus reculés jusqu'en 1789* (4th edn. Paris, 1865) bk. I, bk. XX.

13   Cf. R. H. Super, Notes to Matthew Arnold's 'On the Study of Celtic Literature', *The Prose Works of Matthew Arnold*, ed. R. H. Super, vol.3; *Lectures and Essays in Criticism* (Ann Arbor, 1962), 501.

14   Matthew Arnold, 'On the Study of Celtic Literature [1865/66]', *Prose Works*, ed. R. H. Super, vol.3 (Ann Arbor, 1962), 292f.

15   *Culture and Anarchy*, Ch. 1: 'Sweetness and Light', 212.

16   Ibid., 296f.

17   Seamus Deane, 'Irish Writing and Irish Nationalism', in Douglas Dunn (ed.), *Two Decades of Irish Writing: A Critical Survey* (Cheadle, Carcanet, 1975), 8.

18   'Provincialism the Enemy', *The New Age* 12, 19, 26 July; 2 August 1917. rpt. *Selected prose: 1909–1965*, ed. William Cookson (London, Faber, 1973), 159ff.

19   Ibid.

20   Ibid., 169–72.

21   Ibid., 160–62.

22   Ibid., 169–72.

23   Loc. cit.

24   Cairns Craig, 'Peripheries', *Cencrastus*, No. 9 (1982), 7.

25   Tom Paulin, 'Introduction', *Ireland and the English Crisis* (Newcastle-upon-Tyne, 1984), 19.

26   'Civilisation is made by men of unusual intelligence ... And what man of unusual intelligence in our day, or in any day, has been content to live away from, or out of touch with, the biggest metropolis he could get to?' 'Provincialism the Enemy', op. cit. 172.

27   Hugh Kenner sees internationalism – Pound's 'world citizenship' (cf. *Patria Mia* [1909]) – as a prerequisite for modernism and therefore dismisses writers as Virginia Woolf, William Carlos Williams and William Faulkner as 'provincial writers', or 'regionalists' (Hugh Kenner, 'The origins of modernism', Lecture at madison/Wisconsin 1983). For an exposition of H.D.'s 'dynamic middle position between the internationalism of Pound and the nationalism of Williams', see Susan Stanford Friedman 'Exile in the American grain: H.D.'s diaspora', in D. Collecott (ed.), *H.D. Special Issue: Agenda*, 25, 3/4 (1987/88), 27–50.

28   On the role of London as the epitome of the metropolis for modernism see Malcolm Bradbury, 'London 1890–1920', Malcolm

Bradbury and James McFarlane (eds.), *Modernism 1890–1930*, Pelican Guides to European Literature (Harmondsworth, Penguin, 1976, rpt. 1981), 172–90.

29 Charles Tomlinson, 'The Middlebrow Muse', *Essays in Criticism* 7 (1957), 208–17.

30 Charles Tomlinson, 'Poetry Today', *The Pelican Guide to English Literature*, vol.7 (1967), 458–9.

31 Cf. Krishan Kumar, 'The social and cultural setting', in Boris Ford (ed.), *The New Pelican Guide to English Literature*, vol.8: *The Present* (Harmondsworth, Penguin, 1983, rpt. 1986), in particular the section on 'The nationalization of culture', 25–38. In July 1945, Maynard Keynes had defined two main aims for the Arts Council: 1. 'To decentralize and disperse the dramatic and musical and artistic life of this country, to build up provincial centres and to promote corporate life in these matters in every town and country'; 2. 'To make London a great artistic metropolis'. The Arts Council itself forty years later recognized that while Keynes's second aim 'has been achieved, to a degree even beyond what he envisaged ... his first aim ... has not been adequately realized'. The verdict returned by the Arts Council on forty years of its own work is a sobering one: 'we live as two artistic nations – London and everyone else.' (*The Glory of the Garden: The Development of the Arts in England* [London, The Arts Council, 1984].)

32 John Carey, 'Suburban poetry and the death of myth', Jürgen Schläger (ed.), *Anglistentag: 1983 Konstanz* (Giessen, Hoffmann, 1984), 7–21.

33 Ibid., 8f.

34 Cf. the debate on Tomlinson's article in *Essays in Criticism* (1957), notably the contributions by Ronald Hayman and F. W. Bateson; John Press, 'Provincialism and tradition', *Rule and Energy: Trends in English Poetry Since the Second World War* (Oxford, Oxford University Press, 1963), 90–122; Alan Brownjohn, 'A view of English poetry in the early 'seventies', in Michael Schmidt and Grevel Lindop (eds.), *British Poetry Since 1960* (South Hincksey, Oxford, Carcanet, 1972) 240–49.

35 Charles Tomlinson, 'Poetry today', in Boris Ford (ed.), *The Pelican Guide to English Literature,* vol.7 (Harmondsworth, Penguin, 1967), 458f.

36 Stephen Spender, 'Uncommon poetic language', *Times Literary Supplement,* 5 October 1967, 939f.

37 Hugh Kenner, *The Sinking Island* (London, 1989), 254.

38 Alan Brownjohn, 'A view of English poetry in the early 'seventies', in Michael Schmidt and Grevel Lindop (eds.), *British Poetry Since 1960: A Critical Survey*, op. cit., 240.

39 Cf. e.g. Walter Christaller, *Die zentralen Orte in Süddeutschland*

(Jena, Fischer, 1933); Derwent Whittlesey, *The Earth and the State: A Study of Political Geography* (New York, Holt, 1944).

40 Edward Shils, 'Centre and periphery', *The Logic of Personal Knowledge*, Essays Presented to Michael Polanyi (London, Routledge, 1961), 117f.

41 Johan Galtung, 'Foreign policy opinion as a function of social position', *Journal of Peace Research* 1 (1964), 206–31; cf. 207f.

42 Johan Galtung, 'A Structural Theory of Imperialism', *Journal of Peace Research* 8 (1971), 71–107; cf. 81–3.

43 Michael Hechter, *Internal Colonialism: The Celtic Fringe in British National Development*, 1536–1966 (London, Routledge, 1975; rpt. 1978).

44 Ibid., 10.

45 It provides a frame of reference for some recent numbers in the Field Day Pamphlets series on 'Nationalism, Colonialism and Literature', e.g. for Fredric Jameson's homology of colonialism and modernism via the concept of spatiality in no. 14 (Fredric Jameson, *Modernism and Imperialism*, 11), or Terry Eagleton's contrast of a 'negative collective identity' [of an oppressed group] and 'a positive particular culture without which political emancipation is probably impossible' in no. 13 (Terry Eagleton, *Nationalism: Irony and Commitment*, 16), or Edward Said's attempt to rank William Butler Yeats among the 'great nationalist artists of decolonization and revolutionary nationalism' in no. 15 (Edward W. Said, *Yeats and Decolonization*, 8).

46 Terry Eagleton, *Nationalism: Irony and Commitment*, Field Day Pamphlet no. 13 (Derry, Field Day Theatre Company, 1988).

47 Seamus Heaney, *Preoccupations: Selected prose 1968–1978* (London, Faber, 1980), 57.

48 Ibid., 196.

49 Ibid., 13.

50 Ibid., 136f.

51 Ibid., 137–9.

52 Ibid., 137, no source given.

53 Ibid., 13.

54 Ibid., 150.

55 Ibid., 150f.

56 Ibid., 169.

57 Seamus Heaney, 'The regional forecast', [1986] in R. P. Draper (ed.), *The Literature of Region and Nation* (Basingstoke, 1989), 10–23; cf. 22.

58 Seamus Heaney, 'The murmur of Malvern', *The Government of the Tongue* (London, 1988), 26.

59 Cf. e.g. Tom Nairn, 'Internationalism: a critique', *The Bulletin of Scottish Politics*, no. 1 (Autumn 1980), 101ff.; Cairns Craig,

'Nation and history', *Cencrastus*, no. 19 (Winter 1984), 13–16; Colin Crouch and David Marquand (eds.), *The New Centralism: Britain Out of Step in Europe?* (Oxford, Blackwell, 1989).

60 Cf. e.g. Christopher Harvie, *Against Metropolis*, Fabian tract 484 (London, Fabian Society, 1982).

II
THE PLACES OF CONTEMPORARY POETRY

4

'The centre cannot hold': Place in modern English poetry

JEREMY HOOKER

1

Kim Taplin's *Muniments*, first published in 1987, is a sequence of ten poems about places in Britain where nuclear bases have been sited. As Kim Taplin says in her introductory note, the title has two meanings: 'Muniments are defences'; they 'are also documents preserved as evidence of privileges or rights'. She continues:

> In these ten places, as elsewhere, people have added their lives to the humus of history; and the chronicles, books, essays and articles they wrote about such places and themselves, were muniments in that sense. The writing of any local history tacitly asserts the rights of man and the privilege of being human. There are records, too, of the local plants and animals: they also have their muniments.[1]

Kim Taplin's aim in the sequence is 'to bring home that all places are home'. To this end, she uses documents in which the voices of past generations may be heard, and presents details of the natural world, thus bringing together history and nature, as they interact in the making of place:

> Flint axe, copper dagger, Roman brooch:
> always people there between fen and breck
> alongside the rabbits and plovers and curlews
> scratching the sand.
>
> Ground they broke with plough or spade
> the Celts called breck; but breck goes back
> and to Saxons the word meant waste,
> where water is brackish and bracken grows.[2]
>
> ('III: Lakenheath, Suffolk')

The art of *Muniments* is a naming art; the poems are rich in place names, names of people, creatures and things, words which – as Stuart Piggott has written of David Jones's – are 'radio-active with history'.[3] 'What does it mean to talk about *our country*?' Kim Taplin asks. Her implicit answer is that it means to talk about particular localities, using the words proper to them; as, once, in High Wycombe,

> The grey herb southernwood that has so many names,
> lad's love, that Edward Thomas wrote about,
> they knew as *kiss-i-my-corner*, wren was *tickety*,
> and creeping saxifrage was *thread-of-life*.[4]

Or rather that is what it used to mean. In earlier times places were 'bounded'. But now:

> Kingdoms are boundless
> from the air.
> The Port Way is blocked
> and at night the camp is lighted like a city,
> a disinfected, cultureless, bland city
> of a newer empire.[5]

Muniments uses the constituents of place, human and non-human, natural and historical and mythological, to speak in defence of place, and in defence of the earth. The sequence defends an idea of 'home' against the 'newer empire'. A Christian feminism informs its ecological vision. This is a poetry of the 1980s, which responds to the nuclear threat and the environmental crisis, seen as having a common source in man's abuse of his power. It has affinities with the writings of Gary Snyder and Wendell Berry in America. But it also extends an English poetic tradition, native and modernist, of defending place against placelessness, home against empire, the local and particular against bland megalopolitan uniformity. It is not surprising, therefore, that the main literary influences on Kim Taplin's style in this sequence should be Edward Thomas and David Jones. It is a central tenet of my argument that thinking and feeling about place in English poetry since Wordsworth responds, in different ways and to different degrees, to the pressures of an imperial and increasingly secular civilization, and that within this history, affecting modern English poetry at a deep level, the First World War was a decisive critical phase.

Both Edward Thomas, writing in the 'native' English tradition, the tradition of Hardy and Wordsworth, and David Jones, a modernist in the line of Eliot and Joyce, were profoundly influenced as poets by the First World War. Indeed, there is a sense in which the war could be said to have made them into poets. The war quickened Edward Thomas's sense of *his* England, as distinct from Great Britain: an England with a timeless spirit, which released the patriotic sentiment of his poetry. Unlike Edward Thomas, David Jones survived the war, and in his first writing, *In Parenthesis* (1937), which he began ten years after the end of the war, he developed his idea of 'the genuine tradition of the Island of Britain',[6] which he had experienced with his fellow soldiers in the trenches.

A love of the local and particular has been manifest in English poetry since its beginnings. It certainly is not a modern phenomenon. It was, however, intensified by the First World War, partly in the form of patriotic sentiment, and partly as a defence against the destructive, mechanical forces unleashed by the war. In a larger perspective, within which the First World War is viewed as a critical episode of the historical period beginning with the Industrial Revolution, poetry of place may be seen as frequently bearing an equivocal relationship to empire. Broadly speaking, there is a distinction to be made between poets such as Kipling and Newbolt on the one hand, and Edward Thomas and David Jones on the other, on the grounds that the former constructed ideas of 'home' which colluded with imperial designs, while the latter, in speaking in defence of place, implicitly defended all marginal or peripheral places against all imperial or megalopolitan centres. But this is to speak too generally and too simply, since particular poems of place often reveal complex mixed feelings. Thus *Muniments*, like the poetic tradition to which it belongs, is fed by a nostalgia which both energizes its defensive action on behalf of '*our country*', and projects idealized images of England in the past. In this, it shows the tendency of English poetry since Wordsworth to be at once radical and conservative, and celebratory and critical. Indeed, lyrical poetry – and even the modern epic poems with which I shall be concerned are, primarily, lyrical – might be described as the art of mixed feelings. In what follows I hope to outline some useful ideas about place in relation to centre and periphery in modern English poetry, but also to disrupt beguiling historicist abstractions by attending to what particular poems actually say.

2

In about 1932, Helen Thomas, widow of Edward, began to visit Ivor Gurney who was incarcerated in the City of London Mental Hospital at Dartford, Kent. On her second visit she took with her Edward Thomas's ordnance maps of Gloucestershire, which was Ivor Gurney's beloved county.

> This proved to have been a sort of inspiration for Ivor Gurney at once spread them out on his bed and he and I spent the whole time I was there tracing with our fingers the lanes and byways and villages of which Ivor Gurney knew every step and over which Edward had also walked. He spent that hour in revisiting his home, in spotting a village or a track, a hill or a wood and seeing it all in his mind's eye, with flowers and trees, stiles and hedges, a mental vision sharper and more actual for his heightened intensity.[7]

It is difficult not to see an ironic significance in this poignant episode, in which, as Helen Thomas says, Ivor Gurney had Edward 'as companion in this strange perambulation'. Edward Thomas had died for his country, for the very earth[8] on which he had walked, rather than for the nation state. It would be melodramatic to say that Ivor Gurney had lost his sanity in the same cause, since Gurney had shown signs of mental instability before the war. But the war certainly affected the local attachment which became, ultimately, his greatest source of torment.

There are plenty of place names in Edward Thomas's poems, but Thomas is a less 'local' poet than Gurney. The England of Edward Thomas's poetry is largely what he described, with significant ambiguity, as 'the south country': 'yet is this country, though I am mainly Welsh, a kind of home, as I think it is more than any other to those modern people who belong nowhere'.[9] In weighing Edward Thomas's sense of the south of England as 'a kind of home' we have also to take into account his displacement, as a Welshman born in a London suburb. His ambiguous sense of belonging is partly what distinguishes Edward Thomas's modernity, as it affected the self-consciousness which tormented him as a man and stultified much of his descriptive prose, but contributed to the strength of the poetry. To say this is partly to acknowledge that Edward Thomas's poems are about his quest for identity, more than they are about specific places. But it also has a bearing on his 'Englishness'. To my mind, Edward Thomas published no more poignant book than *This England*, the wartime anthology in which he 'wished to make a book as full of English character and country as an egg is of meat',[10] and in which he included two of his own poems, under the name Edward Eastaway. These poems, 'Haymaking' and 'The Manor Farm', picture a timeless, essential, rural England. This is an ideal which, in his prose, Edward Thomas had contrasted with present-day 'Great Britain, the British Empire';[11] an England which he could worship, and die for.

There are affinities but also marked differences between Edward Thomas's and Ivor Gurney's sense of place. Gurney was essentially a praise-poet, and the object of his praise was Gloucestershire. This was at once his county, where he walked by day and night and in all weathers, and an ideal England, redolent of Roman and Elizabethan continuities; ground of good fellowship, and of musical and literary tradition. Gurney formed the attachment in boyhood, but as he saw his home area from the trenches, it became his sole spiritual resource:

> O does some blind fool now stand on my hill
> To see how Ashleworth nestles by the river?
> Where eyes and heart and soul may drink their fill.[12]

To this country Gurney felt called to be poet, musician, even Psalmist:

> I must play tunes like Burns, or sing like David,
> A saying-out of what the hill leaves unexprest,
> The tale or song that lives in it . . .[13]

Gurney's 'saying-out' of the landscape, in which he plays or sings what it does not express, complements his sense of history, by which he sees the past present in the land.

After the war, and largely as a result of his conviction that England had not 'honoured' him for his services as soldier and poet, the unity of Gurney's vision, the wholeness of his sense of place, suffered a terrible fracturing. This is evident in 'The Mangel-Bury',[14] which begins:

It was after war; Edward Thomas had fallen at Arras –
I was walking by Gloucester musing on such things
As fill his verse with goodness . . .

Gurney (for the speaker is obviously the poet himself) says that
he came upon a straw-thatched heap of mangel-wurzels, which
'looked as part of the earth heaped up by dead soldiers'. The
image suggests the poet's mental and emotional distress, which is
not dealt with directly in the poem – and the poem is more
moving for that – but is compounded by his neurotic obsession
with 'cleanness', revealed in his description of waiting for a
chance to shift the vegetables – 'right to be rolled and hefted / By
a body like mine, soldier still, and clean from water'. Gurney
then describes the farmer who assented to his request to help
him, and the outcome of their work together:

His was the thick-set sort of farmer, but well-built –
Perhaps, long before, his blood's name ruled all,
Watched all things for his own. If my luck had so willed
Many questions of lordship I had heard him tell – old
Names, rumours. But my pain to more moving called
And him to some barn business far in the fifteen acre field.

The conclusion exposes a state of total non-communication. The
farmer assents silently to the poet's request; there is no conversa-
tion between them, and the silence is filled by the poet's fantasies
about the farmer's 'blood's name' and 'lordship' over the land.
The farmer is an ideal figure in Gurney's vision of his country;
there is nothing in the poem to suggest that the ideal exists
outside Gurney's mind.

'The Mangel-Bury' may be contrasted with Edward Thomas's
'As the team's head brass'.[15] The latter is a poem charged with
suspense – the suspense of the lovers' disappearance into the
wood; the suspense of the break from ploughing, during which
the poet and the ploughman talk with each other; the suspense of
the poet's mental state as he wonders whether he will go to
France; the suspense of England at war. The poem is filled with
images of violence, and the poet is associated with 'the fallen elm'
among whose boughs he sits. Every detail of the poem
contributes to its extraordinary tension and poise – which is the
poise of a moment of unity before it all falls apart. Most remark-
able of all is the complete mutual understanding of poet and

ploughman as they share their thoughts in a common language.

In 'The Mangel-Bury', by contrast, the poet is by 'my pain to more moving called' and the farmer 'to some barn business', and the word 'called' is touched with a sense of vocation, as if to say pain is Gurney's calling. He is here a poet with a dream of human communion, in a land where the present is linked by noble blood ties with the past, but he is starved (and perhaps now incapable) of actual human contact. Gurney's predicament, however, is not an isolated one, to be ascribed solely to his psychotic condition. The difficulty of finding a language of shared meaning is common to English poetry in the twentieth century. It is a difficulty that poetry of place usually attempts to overcome, but of which it may also be a symptom. Being rooted in place can evidently be a most unsettling experience.

3

The image of the securely 'rooted' poet does not hold good for any major English poet since the eighteenth century, and those who at first sight seem most rooted – John Clare and Thomas Hardy – prove on examination to owe the intensity with which they apprehend place to their deracination. Not that 'uprooting' is in every case the same. It was however the experience of change in their native landscapes that intensified the sense of place for Clare and Hardy and distanced their sensitized vision from conventional ways of seeing. Neither was either geographically or socially 'stationary',[16] as Gilbert White was. Their close observation never lost the child's-eye view, in which it originated, but rather than being primarily observers of localities that were stable within the seasonal round, they were poets who saw place tragically, in terms of social change and personal loss. Pain in Clare's later apprehension of his native ground is very similar to pain in Gurney's, and is the obverse of possessive ecstasy. Hardy tempered a similar sense of loss with philosophy and his story-teller's art. His tragic vision was strongly influenced by the secularization of thought in his time, by the enchantment of nature as it became, largely through Wordsworth, an object of displaced religious sentiment, and by subsequent disenchantment, as evolutionary ideas divested nature of any kind of religious purpose.

Even in 'Domicilium',[17] his earliest known poem, and his most

Wordsworthian, Hardy separated the human from the non-human:

> Wild honeysucks
> Climb on the walls, and seem to sprout a wish
> (If we may fancy wish of trees and plants)
> To overtop the apple-trees hard by.

Even in youth, apparently, Hardy did not 'fancy' volition in the natural world. 'Domicilium' is accordingly a rudimentary expression of his mature vision, in which – in 'At Castle Boterel' for example – there is an absolute division between human feeling and the primeval land. The home ground of 'Domicilium' is identified with human experience, with time and change. The wild has been 'settled' by the Hardy family, but while wildness still exists at the back of the house, settlement has meant change. Hardy's earliest landscape is thus a frontier between the human and non-human worlds. The poem is also a form of imaginative orientation: from this place the landscapes of a large part of Hardy's subsequent writings can be seen. This is not to suggest that the poem is in any way premonitory; it does however indicate that, from the beginning, 'rootedness' in Hardy was a condition of change and potential conflict.

In *Tess of the d'Urbervilles*, Hardy, contemplating the plight of the young Durbeyfields at the mercy of their feckless parents, retorts angrily upon Wordsworth:

> Some people would like to know whence the poet whose philosophy is in these days deemed as profound and trustworthy as his song is breezy and pure, gets his authority for speaking of 'Nature's holy plan'.[18]

The quotation is from 'Lines Written in Early Spring', in which Wordsworth sets his grief at 'What man has made of man' against his affirmation of a link between Nature and the human soul.

For Hardy, there was no such link. He certainly identified people with places, as, in 'Poems of 1912–13', he identified Emma with the 'red-veined'[19] Cornish rocks, but the link is in human consciousness and feeling only – which exist entirely alone in the universe. The breaking of the Wordsworthian link between Nature and the human soul, which Hardy was of course not alone in effecting, or suffering, has had a profound influence upon subsequent English poetry concerned with landscape or place. It may be seen, for example, in a highly politicized version, in W. H. Auden's idea of the exile or spy, or wanderer among strangers, in the Pennine landscape of his early poems. The break between man and nature, and matter and spirit, also motivates the use of myth by D. H. Lawrence and Ted Hughes and other writers, by which the imagination is energized by contact with the elemental cosmos. What does the break not entail? When W. B. Yeats wrote, in 'The Second Coming', 'Things fall apart; the centre cannot hold', he was using the word in its sense, known in ancient Ireland and elsewhere, of the cosmic centre that binds together earth and heaven and hell. When the world is centreless, place in poetry becomes a locus of the most deep-reaching concerns.

4

David Jones uses quotations from Y Gododdin, an early Welsh epic poem attributed to the sixth-century poet Aneirin, on the title pages of the seven parts of In Parenthesis. His explanation of his choice of fragments of Y Gododdin as 'texts' is 'that it connects us with a very ancient unity and mingling of races; with the Island as a corporate inheritance, with the remembrance of Rome as a European unity'.[20] That unity, in fact, is the subject not only of In Parenthesis but also of David Jones's later writings, The Anathemata and The Sleeping Lord. In political terms, the idea represents a destabilization of English hegemony over the Celtic peoples within the British Isles, a hegemony first established by the Tudors, and its replacement by a different cultural order, Christian and composed of a 'unity and mingling of races'. The alternative order is first shadowed in the writings by the folk-life of the English and Welsh soldiers in the trenches of In Parenthesis.

The relation between centre and periphery is of first importance in the writings of David Jones. It is presented in In Parenthesis as a relationship between opposing but connected forces, which are identified with mechanistic regimentation on the one hand, and the ancient cultural unity re-created by the soldiers on the other. In the later writings the emphasis falls increasingly on an opposition between what David Jones calls 'our placeless cosmopolis'[21] and his idea of sacramental place.

The part played by empire, however, obviates a simple pattern of oppositional thought. For empire is 'robbery',[22] as St Augustine said, but the Roman Empire was also an historical condition of the Christian order. Hence the significance of the tension between Rome and its heterogeneous peoples, and between Rome and Jerusalem, in 'The Wall' and 'The Fatigue' and 'The Tribune's Visitation'. David Jones was well situated to understand the mind of the man who is emotionally attached to place, but adheres with his reason to imperial force and order, which create the 'placeless cosmopolis'. This is the position of the Tribune in 'The Tribune's Visitation', who is both a military spokesman for empire, and a type of the poet with a local allegiance, who belongs to an imperial civilization. (Hence the echoes of Wordsworth and Shakespeare in the poem.)

> I too could weep
>   for these Saturnian spells
> and for the remembered things.
> . . .
> No dying Gaul
>   figures in the rucked circus sand
> his far green valley
>   more clear than I do figure
> from this guard-house door
>   a little porch below Albanus.
> . . .
>   But you are soldiers
> with no need for illusion
> . . .
>   you *shall* understand
> the horror of this thing.[23]

David Jones's understanding of his own position, as a man belonging to a centralist and imperialist state but with a primary attachment to one of the peripheral cultures – the Welsh – whose identity it suppresses, gave him profound insights not only into the conflict between place and placelessness, and centre and periphery, but also into the conflict as it helps to shape the English poetic mind. David Jones celebrated and commemorated 'the remembered things'. He was a praise-poet, like Aneirin, but his poetic strength derived from his struggle to fulfil that role, in a society far more complex than Aneirin's, and inimical to his sacramental vision.

Basil Bunting, also, in *Briggflatts*, invokes the poets of the Old North:

> I hear Aneurin number the dead and rejoice,
> being adult male of a merciless species.
> ...
> Clear Cymric voices carry well this autumn night,
> Aneurin and Taliesin, cruel owls
> for whom it is never altogether dark, crying
> before the rules made poetry a pedant's game.
> Columba, Columbanus, as the soil shifts its vest,
> Aidan and Cuthbert put on daylight,
> wires of sharp western metal entangled in its soft
> web, many shuttles as midges darting;
> not for bodily welfare nor pauper theorems
> but splendour to splendour, excepting nothing that is.[24]

Briggflatts is 'an autobiography', and one of its shaping emotions is remorse for 'love murdered'; but it, too, is a praise poem, and its design embraces far more than personal experience, 'excepting nothing that is'. Or rather Bunting, like David Jones, begins with the actually loved and known, with imagination working through sensory experience, and binds the personal into a design that is a shape of universal order:

> Tortoise deep in dust or
> muzzled bear capering
> punctuate a text whose initial,
> lost in Lindisfarne plaited lines,
> stands for discarded love.[25]

Bunting's 'initial' in *Briggflatts* 'stands for discarded love', and the poem, by analogy with the sixth-century Lindisfarne Gospels,[26] is a text which weaves the whole of creation into its design. Nor does it except cruelty or defeat. On the contrary, *Y Gododdin* is a foundation of the Celtic literary tradition because it commemorates a defeat and praises the defeated, and Bunting in *Briggflatts*, partly through the figures of the mason and of Eric Bloodaxe, raises a monument to a lost love and a lost independent kingdom, Northumbria, which nevertheless achieve a transcendent existence through loss. And, as both David Jones and James Joyce associated the unity of form and content they sought in their writings with the Book of Kells, so Bunting chose the Lindisfarne Gospels as an analogue of his poem.

But the illuminated book from Northumberland is more than an analogue of the form of *Briggflatts*, as Northumberland is more than a poetic 'setting'. The poet, like the medieval illuminator and the mason, is one who shapes, and, like the musician, he makes a shape with sounds. Thus land and sea are wrought within the poem, as corresponding verbal textures and sounds. And for Bunting, shape and music incarnate universal order, in which waves carve the 'text' on the skerry and

> Silver blades of surf
> fall crisp on rustling grit,
> shaping the shore as a mason
> fondles and shapes his stone.[27]

Bunting was a Quaker; he had 'no use for religion as church forms or as believing as historical fact what are ancient parables', but he did 'believe that there is a possibility of a kind of reverence for the whole creation'.[28] In this sense, *Briggflatts* is a religious poem.

So are *Four Quartets* and *The Anathemata*, which are also responses to the crisis of English national identity in the context of the Second World War. All three poems – the major English long poems of the period since 1944 – are also crucially concerned with places – for example, East Coker, Little Gidding, Briggflatts, medieval London, Wales – which are, in one way or another, spiritual 'centres'. In this sense, all are responses, not only to a national crisis but to the catastrophe overtaking a civilization, about which Yeats wrote in 'The Second Coming'. In so far as the three poems are political – and all are, *Briggflatts* least overtly – their politics have to be understood in terms of a primary religious concern. It is as a locus of the root meaning of 'religion' – that which binds together man and God, and the whole creation – that place embodies ideas of the centre in these poems.

5

The idea of absolutely binding relationships is a key concept in English Romantic poetry. It is ultimately by virtue of the link between Nature and the human soul that Wordsworth sees the poet as a carrier of 'relationship and love'.[29] But if for

Wordsworth and Coleridge the ties that bind are a fundamental source of values, others see 'bonds' negatively. Thus, for William Blake, the idea is associated with imagery of snares and prisons and chains and manacles, all of which are products of the human mind. Blake's great theme is slavery: man's determination, manifested in the science and philosophy, the wars and industrial revolution, of Blake's time, to enslave himself and others to a destructive social and mental system. And Blake's whole effort is to oppose slavery with imagination, which liberates and enlarges and is the divine faculty in man. Despite the social criticism of Goldsmith and Crabbe and Clare, rural poetry of place in England tends towards a radical conservatism, as one might expect given the relative stability of country life, the inclination of rural writers to look to the past rather than the future for their images of an ideal society, and the regularity of elemental rhythms. Not suprisingly, therefore, Blake, a great urban poet, has had few followers in England, few, that is, who have perceived, with an equivalent intelligence, the city as a mental construct. Blake saw the beginnings of urban industrialism as an inherently unstable process, born in the mind of the authorities of State and Church, and imposed upon the human and natural 'materials'. But the process of making, will-driven and utilitarian and exploitative, is also a process of unmaking, vulnerable alike to nature and the mind's capacity to see differently.

Roy Fisher has strong affinities with European and American modernist writers and painters and musicians (for he is also a jazz musician, and jazz has affected his sense of poetic sequence and improvization), but these should not be allowed to obscure the fact that the main influence upon his way of seeing is Blake.

A debt to Blake may be less evident in *City*, first published in 1961, than in some of Fisher's later work, notably *A Furnace* (1988), but *City* is an intensely visual poem, in which the poet both perceives and suffers the instability of his urban world:

> Brick-dust in sunlight. That is what I see now in the city, a dry
> epic flavour, whose air is human breath. A place of walls made
> straight with plumbline and trowel, to dessicate and crumble in
> the sun and smoke. Blistered paint on cisterns and girders, crack-
> ing to show the priming. Old men spit on the paving slabs, little
> boys urinate; and the sun dries it as it dries out patches of

damp on plaster facings to leave misshapen stains. I look for
things here that make old men and dead men seem young.
Things which have escaped, the landscapes of many childhoods.

Wharves, the oldest parts of factories, tarred gable ends rearing
to take the sun over lower roofs. Soot, sunlight, brick-dust; and
the breath that tastes of them.[30]

What the poet ('I') sees here are not things or surfaces alone, but
an interaction of the sun's creative and destructive power and
human making; and the latter is present both as 'breath', with its
associations of 'epic' and subjective imagining ('the landscapes of
many childhoods'), and structures that are decaying. The child-
hood landscapes that have 'escaped' are as much 'things' of the
city as are walls and cisterns and girders and paving slabs. But
the former cannot be seen, and the poet as perceiver is at least as
baffled by his urban environment as he is its seer.

It could be said that there are two modes of perception in City:
that of the poet who 'reads' the visible, perceiving – often surre-
alistically – fugitive meanings; and that of the poet as critical
observer of the civic authorities' 'power of will'.[31] The problem
with this view of Fisher's way of seeing in City, however, is that
it makes it more deliberate, less anarchic, and less involuntarily
voyeuristic, than it is. For all its wit and clarity, there is a kind of
bewildered, numbed pain in City. The cause of this seems to be
the poet's refusal or inability to escape from an alienating envir-
onment, in which he is not free to exercise his will or
imagination, but is a victim of his own disconnected vision,
which is shaped by the power behind the rigid yet decaying struc-
tures of his urban world. 'Most of it has never been seen',[32]
Fisher says of Birmingham, which, significantly, he does not
name. In more ways than one, City enables us to 'see'
Birmingham as it has never been seen before.

Returning to the same 'materials' some twenty-five years later,
in A Furnace, Fisher was no longer under the constraint that
afflicted him when writing City. At the risk of foreshortening
Fisher's poetic development, I would guess that the freedom arose
from his subsequent discovery of what to do, imaginatively, with
his Blakean perception that: 'The human mind makes the
world'.[33] A Furnace is dedicated 'To the memory of John Cowper
Powys'. Powys, perhaps the greatest follower of Blake in the

twentieth century, exercised his belief in the creative and destructive power of the human mind, with its aboriginal freedom rooted in Nature. In his Preface to A Furnace, Fisher acknowledges his debt to Powys's writings 'for such understanding as I have of the idea that the making of all kinds of identities is a primary impulse which the cosmos itself has; and that those identities and that impulse can be acknowledged only by some form or other of poetic imagination'. Fisher also draws attention to Powys's description, in Atlantis, of a lost poem in which landscape is 'superimposed upon landscape rather than rhythm upon rhythm', and says that he, too, in A Furnace, has 'set one landscape to work with another'.[34] The landscapes are those of Birmingham and north Staffordshire. Thus the 'world' of A Furnace is in more than one sense larger than that of City, not only because it opens on a wider tract of country, with roots in history and myth, but also because nature in the poem is a source of imaginative energy, transformation, and renewal. This is the crucial difference between A Furnace and City, in which imagination is without power in the world it perceives. The freeing and empowering of imagination in Fisher's writing also owes something to a Powysian sense of cosmic dualism, especially in respect of life-in-death and death-in-life. It is rather the disconnection between the living and the dead, and between mind and matter, that makes City a static poem, with the poet as observer frozen in his alienated state, whereas A Furnace is magically (in the Powysian sense) fluid and metamorphic. Fisher certainly pays his debt to Powys in the poem; and he does so by *using* ideas learned from Powys, and in a poetic language that is quite unlike Powys's.

As Blake brought his imagination to bear upon the urban industrial world in an early phase of its development, exposing the mental system by which Church and State tyrannized over their human subjects, so Fisher in A Furnace reveals the collapse of that system, in the decaying edifice of Birmingham and other cities, and the subsequent release of a sense of imaginative possibility, and the natural energy that empowers it. Here, as it were, the sun that interacts with the brick-dust in City, has become the Heraclitean fire that flames out in a myriad identities. The result of urban decay is horrific, as 'Puritan materialism dissolves its matter', leaving 'glassy metaphysical void'.[35] In this aspect of its

vision, *A Furnace* has affinities with another Blakean long poem
of recent time, George Oppen's *Of Being Numerous*. But Fisher
shares with Powys a sense of ancient images that are not dead:
'*like dark-finned fish embedded in ice/they have life in them that
can be revived*'.[36] The presence of imaginative power in the land-
scape releases the lyricism that has always been an element in
Fisher's writing, but now achieves a magical quality comparable
to Geoffrey Hill's and Basil Bunting's renderings of their
'charged' landscapes. For example, in Fisher's presentation of an
area of north-west Staffordshire connected with the composition
of *Gawain and the Green Knight*:

> Gradbach Hill, long hog's back
> stretching down west among taller hills
> to the meeting of Dane river
> with the Black Brook skirting its steeper side,
> the waters joining
> by Castor's Bridge, where the bloomery
> used to smoke up into the woods
> under the green chapel;
> the hill,
> stretching down west from Goldsitch
> a mile from my side yard, shale measures
> on its back and the low black spoilheaps
> still in the fields,
> darkens to an October sunset
> as if it were a coal,
> the sun sinking into Cheshire, the light
> welling up slow along the hillside,
> leaving the Black Brook woods
> chill, but striking for a while
> fire meadows out of red-brown soft-rush,
> the dark base, the hollows, the rim swiftly
> blackening and crusting over.[37]

6

Roy Fisher uses myth not as a system of belief, but with a sense
of its imaginative function, and its provisional and historical
nature, as if to say, '*This* is what the human mind does, *this* is
what it is capable of'. Whether there is a more mystical dimen-
sion to *A Furnace* is open to question,[38] just as it is in Powys's

writings too. Ted Hughes, by contrast, commits himself to the truth of myth, invoking non-human powers, and abstracting a pattern of conflict between Man and Earth from the long history of human occupation of the land. Thus, he describes his landscape in *Remains of Elmet* in this way:

> The Calder valley, west of Halifax, was the last ditch of Elmet, the last British Celtic kingdom to fall to the Angles. For centuries it was considered a more or less uninhabitable wilderness, a notorious refuge for criminals, a hide-out for refugees. Then in the early 1800s it became the cradle for the Industrial Revolution in textiles, and the upper Calder became 'the hardest-worked river in England'.
>
> Throughout my lifetime, since 1930, I have watched the mills of the region and their attendant chapels die. Within the last fifteen years the end has come. They are now virtually dead, and the population of the valley and the hillsides, so rooted for so long, is changing rapidly.[39]

Hughes envisages the whole process of place-making in the Pennine valley as a form of warfare, in which man overcame earth's primal energy in order to make himself a slave. Now,

> The upturned face of this land
> The mad singing in the hills
> The prophetic mouth of the rain
>
> That fell asleep
>
> Under migraine of headscarves and clatter
> Of clog-irons and looms
> And gutter-water and clog-irons
> And clog-irons and biblical texts
>
> Stretches awake, out of Revelations
> And returns to itself.[40]

In this perspective, industrial history in the valley is seen as a dream of slaves, from which the land is awaking. The slavery is self-imposed, through religion and industry, and its fruit is death. Hughes describes an elemental erasure of the human ('A slow fire of wind / Has erased their bodies and names',[41]) which leaves 'This harvest of long cemeteries'. In Blakean fashion, *Remains of Elmet* enacts a myth of war between two religions: that of the mills 'and their attendant chapels', and the aboriginal religion of the Earth Goddess. Thus the Chapel is 'Mount Zion's gravestone slab'. It shuts out its enemy, Nature; but Nature cannot be excluded, and a cricket lodged in the wall has men 'Riving at the religious stonework/With screwdrivers and chisels'. To Hughes, this religion, with its hysterical fear of Nature and worship of death, reduces the sacred to a miserable portion of its divine substance:

> And Christ was only a naked bleeding worm
> Who had given up the ghost.[42]

Christ's counterpart in *Remains of Elmet* is the Ancient Briton, son of the Earth Mother, but imprisoned in the womb that bore him, as the people of the valley are imprisoned in ideas that divide them from the creation they are part of:

> We needed that waft from the cave
> The dawn dew-chilling of emergence,
> The hunting grounds untouched all around us.
>
> Meanwhile his pig-headed rock existed.
> A slab of time, it surely did exist.
> Loyal to the day, it did not cease to exist.
>
> As we dug it waddled and squirmed deeper.
> As we dug, slowly, a good half ton,
> It escaped us, taking its treasure down.
>
> And lay beyond us, looking up at us
>
> Labouring in the prison
> Of our eyes, our sun, our Sunday bells.[43]

Donald Davie is an older contemporary of Ted Hughes, from the same area of Yorkshire, but Davie's 'north' is quite different from Hughes's. As Davie writes in 'Westmorland', from *The Shires*:

> It's a chosen
> North of the mind I take my bearings by,
> A stripped style and a wintry.[44]

This ' "north" is a metaphysical or else a metaphorical place',[45] which derived from Davie's Baptist childhood and upbringing in Barnsley. It is a source of the 'Calvinist aesthetic' of 'simplicity, sobriety, and measure',[46] that Davie has written about since his return to Christianity, in his fiftieth year, but which names qualities that he sought as a poet from the start.

The landscape of Davie's *Essex Poems* is a landscape of the 'north', in the metaphysical or metaphorical sense. Thus, the 'bare Epiphany' of 'January' –

> In a field between
> The Sokens, Thrope and Kirby, stands
> A bare Epiphany.[47] –

is, so to speak, an epiphany more by virtue of its northern bareness than of the Essex location and place-names. Indeed, although Davie has a strong geographical imagination, he is not especially a poet of place; his concern is less with particular localities than with the national culture. More specifically, his subject in *Essex Poems* is death – as personal loss, and as the 'death' that he sees afflicting the nation. In *Thomas Hardy and British Poetry*, Davie writes:

> Facing (and out-facing) death is as necessary in socialist Britain as in capitalist America or communist Russia; and there, in the fact of death and the term it sets to all our exertions, is the place where we escape at last the attentions of the bureaucrats, the philanthropists, and the moulders of opinion, and need the hard rigidity which only monumental art can give us.[48]

There are poems in *Essex Poems* about the death of Davie's father, and the death of his close friend, Douglas Brown, and other deaths, but the whole sequence could be described as 'deathfearing', by analogy with Davie's later *To Scorch or Freeze* (1988), in which 'god-fearing' is the shaping emotion. Place in *Essex Poems* is closely associated with death, as Davie faces loss and the prospect of death, and looks for 'the hard rigidity which only monumental art can give', in a world of flux. The choice that surfaces in a number of poems is between Christianity and the 'peace' of art.

Davie moves between lyricism and a more didactic mode, depending on whether he is quarreling primarily with himself or with his nation, whose 'failure' he is bitterly aware of:

> Landscapes of supertax
> Record a deathful failure
> As clearly as the lack
> Of a grand or expansively human
> Scale to the buildings of Ilford.[49]

The sequence expresses what Davie was to assert in *Thomas*

Hardy and British Poetry: 'Our poetry suffers from the loss, or the drastic impoverishment, of the traditional images of celebration'.[50] The 'deathful failure' of his nation is manifested in an acute linguistic constriction of which Davie is aware in himself. As he wrote in another poem of the time:

> Death, an authentic subject,
> Jaime Sabinès has
> Dressed with the yew-trees of funereal trope.
> It cannot be his fault
> If the English that I feel in
> Feels itself too poor
> Spirited to plant a single cypress.
> It is afraid of showing, at the grave-side,
> Its incapacity to venerate
> Life, or the going of it. These are deaths,
> These qualms and horrors shade the ancestral ground.[51]

Unlike the Mexican poet, Jaime Sabinès, Donald Davie feels that his language, 'the English that I feel in', is 'too poor/Spirited' – too weak in a sense of the sacred – to venerate either life or death. Davie's response to this predicament was initially to seek in exile, in America, the great non-human spaces that inspired in him a sense of awe, and, a little later, to return to the Christian religion. Davie thus enriched his language from traditional sources of feeling and dogma, enlarging his capacity to venerate, to the point at which, in *To Scorch or Freeze*, he could join his modern voice to the 'god-fearing' Psalmist's songs.

7

Edward Thomas described Richard Jefferies, in relation to his native Wiltshire, as 'the genius, the human expression, of this country, emerging from it, not to be detached from it any more than the curves of some statues from their maternal stone'.[52] The idea that man is 'Earth-born' is an ancient one. Mircea Eliade writes:

> Even among Europeans of today there lingers an obscure feeling of mystical unity with the native Earth; and this is not just a secular sentiment of love for one's country or province, nor admiration for the familiar landscape or veneration for the ancestors buried for generations around the village churches. There is also something quite

different; the mystical experience of autochthony, the profound feeling of having come from the soil, of having been born of Earth in the same way that the Earth, with her inexhaustible fecundity, gives birth to the rocks, rivers, trees and flowers. It is in this sense that autochthony should be understood: men feel that they are *people of the place*, and this is a feeling of cosmic relatedness deeper than that of familial and ancestral solidarity.[53]

Thomas's image of Jefferies may be related to Eliade's definition of 'autochthony'. It is an attractive image, and it expresses a powerful feeling, as other artists and writers also testify – Ivor Gurney, for example, though Gurney apprehended his relatedness to place not in terms of sculptural form, but of musical and poetic expression. The image is a myth, of course. But I do not want to end these reflections on 'place' in modern English poetry by asserting that the image is *only* a myth. In any case, there is, as David Jones says, myth that 'proposes for our acceptance a truth more real than the historic facts alone discover'.[54] The feeling that Thomas identified with Jefferies, and Gurney expressed in *his* sense of being Gloucester-born, is part of the answer to Kim Taplin's question: 'What does it mean to talk about *our country*?' It means to have that feeling, or a similar one. But it is evident, I think, that the image of the writer as 'the genius' of his country, emerging like a statue from its 'maternal stone', is *also* a myth. Jefferies, who said that in order to know a place, 'It is necessary to stay in it like the oaks',[55] was not 'a stationary man', like Gilbert White. Much of Jefferies's writing about Wiltshire was retrospective, and written elsewhere. More significantly, his acute sense of seeing was heightened by the passionate intellectual and spiritual quest that separated him from nature. In concluding these reflections, I want to affirm the many diverse *uses* of place by different poets – and of course, I have considered only a few, partially, here. But I want also to suggest that, in English poetry of place since Wordsworth, 'the mystical experience of autochthony', or some sense of it, where it occurs, relates to the disruption of the other sense of love of country, and veneration for buried ancestors, that Mircea Eliade describes. That is to say, the enchantment of place in modern English poetry owes a significant debt to the poet's disenchantment with the national or imperial culture. Or, to put it another way, the failure of central binding relationships – between poetry and patriotism, and between the past and the present, the living and the dead – has put great pressure on particular places as the locus of *all* meaning. Where modern English poetry has renewed itself from 'peripheral' regional or local sources, it has usually been in response to disintegration and emptiness at the 'centre' of the culture, rather than from poets simply drawing nourishment from the ground where they 'stay', like the oaks.

Notes

1 Kim Taplin, *Muniments* (London, Jackson's Arm, 1987), 3. The sequence was reprinted in Kim Taplin's *By the Harbour Wall* (Petersfield, Enitharmon Press, 1990).

2 Ibid., 9.

3 Stuart Piggott, 'David Jones and the past of man', *Agenda*, David Jones Special Issue, Autumn–Winter 1973–4, 62.

4 'IV: High Wycombe, Buckingshamshire', *Muniments*, 11.

5 'II: Upper Heyford, Oxfordshire', ibid., 8.

6 David Jones, *In Parenthesis* (London, Faber, 1963), x.

7 Helen Thomas, *Time & Again* (Manchester, Carcanet, 1978), 111–12.

8 ' "Do you know what you are fighting for?" He stopped, and picked up a pinch of earth. "Literally, for this." He crumbled it between finger and thumb, and let it fall.' Eleanor Farjeon, *Edward Thomas: The Last Four Years* (London, Oxford University Press, 1958), 154.

9 Edward Thomas, *The South Country* (London, Dent, 1932), 7.

10 Edward Thomas (ed.), *This England* (London, Oxford University Press, 1915), note.

11 *The South Country*, op. cit., 75.

12 'Above Ashleworth', *Collected Poems of Ivor Gurney* (Oxford, Oxford University Press, 1982), 53.

13 'Larches', ibid., 132.

14 *Collected Poems of Ivor Gurney*, op. cit., 163

15 *The Collected Poems of Edward Thomas* (Oxford, Oxford University Press, 1981), 108–109.

16 See Gilbert White, *The Natural History of Selborne* (1788), *passim*.

17 Thomas Hardy, *Selected Poems* (Harmondsworth, Penguin Books, 1978), 51–2.

18 Thomas Hardy, *Tess of the d'Urbervilles* (Harmondsworth, Penguin Books, 1978), 61–2.

19 'The Going', Hardy, *Selected Poems*, op. cit., 370.

20 *In Parenthesis*, op. cit., 191–2.

21 David Jones, *The Dying Gaul* (London, Faber, 1978), 58.

22 Cited by David Jones in *The Anathemata* (London, Faber, 1952), 85.

23 David Jones, *The Sleeping Lord* (London, Faber, 1974), 52–4.
24 Basil Bunting, *Briggflatts* (London, Fulcrum Press, 1966), 31–2.
25 Ibid., 21.
26 In view of Basil Bunting's years in Persia and his deep interest in Persian culture, the following comment by an art historian is of particular interest: 'an ornamental page from the Lindisfarne Gospels is as richly inventive and exciting as a fine Persian carpet'. Michael Gough, *The Origins of Christian Art* (London, Thames and Hudson, 1973), 191.
27 *Briggflatts*, op cit., 36.
28 Dale Reagan, 'Basil Bunting obiter dicta', in Carroll F. Terrell (ed.), *Basil Bunting: Man and Poet* (Maine, The National Poetry Foundation, 1980), 271.
29 Preface to *Lyrical Ballads* (1802).
30 Roy Fisher, *Poems 1955–1987* (Oxford, Oxford University Press, 1988), 20.
31 op. cit.
32 Ibid., 23.
33 Robert Sheppard, *Turning the Prism: An Interview with Roy Fisher* (London, Toads Damp Press, 1986), 13.
34 Roy Fisher, *A Furnace* (Oxford, Oxford University Press, 1986), vii. See John Cowper Powys, *Atlantis* (London, Macdonald, 1954), 336.
35 *A Furnace*, op. cit., 35.
36 Ibid., 12. The quotation is from John Cowper Powys, *Maiden Castle* (London, Macdonald, 1966), 167.
37 *A Furnace*, op cit., 10.
38 'I think we should at least pause to ask if *A Furnace* does not arrive, finally, at a heterodox mysticism. Is its aim to annul the natural fact of death? To offer a prospect of transcendence?' Andrew Crozier, 'Signs of Identity: Roy Fisher's *A Furnace*', *PN Review* 83, 32.
39 Ted Hughes, *Remains of Elmet* (London, Faber, 1979), prefatory note.
40 'The Trance of Light', ibid., 20.
41 'Walls', ibid., 33.
42 'Mount Zion', ibid., 82.
43 'The Ancient Briton Lay Under His Rock', ibid., 84.
44 Donald Davie, *Collected Poems* (Manchester, Carcanet, 1990), 269.
45 Donald Davie, *These the Companions* (Cambridge, Cambridge University Press, 1982), 19.
46 Donald Davie, *A Gathered Church* (London, Routledge & Kegan Paul, 1978), 25–6.
47 Davie, *Collected Poems*, op cit., 139.
48 Donald Davie, *Thomas Hardy and British Poetry* (London, Routledge & Kegan Paul, 1973), 182.

49   'Thanks to Industrial Essex', Davie, *Collected Poems*, op cit., 145.
50   Davie, *Thomas Hardy and British Poetry*, op. cit., 72.
51   'Epistle. To Enrique Caracciolo Trejo', Davie, *Collected Poems*, op.
     cit., 164.
52   Edward Thomas, *Richard Jefferies: His Life and Work* (London,
     Hutchinson, 1909), 1.
53   Mircea Eliade, *Myths, Dreams and Mysteries* (London, Collins
     Fontana Library, 1968), 165.
54   David Jones, *The Anathemata*, op. cit., 124.
55   Richard Jefferies, 'Meadow Thoughts', *The Life of the Fields*
     (London, 1884).

Further reading

Davie, Donald, *Thomas Hardy and British Poetry* (London, Routledge
   & Kegan Paul, 1973).
Davie, Donald, *Under Briggflatts* (Manchester, Carcanet, 1989).
Fietz, Lothar, Hoffmann, Paul and Ludwig, Hans-Werner (eds.),
   *Regionalität, Nationalitat und Internationalität in der zeitgenöss-
   ischen Lyrik* (Tübingen, Attempto Verlag, 1992).
Galbraith, Iain (ed.), *Britische Lyrik der Gegenwart*. Eine zweisprachige
   Anthologie (Mainz, E. Weiss, 1984).
Heaney, Seamus, *Preoccupations* (London, Faber, 1980).
Hooker, Jeremy, *Poetry of Place* (Manchester, Carcanet, 1982).
Hooker, Jeremy, *The Presence of the Past* (Bridgend, Poetry Wales Press,
   1987).
Jones, Peter and Schmidt, Michael (eds.) *British Poetry Since 1970: a
   critical survey* (Manchester, Carcanet, 1980).
Longley, Edna, *Poetry in the Wars* (Newcastle upon Tyne, Bloodaxe
   Books, 1986).
Matthias, John, *Reading Old Friends* (Albany, State University of New
   York Press, 1992).
Smith, Stan, *Inviolable Voice: History and Twentieth Century Poetry*
   (Dublin, Gill and Macmillan, 1982).

5

Prints of Wales: Contemporary Welsh poetry in English

M. WYNN THOMAS

1

What exactly is Wales's current position on the cultural map of
Britain? This is a particularly sensitive question for those writers
from the territory (country?/principality?/region?) who write in
English, because they find themselves and their words entangled
in a skein of conflicting answers. Wales is, for some, a separate
cultural entity centred not on a distant London but on its own
distinctive concerns. This view is most convincingly advanced by
those who value the Welsh language as the great preservative of
difference, a language whose irreducible foreignness would be
difficult for any outsider to deny. But the very existence of Welsh
not only as a living language but as a continuing active element
in Wales-wide culture has been seriously jeopardized by the
general indifference or hostility to it of the English-speaking
majority of the Welsh population. The mind-set of that majority
is made visible, some would say, on the rooftops of south Wales
that, as Peter Finch has acidly noted, 'point [their] aerials at the
Mendip hills'.[1] These aerials are the compass needles of contem-
porary Wales, pointing steadily towards the magnetic pole of
popular culture which is of course located in England. They are
also pointers to the political outlook of a people whose anti-
devolution vote in 1979 and subsequent loyalty to a
London-based system, in spite of the 'smashed south' (in John
Tripp's words)[2] that was the result of the Thatcher years, proved
them to be still unreconstructed British centralists at heart.

2

Although English-language writers in Wales have, over the last fifteen years, been on the whole unwilling to align their poetry to these aerials, they have also by and large been reluctant to point their poems clearly in any alternative direction. This is especially true, although to varying degrees, of those poets (Bush, Curtis, Davies, Minhinnick, Pugh, etc.) who came to prominence during this period. The generation gap between them and their seniors was made vividly clear when R. S. Thomas published *Welsh Airs* in 1987.[3] In this collection he reprinted many fierce, uncompromisingly committed political poems from the sixties, poems that lamented, lacerated and lambasted a supine people. Engaging as they very directly did with specific issues – the decline of the language, immigration, the tourist invasion, the Investiture – these seemed yesterday's tired poems to some of the young Turks of the eighties.

When Robert Minhinnick came to do a bit of lambasting of his own, it was the sixties generation, which had given itself such tiresomely Welsh airs, that he singled out for attack. Ridiculing what he saw as their 'psychedelic cultural optimisms',[4] their misty-eyed reference to remote Welsh history, their cliché-trove of romantic images, their gung-ho nationalism and their psychological hang-ups about their monolingualism, he claimed that poetry in Wales had at last come of age in his own time. The political maturity of this body of work was evident, he added, in its scrupulous determination to allow the unglossed details of contemporary life to enter the poem and to speak for themselves.[5] Minhinnick revealed that one of his heroes was the late John Tripp, an early admirer of R. S. Thomas and callow imitator of his political rhetoric, who turned during the seventies from his original fustian to writing cynically observant poems about the seedy physical and cultural landscape of his native south Wales.[6] Tripp was, without doubt, a significant transitional figure, and Minhinnick was shrewd to spot it. Tripp's 'Connection in Bridgend', for instance, could be seen as one of the seminal poems of the eighties. Stuck in the bus café 'I watch/nothing happening in Bridgend' – nothing in particular that is, or nothing perhaps but serendipitous particulars. Genially bemused by their lack of interconnection (what are the Pakistanis doing here, the Sikhs, the Chinese?), he savours his sandwich a philosophical bite at a time and concludes 'We are in it/together, until the last buses go out.'[7] A bus station is I think an appropriate setting for an Anglo-Welsh poem of the eighties – a period when, I shall shortly be suggesting, several leading poets were intent on catching a society in transit. And Tripp's acceptance (weary but kindly in his case) of a merely coexistential and contingent togetherness existed throughout the decade in creative tension with various versions of settled belonging.

One definition of such belonging is of people 'keep[ing] house in a cloud of witnesses'.[8] The Welsh poet Waldo Williams's celebrated image is a reminder of the astonishing amount of creative energy that has been invested by Welsh writers and intellectuals, from D. J. Williams to Raymond Williams and from Dylan Thomas to Dafydd Elis Thomas, in attempts to imagine community. This is not the place to explore the vast socio-historical hinterland of the idea – to enquire into the internal relationships between it and alienation, to consider it as a species of nostalgia, to discriminate between the rural and the industrial, the progressive and the reactionary forms of the phenomenon, etc. – relevant though all this undoubtedly is to the Welsh case. To keep the concept manageable and focused, it will be convenient to keep that trope of the house in mind, a trope whose centrality to Anglo-Welsh culture could be traced way back to Dylan Thomas's 'Fern Hill' and Vernon Watkins's 'Returning to Goleufryn'.[9]

3

When he gave up the care of his last parish, R. S. Thomas retired from remote Aberdaron to a 400-year-old cottage in the neighbouring peninsular countryside of Llŷn In 1988 the cottage entered his poetry as the equivalent of Yeats's tower – a fastness for an imagination besieged by the aggressively uncongenial world of contemporary Wales. Here his soul could select its own society, then close the door. The cottage 'remembered centuries of Welsh tenancies' and 'was a sounding-box in which the sea's moods made themselves felt'.[10] Sea (as synecdoche for nature) and history – taking his bearings from these formidable co-ordinates, Thomas was able to mount a contentious campaign

against the creep of Anglicization, while steadily producing great
religious poetry which has significant, though hidden, social
aspects. However, having found strong (but independent-minded)
allies among pro-nationalist Anglo-Welsh poets of the late sixties
and early seventies, R. S. Thomas exerted by contrast a signifi-
cant negative influence on the generation of the eighties. Younger
English-speaking poets raised in post-industrial south Wales
objected to the absolutist terms and tone in which Thomas
excluded them from Welshness. The endlessly vexed question of
the appropriate language for modern belonging was raised even
in Thomas's 'native' area of Llŷn – not by new English settlers
but by Welsh-speaking youngsters as reported in a poem by
Christine Evans. Evans, who was raised in England but married
into a Welsh-speaking family and 'converted' to the indigenous
culture, found her guilt at teaching English literature to local
youngsters was itself perplexed by their reaction. Manon, 'riding
a name out of myth', finds in this her second language the native
idiom of her young imagination, claiming 'she heard no echoes,
never sang/in her own language'.[11]

Having left her native Cardiff to settle in the old family home in
rural Cardiganshire, Gillian Clarke would at first sight seem to
have ended up during the eighties in a situation broadly parallel to
that of R. S. Thomas. Her 'Cofiant' (modelled on a uniquely Welsh
form of memorial volume which is a cross between biography and
selected writings) is full of the aura and mystique of houses that
literally carry the fingerprint of the past, that are layered with
memories and are genealogies rendered in stone.[12] She has a
particular interest in tracing her own line of descent as maker
through the female line of her family. Her memorable 'Letter From
a Far Country' memorializes the women of the past in densely
textured terms produced by interweaving anger at their restricted
roles, appreciation of the way they patiently mended the fabric of
domestic life, and qualified admiration for their selfless service.[13]
The experience of social embeddedness that Clarke has gained
partly through her sense of solidarity with the historical life of
women in a particular place obviously sets her apart from
Thomas, while her emphasis on the unappreciated creativity of
ordinary work unexpectedly brings her close to those many male
Welsh writers, such as Duncan Bush ('Navvies'),[14] who have
responded to the post-industrial age of technology by elegizing the

passing of the heroic age of labour. She connects again with R. S. Thomas, though, through her conviction that, being Welsh and a woman, she is doubly bound (in the name of both conscience and art) to keep her distance from much that centrally concerns writers in England. Her style of handling what, from a British 'establishment' perspective, might appear to be her marginalized status is instructively different from Dannie Abse's way of dealing with a related situation. Abse, who enhanced his international (and internationalist) reputation during the eighties, has always thrived on a carefully fostered image of being the eternal outsider. A Jew in Wales, Welsh in England, a doctor amongst writers and a writer amongst doctors, Abse has used his poetry not, like Clarke, to find a home in a specific social and natural landscape, but rather to create a living space for his imagination by constantly playing one of his identities off against another.[16] It seems appropriate that he divides his time between a house in London and one in the Vale of Glamorgan, as if his absence from the one were always implicit in his presence at the other.

4

Abse's paradoxical commitment to the provisional and his long-standing cultivation of non-alignment as an art form, may well have provided younger writers (like Tony Curtis)[17] over the past decade with a mature model of suppleness to set against the perceived rigidities of an earlier 'committed' generation. But before we examine what might be termed 'the new freedom' (or perhaps 'the new pragmatism'), attention must be paid to the work of two poets, Tony Conran and Jeremy Hooker, who for more than two decades have been the major cultural theorists of English-speaking Wales. Conran has written a poem about visiting the cottage on Skye where Sorley MacLean lives 'among the presentative past of his people', and about the fern he brought away with him to Wales:

> Rock. And a great music.
> Apprehension
> Of the fern resonating
> To the taut scansion
> . . .
> Of that ground.[18]

The idea of poetry as mediating community (Skye as 'voiced' by MacLean), and of a poem as being a 'tryst' (here the means of bringing Conran into intimate social communion with MacLean) – these are two important concepts for Conran and they play an important part both in his theorizing and in his creative work. Believing modern Anglo-American writing to be vitiated by the Romantic cult of individualism, which elevates artistic sensibility above general social experience, Conran has found an alternative model for poetry in the great Welsh poems from the sixth century to the present which he published in translation in 1966.[19] According to Conran, the key artistic forms of this literature, both ancient and modern, are forms of collective experience: so, for instance, the 'praise tradition' consists of poems that embody, in the idealized person of the eulogized subject, values that inform and sustain a whole society. On this reading, poetry becomes an important social ritual, a bonding ceremony, and Conran has written interestingly about the ritualistic arts, relating poetry both to dance and to stylized forms of worship.[20]

That impressive public poetry can be generated by this theory was proved when Conran wrote an elegy for the Welsh guardsmen killed at Bluff Cove during the Falklands/Malvinas war. Using the short, seven-syllable line of the classical Welsh *cywydd* form and modelling both his narrative and his archaically stylized diction on a great sixth-century poem (*Y Gododdin*) mourning a tiny Welsh war-band wiped out by a giant enemy force, Conran fashioned a powerful modernist elegy, sensitively balanced between admiration of the soldiers' courage and anger at their being first Thatcher's dupes and then her victims.[21] Informing the whole poem is an awareness of how the whole episode at Bluff Cove was the culmination of decades of systematic dismantling of Welsh industry, and of centuries during which soldiers recruited from poverty-stricken Wales had been used by England as the expendable shock troops of empire. Elsewhere in his poetry Conran has successfully fused the public and the personal modes, as in the 'gift poem' he presented, on behalf of the Welsh people, to Pedro Perez Sarduy, a poet from Cuba. The poem, modelled on the *llatai* convention from classical Welsh tradition, aims to 'speak / . . . Of the Welshness of Wales / Now, on this spot'.[22] And indeed all Conran's poetry is an attempt to construct a poetry in English that will be uniquely and inalienably Welsh *not* by virtue of transitory instances of pseudo-*cynghanedd* (the kind of assonantal and consonantal patterning that many Anglo-Welsh poets go in for, believing it to be somehow intrinsically Welsh), or through a limiting obsession with Welsh subjects, but by virtue of a grammar – of literary forms, syntax and discourse – that corresponds to the deep structure of an old, distinctively Welsh 'civilization'.

A similar preoccupation with what differentiates Anglo-Welsh literature from English writing has been central to the work of Jeremy Hooker, a poet from Southampton whose long stay at Aberystwyth sensitized him to both the potential and the plight of Welsh culture. As well as exploring suggestive parallels between Anglo-Welsh poetry and 'the poetry of place' in Ireland, Scotland, the regions of England and parts of the United States, Hooker has persuasively argued that Welsh writing in English has its own socio-cultural *Gestalt* – that certain literary forms and conventions occur and recur both in Welsh-language and in English-language writing because they correspond to underlying social configurations that are constants in the culture.[23] By demonstrating this while still patiently attending to the quiddity of a whole range of contemporary Anglo-Welsh poets, Hooker has done much to create a generous sense of a separate, single, but internally diversified, world of Anglo-Welsh writing. Particularly struck by the egalitarianism that characterized both traditional Welsh-speaking culture and the now dying culture of Welsh industrial society, Hooker has noted a corresponding, un-English emphasis on shared experience in the poetry. For him, typical Anglo-Welsh genres include the portrait poem (most notably evident in John Ormond's sympathetic studies of individuals from the working village of Dunvant where he grew up, but also a feature of the work of Roland Mathias, Mike Jenkins and many others); the poem that (in the work of Bush, Curtis, Mike Jenkins, Mathias, Minhinnick, etc.) almost guiltily speaks for those in society who have no voice; poetry variously deriving from what Minhinnick has called a 'violent need to praise';[24] the poetry of memory; and highly crafted poems that are at once literary artefacts and social objects (Hooker cites works by Leslie Norris, John Ormond and Christopher Meredith). Even landscape is turned by Anglo-Welsh poets into a subtle language for the expression of social feeling, as Hooker points out by

contrasting the isolated and self-divided Edward Thomas's poems
with the nature poetry of a Ruth Bidgood who is 'more settled in
her place, and more interested in permanent features than in
using it to reflect inner states'.[25] And a rapt sense of the vision-
ary company of living forms informs Jean Earle's 'Woollen Mill'.
One of the most perfect poems of the last fifteen years, it reminds
one both of the social mysticism of Waldo Williams and the
cosmic mysticism of Henry Vaughan – with the latter irresistibly
brought to mind when Earle wondrously remembers two fish left

> On the window sill – and they burned light.
> Drew it into their stillness
> Like a great cry. Blinding silver.[26]

5

Living in Brynbeidog cottage, Llangwyryfon, Hooker always felt
an otherness in the very landscape around him which he wanted
to honour, but could not, in his own English tongue.[27] His
sympathy with Anglo-Welsh writers was, therefore, founded on
the feeling that they were insiders condemned nevertheless to be
eternal outsiders in Wales, rather like him. This, however, was
precisely the view of their situation that several of the eighties
generation impatiently rejected. They saw their poems as taking
the full stress of life in post-industrial Wales. A striking case in
point is that of Robert Minhinnick, some of whose best poems
have been about breakdown, in the psychological, social and
cultural realms. His preferred way of dealing with it is not to
moralize but to exploit, in livid language and through convulsive
spurts of anapaestic rhythm, the vividness of experience that an
exploded mental or social order produces. With its combination
of high-risk, polychromatic images and desolate subject-matter,
his poetry is like the iridescent rainbow-stain of oil on a derelict
garage floor. Dissatisfied with the subtly nuanced, ruminative
tone that dominated Anglo-Welsh poetry for a period,
Minhinnick has turned back for his models to Dylan Thomas and
to the early, thirties, work of Alun Lewis and Glyn Jones. By
playing with what, referring to derelicts, he has called 'the
gelignite of experience',[28] Minhinnick allows 'the yeast of fear'[29]
to work in his imagination. By refraining from generalizing

comment, he aims to let his poems 'take their colour and depth from the actual minutiae of the crises they confront.'[30]

In his poem, 'The House', Minhinnick significantly sees himself not as cohabiting with a comforting past, but as having to match himself against the house's fifty years:

> I must establish my own
> Permanence. For territory is not
> Bought or sold but fought over. [31]

His reaction to the more presumptuous of the claims of Welsh history is encapsulated in these phrases. A similarly rebellious spirit of self-assertion works itself out in rather different terms in Tony Curtis's writing, even though he (again like Minhinnick) still strongly and unsentimentally feels the counter-attraction of a vanished way of life, sensitively honoured in several fine poems about the death of his father. The two inclinations, outwards and backwards, are beautifully harmonized in 'Lines at Barry' where Curtis remembers that his grandfather had, in his time, also struck out on his own, when he ventured to row all the way from Fishguard to Barry in search of work. Recalling the adventure involves, for Curtis,

> this drawing from memory of lines
> where, steely-silver, what we are now
> touches everything that made us,
> and is dangerous, and shine.[32]

This sense of the past as an unpredictable potency within the present is consistent with Curtis's general sense of modern life as being constantly vivified by risk.

Curtis is conspicuously a poet of the new freedom, refusing to be tied to a particular place, always seemingly on the wing from form to form and from Dyfed to Vermont to wherever next. Indeed in his writing travel is as much metaphor as fact. In 'Trains', for instance, he declares that

> people can talk on trains:
> capsule between poles of the familiar rooms
> . . . words like wheels measure distances.[33]

There is a part of him that comes alive only in transit, that is exhilarated by its own restlessness and is proud of its tough-minded knowledge that the world at large 'is made by accidents'. But there is another part that is attracted to a countervailing stability. Of the two speakers, male and female, in 'Field of wheat', the former sees a naked violence everywhere in the landscape while the latter works it all into a specifically localized pattern of love.[34] Clearly Curtis's poetry is a continuation of this dialogue, as instanced in 'Families' where the scratching, scurrying, frenetically breeding creatures in the attic (bats, rats?) represent 'a dirt, a life' that keeps up a literally running commentary on loving family life. 'Our words build walls, bridges', while 'they travel the night'.[35] But in his poems Curtis's words also travel the night, breaking through walls and crossing boundaries not in an effort to reach a final destination but in an attempt to learn the necessary arts of modern survival.

Although for Curtis Wales is, in one sense, the family home, the familiar territory where his travels begin and end, in another sense it is itself a country in transit. Gwyn A. Williams's view of Welsh history down to the very present as a continual improvisational process of unmaking and remaking[36] speaks very directly to Curtis: his mother was a Lancashire lass but his father came from south Pembrokeshire, and his paternal grandfather came to west Wales from Berkshire whereas his maternal grandfather moved from north Wales to the north of England. Of such 'flight patterns' has Wales traditionally been made and remade – a phrase borrowed from the title of John Davies's most recent book in which a poetry that is dense with intelligence offers us striking variations on the contrasting themes of social mobility and cultural stability. The volume is divided into a section on the United States and a section on Wales – which is in its turn subdivided between poems about Davies's present home area of the northern coastal resorts and poems about the very different valleys of the industrial south where he was raised. Several Anglo-Welsh poets have enjoyed bypassing England and connecting Wales directly with the wider world, and Davies has long been a master at this manoeuvre. For him the United States is fascinating partly because 'difference haunts too, offering / another self to visit, at least a different slant'.[37] But ever since *The Visitor's Book*[38] he has also been taken by the way 'new accents echoed yours', finding suggestive parallels in that book between the remnants of Native American culture in Washington state and the declining Welsh-language culture of his native country.

Davies's poems offer us an ambivalent assessment of diaspora, the state of chronic self-dispersal that characterizes much of modern existence. In several fine poems about refugees who have settled in north Wales he speculates on the relationship between an unremarkable present and an exotically 'foreign' past, as he does elsewhere when he ponders how an American chicken-farmer connects his settled life in Washington to the experiences of his young wartime self in England. Davies can relate to these examples of internal discontinuity and multiple selfhood both because he has himself become a kind of stranger to his own early background, and because in a sense his own being is centrally divided between Wales and the United States. Whereas his brother has simply resolved such conflicting claims on the affections by opting wholeheartedly for America, Davies remains in flight between different locations and out of this personal dilemma he has made a poetry that speaks very directly to contemporary Welsh experience. His flight patterns trace out paradigms for several forms of psychosocial dislocation – the transition from industrial to post-industrial society, from community to the nuclear family, from faith to scepticism, from a closed to an open society, from Welsh-language culture to – what? The bewilderments that accompany this last transition are sympathetically caught in a poem where the plight of a Welsh-speaking north Wales is epitomized by an old farmer's visit to hospital:

> At the hospital, thickset
> like an old coat stuffed with bracken, someone lurched
> from a lift to a board blaring with ward names, offices
> and the message *You Are Here*. But he was not.[39]

6

Where, for that matter, some critics have recently asked with the likes of Davies, Curtis and Minhinnick in mind, is most contemporary Anglo-Welsh poetry situated?[40] It certainly is not located in 'Wales', they assert, if that proper noun is taken to be not merely a geographical expression, or an identity tag for an Anglo-British region, but rather the name of a separate country with its own cultural integrity. Only the influence, direct or otherwise, of the Welsh language, they continue, has for the past several generations made possible a credibly 'Welsh' culture and literature in English. The current problem is, therefore, as obvious as it is urgent: how to write about an increasingly Anglicized life in Wales without writing an Anglophone (or frankly English) poetry. In so far as the language and culture of Welsh Nonconformity continued for a century to interact with English to produce in the south Wales mining valleys a distinct- ively non-English milieu, it was meaningful to claim that a Welsh literature in English came out of that region. However, the mate- rial base of that society has long since been removed. The Valleys are dead and the values of coalfield society live on, if at all, only in the sketchy communitarianism and the token socialism of what is essentially a modern consumer society. So what is left in those parts that is not to be found in England? And what is written about Wales that cannot reasonably be called English literature?

The Jenkinses, Mike and Nigel, are two poets who have linked the decline of Welsh to the decline of a Welsh society. A native of Aberystwyth, Mike Jenkins is nevertheless a poet of his adopted Merthyr. The oldest industrial town in Wales and one of the oldest in Britain, Merthyr is also the epitome of present-day post- industrial blight and poverty. The Merthyr Rising, the Chartists, Keir Hardie and other epic subjects from Merthyr's extraordi- nary past are not even distant memories on the run-down Gurnos council estate from which many of schoolteacher Jenkins's pupils come. In many of his poems he gives sympathetic voice to their desolating stories, sometimes speaking in their 'own' terms, accent and dialect: 'Our streets woz named after trees / to make 'em sound natural, innit?' says his 'Gurnos Boy'. 'But ew mostly 'ave Nature by year / when ew tread in some shit'.[41] Whenever Jenkins's outraged imagination is overwhelmed by anger instead of being powered by it, his poems tend to harangue the reader, but at his best he is the Idris Davies of his time and place, producing painfully memorable images of the courage, resource- fulness and despair that are bred from dereliction. His sense of the internal connection between England's cultural imperialism and its industrial exploitation of south Wales is well brought out in 'Letters to Indrek' (an Estonian poet).[42] Through elliptical

phrases and brusquely short lines that capture an edgy abrupt-
ness of speech, Jenkins invites Indrek to join him in a search of a
polluted landscape (both Estonian and Welsh) for the hidden
'springs our languages/come from'.

If scarred, decayed Merthyr is one of the faces of post-
industrial Wales, the thriving consumer society of the coastal belt
is another, and Nigel Jenkins has been regularly provoked into
satire by its bland lack of Welsh character. 'Never forget your
Welsh' is a sequence that takes its title from a recent Welsh beer
advert which reeked of the back-slapping, rugby-club convivial-
ity of south Wales. Like R. S. Thomas, Nigel Jenkins associates
this boyo culture (promoted, he believes, by the likes of Max
Boyce – 'old bopa Max, the white man's Welshman') with a cosy
provincialism of outlook that has traditionally been hostile to
any genuine manifestation of Welsh independence, particularly
the Welsh language. Influenced by William Carlos Williams and
other poets from the United States (where he has worked as a
circus hand), Jenkins has constructed a sequence in the form of a
collage of discourses. His own contemptuous epigrams on Welsh
thinking ('the Daily Mail / owns my / brain') are mixed in with
showbiz gush ('some of the happiest years of Petula Clark's life /
were spent in Wales') and mock newspaper headlines ('Roddy
fucks royal in Bahamas / another first for Wales'), while sombre
lines from the great sixth-century poem *Y Gododdin* recur
throughout the poem, tolling the knell of a parting Welsh
society.[43]

Modern south Wales is nothing if not a cosmopolitan society,
as demonstrated by Peter Finch's imaginary telephone directory,
where Abed, Ital is followed by Aberaman Original Band.[44]
Because of his longstanding delight in experimental poetry –
concrete, visual, typewriter, 'found', 'made', etc., etc. – Finch is
usually treated as if he were only accidentally Welsh, being essen-
tially a strongly visual-arts-influenced member of the inter-
national avant-garde. This is at best a half-truth. His maverick
poems are quintessentially Welsh wordscapes in the sense that
they are the product of a society in which 'the language issue'
(Welsh versus English) is a primary fact of life that makes the
English language visible and tangible in a way it rarely can be in
'purely' English society. Even Finch's exuberant Dadaist demon-
strations of the wild arbitrariness of language carry a political

charge in the Welsh context, since they undermine that assumption of the 'normality' and 'authority' of English (and the corresponding 'abnormality' and 'inferiority' of Welsh) that has prevailed in Wales. Indeed, of all Anglo-Welsh writers it is Finch who in a way best understands how the (crazy) matter of language is of the very essence in contemporary Welsh experience.

Virtually the only other poet to have realized this in something like Finch's terms is Oliver Reynolds, whose *Skevington's Daughter* includes a fascinating section of poems based on, or relating to, Welsh words and expressions. Reynolds is sadly the only example to date of a writer alert enough to capitalize on the immense postmodernist potential of the Welsh politico-cultural situation by ingeniously wording his experiences as a Welsh learner:

> Each has his reason to be here
> Speaking through declenched teeth:
> I'd thought it time to stop
> Welshing on the language.[45]

That words are literally a sensual body-language is realized when Reynolds is taught to pronounce 'Ch' by tightening the palate over the consonant; that in Wales the search for cultural roots inescapably involves learning the etymology of Welsh landscape is appreciated in 'Dysgu'; and that the word for 'poetic inspiration' is appropriately of feminine gender in Welsh is recognized in 'Awen II' as one of that language's great strokes of genius.[46] Reynolds's punning, mannered style is not simply that of a Welsh Martian, or of a Welsh mountebank: it is the sign of a writer who knows he needs to keep all his wits about him when dealing with a modern Wales whose mutations are as bewildering as those of the Welsh language.

7

Anglo-Welsh poetry points in no single clear direction, but it does refuse to align itself to the television aerials that point towards the Mendips. That, perhaps, is the best way of putting it. In other words there is an oppositional spirit at work, not because the poets feel distant from some centre but because they feel Wales to be different from elsewhere. It is not a remoteness from London that concerns them but a feeling that Wales is some place other than England, even if their sense of that place is not consistent or clear and even if for some of them its otherness is minimal – the residue of a once clearly separate history. And yet, in spite of the great differences of outlook among them that has been demonstrated in this chapter, contemporary Anglo-Welsh poets would seem to fall into two very broad categories. There are those who conceive of Wales in terms of some sort of alternative society – alternative, that is, to what is commonly perceived as the Anglo-American norm. And there are those whose primarily pragmatic interest in Wales relates more to their appreciation, as artists, of an international modernity with the merest hint of a Welsh inflection. The first group ranges from R. S. Thomas (whose alternative society is bound up inextricably with the Welsh language) through the various kinds of organicist communitarians (a crude phrase, unfortunately, to apply to Gillian Clarke, Tony Conran, Jeremy Hooker), to radical socialists (like Mike Jenkins and Nigel Jenkins). The second group includes John Davies (some of whose work falls, though, into the first category), Tony Curtis, Peter Finch (also a more ambiguous case than appears at first sight), Oliver Reynolds and Robert Minhinnick. And, allowing for disagreements, it is Minhinnick's recent statement which would seem finally to speak – though in different accents – for both groups:

> Wales is a country of strongly creative frictions ... the rural and the industrial, traditional industry and new technology, the English and the Welsh languages, a past representing an emphatic and unique cultural identity and a present in which that identity might become irreversibly eroded.[47]

Notes

1   Peter Finch, *Poems for Ghosts* (Bridgend, Seren Books, 1991), 55.
2   John Tripp, 'Roots', *Selected Poems* (Bridgend, Seren Books, 1989), 19.
3   R. S. Thomas, *Welsh Airs* (Bridgend, Poetry Wales Press, 1987).
4   'Our last Romantic: a reading of John Tripp', *Poetry Wales*, vol. 22, no. 1, 29.
5   See, for instance, 'My petition to the zoo keeper', *Planet* 90 (December, 1991/January, 1992), 13–17; 'Writing out of real experience', John Osmond (ed.) *The Future of the Word* (Cardiff, Welsh Union of Writers, 1985), 25–6.
6   Nigel Jenkins, *John Tripp* (Cardiff, University of Wales Press,

1989).

7 *Selected Poems*, op. cit., 152.

8 The phrase in Welsh is 'Cadw tŷ mewn cwmwl tystion', 'Pa beth yw dyn?', *Dail Pren* (Llandysul, Gwasg Gomer, 1956; trydydd argraffiad, 1971), 67.

9 'Fern Hill', Walford Davies and Ralph Maud, (eds.), *Dylan Thomas: Collected Poems 1934–1953* (London, Dent, 1988), 134–5; 'Returning to Goleufryn', Ruth Pryor, (ed.), *Vernon Watkins: Collected Poems* (Ipswich, Golgonooza Press, 1986), 103–104.

10 R. S. Thomas, *The Echoes Return Slow* (London, Macmillan, 1988), 104.

11 'Second Language', *Cometary Phases* (Bridgend, Seren Books, 1989), 60–61.

12 'Cofiant', in *Letting in the Rumour* (Manchester, Carcanet, 1989), 63–79.

13 'Letter From a Far Country', in *Selected Poems* (Manchester, Carcanet, 1985), 52–64.

14 Duncan Bush, *Salt* (Bridgend, Poetry Wales Press, 1985), 30–41.

15 For Gillian Clarke's 'reading' of R. S. Thomas, see 'The Poet', in *The King of Britain's Daughter* (Manchester: Carcanet, 1993), 67.

16 Dannie Abse, *White Coat, Purple Coat: Collected Poems, 1948–1988* (London, Hutchinson, 1989).

17 Tony Curtis, *Dannie Abse* (Cardiff, University of Wales Press, 1985).

18 'A Fern from Skye', *Blodeuwedd* (Bridgend, Poetry Wales Press, 1988), 32–7.

19 *The Penguin Book of Welsh Verse* (Harmondsworth, Penguin Books, 1967); revised and augmented edition published as *Welsh Verse* (Bridgend, Poetry Wales Press, 1986).

20 'The debatable land', *Planet* 90, 55–65.

21 'Elegy for the Welsh dead', *Blodeuwedd* (Bridgend, Poetry Wales Press, 1988), 14–15.

22 'A square of grey slate', ibid., 21–4.

23 Jeremy Hooker, *The Presence of the Past* (Bridgend, Poetry Wales Press, 1987); see also *The Poetry of Place* (Manchester, Carcanet, 1982), especially 159–90.

24 'Dawn: Cwrt y Felin', in *A Thread in the Maze* (Llandybïe, Christopher Davies, 1978), 46–7.

25 *The Presence of the Past*, op. cit., 169.

26 *Selected Poems* (Bridgend, Seren Books, 1990), 143–5.

27 These difficulties issue as poetry in *Englishman's Road* (Manchester, Carcanet, 1980).

28 *A Thread in the Maze*, op. cit., 44.

29 Ibid., 30.

30 *The Future of the Word*, op. cit., 25.
31 'The House', in Meic Stephens, (ed.), *The Bright Field: an anthology of contemporary poetry from Wales* (Manchester, Carcanet, 1991), 221–2.
32 'Lines at Barry', *Selected Poems* (Bridgend, Poetry Wales Press, 1986), 32–3.
33 *Selected Poems*, op. cit., 59.
34 Ibid., 14.
35 *Selected Poems*, 76.
36 'Wales is not a thaumaturgical act, it is a process, a process of continuous and dialectical historical development, in which human mind and human will interact with objective reality. Wales is an artefact which the Welsh produce: the Welsh make and remake Wales day by day and year after year. If they want to.' Gwyn A. Williams, *When Was Wales?* (London/Cardiff, BBC publications, 1979), 23.
37 John Davies, 'Starting Point', *Flight Patterns* (Bridgend, Seren Books, 1991), 49.
38 John Davies, *The Visitor's Book* (Bridgend, Poetry Wales Press, 1985).
39 'North', *Flight Patterns*, 61.
40 'Where next?', *Planet* 91 (February/March 1992), 3–10; Greg Hill, 'Drowned Voices', *Planet* 92 (April/May 1992), 61–70.
41 Mike Jenkins, *A Dissident Voice* (Bridgend, Seren Books, 1990), 40.
42 Ibid., 50–1.
43 Nigel Jenkins, 'Never forget your Welsh', *Acts of Union* (Llandysul, Gomer Press, 1990), 90–6.
44 Peter Finch, 'South-East Wales As Characterised By Its Phone Book', *Selected Poems*, 103–4.
45 Oliver Reynolds, 'Dysgu', *Skevington's Daughter* (London, Faber, 1985), 63.
46 Ibid., 70.
47 Susan Butler (ed.), *Common Ground: poets in a Welsh landscape* (Bridgend, Poetry Wales Press, 1985), 187.

Further reading

Cary Archard (ed.), *Poetry Wales: 25 years* (Bridgend, Seren Books, 1990).
John Barnie, *The King of Ashes* (Llandysul, Gomer Press, 1989).
Susan Butler (ed.), *Common Ground: poets in a Welsh landscape* (Bridgend, Poetry Wales Press, 1985).
Tony Curtis, 'Grafting the sour to sweetness: Anglo-Welsh poetry in the last twenty-five years', in Tony Curtis (ed.), *Wales: the Imagined Nation: studies in cultural and national identity* (Bridgend, Poetry Wales Press, 1986), 97–126.

Jeremy Hooker, *The Presence of the Past* (Bridgend, Poetry Wales Press, 1987).

'Is there a women's poetry?' *Poetry Wales* 23.1 (1987), 30–55. Symposium with contributions from Sheenagh Pugh, Gloria Evans Davies, Christine Evans, Sally Roberts Jones and Val Warner.

Bobi Jones, 'Demise of the Anglo-Welsh?' *Poetry Wales* 28, iii (January 1993), 14–8.

Meic Stephens (ed.), *The Bright Field: an anthology of contemporary poetry from Wales* (Manchester, Carcanet, 1991).

6

The multi-screen cinema: Poetry in Welsh 1950–1990

GARETH ALBAN DAVIES

1

There is a poem by Pennar Davies that tells us a great deal about what has happened to Welsh poetry since the last war. It is called 'Gwynt a Môr' ('Wind and Sea'), and takes as its point of departure and inspiration the roar of a great wind at night. The theme itself reminds Pennar of a well-known poem by John Morris Jones, who at the beginning of the century was one of those who set about rejuvenating both the Welsh language and its poetry. The way in which Pennar recalls that earlier poem signifies the contrast I am after:

> I remember the scholar-poet
> who would pontificate in our deceased Renaissance
> and emulate Heine
> in a sweetly sad lyric,
> telling of the wind weeping
> by his little window and pretending to hear
> his own Thespian lament
> in the wind's moan.

What Pennar lamented was the easy Romantic sentiment that had characterized much of even the best verse of the earlier period. Pennar himself found no sympathetic echo in the wind's voice, but rather a mocking laughter 'that such a gap yawned/ between hope and its prize'. Indeed, Pennar continues:

> Wave and spume laugh so as not to cry,
> they weep because every goodness
> gives birth to devastation.[1]

The reason for that rejection of an older, easier and cosier sentiment is easily identified. It lies in the history of two world wars, of the Holocaust, of Vietnam, of man's immense hatred of his fellow-man. That significant change of prevailing mood haunts modern Welsh poetry, as it does that of other nations. Inevitably too, such change must affect not only theme and mood, but the very substance of poetry, its language and rhythms. In that sense the 1950s was the period when conflict was at its height between the old and the new. The lyric as it had developed in the able hands of John Morris Jones, W. J. Gruffydd and others – coupled as it was with a ruthless revolution that established a new linguistic purity – eventually brought about a suffocating ortho-doxy that brooked no dissent. It was not that the earlier tradition had failed to create outstanding poetry; indeed, one of its masters, R. Williams Parry, who had composed perhaps the most famous poem in the old idiom 'Yr Haf' ('The Summer') (1910), produced his second and authoritative volume of poetry in 1952, entitled *Cerddi'r Gaeaf* ('The Songs of Winter'). He would become the darling of the sixties, the epitome of what Welsh verse should be. But it was difficult to get away from the strait-jacket of his sonnets, and the bittersweet nostalgia that filled his verse. For instance, his beautiful and untranslatable poem 'Clychau'r Gog' ('Bluebells') opens:

> Dyfod pan ddêl y gwcw,
>   Myned pan êl y maent,
> Y gwyllt atgofus bersawr,
>   Yr hen lesmeiriol baent;
> Cyrraedd, ac yna ffarwelio,
>   Ffarwelio, – Och! na pharhaent.[2]

> [They come when the cuckoo comes,
> They go when he leaves,
> The wild memory-laden fragrance,
> The old intoxicating paint;
> Arriving, and then saying farewell,
> Farewell, – Oh! that they would stay!]

He was difficult to improve upon, but, alas, so treacherously easy to imitate.

2

Pennar Davies was no innocent when it came to the conflict between an older tradition and the one which began to shake free in the fifties. He had originally come to the fore as a young and – dreadful to relate – obscurantist poet writing in the English language. His Welsh, like that of a number of modern Welsh poets, was an acquired idiom, and part of his discovery of a new, yet original identity. He was set apart by one other feature. A scholar trained at both a British and an American university, and married to a German woman, he epitomized the breadth of culture, of linguistic and historic awareness, that was certainly not a feature of the characteristic Welsh poet of the period, who was more familiar with his square mile, nourished on a simple lyric pottage, and considered English to be his only foreign language. In this regard Pennar was not a lone figure, but what he represented was certainly different from the run-of-the-mill bard, and in other ways, as we shall see, he characterized important features of the new poetry.

Pennar's definitive choice of the Welsh language as his future medium of expression mirrors another problem that faced the Welsh writer. Aneirin Talfan Davies in a review written in 1957 would refer back to it. He recalls how W. J. Gruffydd, one of the leaders of the earlier renaissance, had acknowledged the natural pull from England, and the fact that her literary life was more adventurous and varied than anything which Wales might offer. Gruffydd, nevertheless, had chosen to stay with the minority language. One of the striking features of Welsh letters in the sixties and subsequently is that the decision no longer offered itself as a matter of choice, but as a declaration of identity. Aneirin Talfan in a lecture given in 1958 encapsulated the shifting mood. The artist's choice of language should not be subject to outside criticism. Did he, or she, have any real choice in the matter? It would be an 'abnormal act' for the Welsh-speaking artist to write in English. It was not just a question of language, but of all that went with it:

> Language is the storehouse of the wisdom of the centuries – centuries of common experiences that spring from living together, suffering together, and sharing in a common joy.[3]

He noted, furthermore, that James Joyce's and Dylan Thomas's choice of a 'foreign language' as their medium had caused the overdominance of expression over content in their work. He contrasted them with Kierkegaard who had insisted on writing in his own native Danish, rather than in German.

In an essay in a collection entitled *Y Chwedegau* ('The Sixties'), which was published in 1970, Bedwyr Lewis Jones gave voice to the new confidence in Welsh letters. He noted the contrast between the smallness of a linguistic constituency that was roughly of the same size as Leeds or Sheffield, and the fact that it produced such an abundance of lively writing. He attributed this partly to the fact that the Welsh language was under siege, noting that this has produced a 'cultural dynamic that Western civilization today cannot afford to lose'.[4] That dynamism, particularly in poetry, has continued into the nineties, and it is fair to ask what the reasons are for it.

Part of the answer is the change in the mechanism by which Welsh books are produced and distributed. Before the 1950s few books appeared, and in an uncertain market the very small number of printer-publishers in Wales were naturally not keen to make outlays that produced little or no return. The situation began to change with the decision to make a small amount of public money available in the mid-fifties for distribution among publishers to enable them to produce Welsh books for adults. In the county of Cardiganshire, and then elsewhere, the travelling library service increased the readership of Welsh books considerably, thus ensuring also a firm core of sales. Then in 1961 Y Cyngor Llyfrau Cymraeg (The Welsh Books Council) was established, which rapidly and completely transformed the publishing and distribution scene. The number of Welsh books overall increased from one hundred in 1950, to 539 published in 1991. As for poetry, a similar transformation occurred: from eleven volumes in 1950, to nineteen in 1991, with a higher plateau in the mid-twenties during the previous decade. We must not forget, in the case of poetry, the additional support given by the Literature Panel of the Welsh Arts Council, established in 1967, which awards grants for the publication of works of specific literary value. We shall see later, success or failure in gaining a grant has itself created a divide between two sorts of poet – or at least, this is the way in which a certain kind of poet prefers to view himself or herself.

The Arts Council was instrumental, too, in establishing and funding Yr Academi Gymreig (The Welsh Academy), which has given poets a common home, and a public platform by which their verse (in both English and Welsh) can reach a wider public. One of the Academy's more interesting publishing ventures has been a series of volumes of translations into Welsh of poetry from other countries. The poetry of Germany, Spain, China, Gaelic Scotland and Classical Greece and Rome are already represented, and there are separate volumes on Rilke, Zbigniew Herbert, and the French Symbolist poets. The Arts Council, through an enlightened commissioning policy, has enabled Cyhoeddiadau Barddas (Poetry Publications) to pursue its own independent policy of publishing poetry, verse anthologies and critical studies, under the shrewd and inspired editorship of Alan Llwyd. The most eminent of younger contemporary poets, he is also the editor of a monthly journal *Barddas*, which publishes poetry in the alliterative metres mainly – a class of poetry to which we shall return – but contains, in addition, articles on a far wider range of poetry both native and foreign, reviews, as well as essays in literary criticism and critical theory.

The increased liveliness of the literary activities of the annual National Eisteddfod has lifted the profile of poetry, which has always been a popular medium of expression in Wales. Furthermore, a series of national poetic contests known as *Talwrn y Beirdd* ('The Poets' Cockpit'), which is regularly broadcast by Radio Cymru and culminates at the Eisteddfod, has increased public awareness of poetry and its enjoyment. In the fifties and sixties the BBC acted as a commissioning agent for new poetry, usually in the form of long poems, but this policy has unfortunately ceased. Indeed, only fitfully now do they provide arts programmes that give attention to the poetic scene. The same criticism can be aimed at Welsh-language television (S4C). On the one hand, it has made a very positive contribution to Welsh culture by broadening its range of interests and activities, but on the other, this has happened at the expense of letters, which are deemed to be a minority interest, and have in any case less visual potential. At the present time, however, the very lively and technically excellent arts magazine *Graffiti* does regularly feature the work of individual poets, often providing an appropriate visual accompaniment to the verse. It is very much to be hoped that such experimentation will lead eventually to the production of a number of video-presentations of modern Welsh poetry.

3

The Welsh poetic scene may be likened to a multi-screen cinema showing three different shows to three separate audiences. To complete the image, we have to imagine that some in the audience are looking at two, even three, of these shows at the same time; whilst certain other members of a different studio audience sometimes put their heads in, just to protest raucously that what their rivals are looking at is not proper cinema anyway. The latter feature indicates how the word has replaced the sword in Welsh tribal warfare. Unfortunately, such activity often dissipates energies that could have been better directed. Nevertheless, when prejudices have been plucked out and the damage from wounding words cauterized, what remains can be a sensible and interesting critical debate.

What exactly is going on in these three different shows? The first, and historically the most important, is a vestige of a popular appreciation of poetry that can be traced back to the Middle Ages and our earlier Celtic inheritance. Its survival even in the English-speaking parts of Wales is demonstrated by the public interest in the ceremony of the crowning and chairing of the winning poets at the National Eisteddfod; likewise the hero's welcome given on their return to their *Heimat*. The nature of that poetry-loving society and its characteristic culture was described by Dafydd Glyn Jones in a notable lecture, 'Some Recent Trends in Welsh Literature' in 1971. Welsh culture, he noted, was:

> that remarkable amateur endeavour which, nurtured by a great common desire for self-betterment, on the part of a society with no economic power and meagre material resources, grew hand in hand with political radicalism, on ground well prepared by Protestant Nonconformity.[5]

It was, he added, 'a democratic, middlebrow and utilitarian culture, one in which all experience gravitated towards a middle ground'.

This was the culture that produced *y bardd gwlad* ('the country poet'). He is not exclusively the creation of the country-

side, since he – or more unusually, she – might, even in the recent
past, be found also in the Welsh-speaking mining, quarrying and
metal-industry areas of north and south Wales. However, even in
those places people's roots were nostalgically felt to be in the
rural hinterlands where the family had originated. Not unexpect-
edly, the poetry that characterizes this tradition is simple,
old-fashioned, and its images are drawn from a rural life both
real and imagined. The style and themes of the poetry of the
Welsh Renaissance of the early part of the century gradually
trickled into this lyricism, but at such late date that they had lost
their innovative force. Another style of poetry was practised too,
that of the medieval poetic tradition in *cynghanedd* (the allitera-
tive metres), particularly the four-line epigrammatic stanza *yr
englyn*, and the part-narrative, part-descriptive poem based on
rhymed couplets, *y cywydd*.

The poetry of *y bardd gwlad* is characteristically one of cele-
bration – a wedding, an epitaph, a local concert, the
competitions of a local eisteddfod or chapel meeting. It is also the
poetry found in *colofn y beirdd* ('the poets' column') of certain
Welsh weeklies. The alliterative forms are frequently used to
mark events in the rural calendar – ploughing, the seasons, the
farm and its animals and implements. All this suggests a poetry
that is slight – but it is often beautiful and well turned. Indeed,
some of the best-known *englynion* are a product of this unso-
phisticated society that keeps its sophistication for its verse. It is
very much a poetry of public performance, being in that sense a
continuation of the medieval tradition, when poems of praise
were recited or sung at the houses of the poets' patrons.
Todayequally, there is an implied, even collusive, celebration of
the community itself. The relation between poet and audience is
central, and the success of performance depends on the latter's
relative competence to appreciate and to discriminate, a particu-
larly important matter when it comes to the subtleties and
intricacies of the alliterative metres.

It is very easy to dismiss this poetry as a mode of rural func-
tionality, and nothing more. That would be a serious mistake, for
it remains, even today, one of the bases on which a more dedi-
cated poetry is set. Alan Llwyd, in his monumental *Barddoniaeth
y Chwedegau: Astudiaeth Lenyddol-hanesyddol* ('The Poetry
of the Sixties: A Historico-literary Study') (1986), used a

memorable image: the rural tradition helped create the greater
poets, 'like tiny waves that carry the great current'.[6] For instance,
two of the best-known poets today in the alliterative metres, Dic
Jones and Donald Evans, have remained part of that rural tradi-
tion, as were their equally famous predecessors in
mid-Cardiganshire. That society still provides a significant
readership for Welsh poetry, thus maintaining the liveliness of the
lyrical tradition; but on the negative side, it must be admitted
that many of these readers remain impervious, even hostile, to
the new-fangled poetry – as they would see it – produced by a
very different sort of poet. The fact that such poets are typically
the product of a college education sets them apart from the
society from which they may well have originally emerged.
Probably too, they will have moved away to an urban environ-
ment, thus impoverishing the cultural life of the local community.

4

The second studio show to which I referred is the eisteddfod, that
is to say, the festival dedicated usually to all the arts, but in
which, traditionally, poetry has played a central role. I have
already mentioned the local eisteddfod, an annual event based on
a small area, or a particular chapel: alas, many of these have
disappeared in the last decade or so. Then there is the regional
eisteddfod, like that of Powys, or of Anglesey. The annual Urdd
Eisteddfod (run by the Welsh League of Youth) has signally
succeeded in promoting the talents of generations of younger
poets, male and female.

At the top of the pyramid we find *Yr Eisteddfod Genedlaethol*
('The National Eisteddfod'), a festival that nowadays lasts some
ten days, and is held at the beginning of August each year in a
town or area alternatively in north and south Wales. The core of
the Eisteddfod is essentially a series of competitions – musical,
artistic, literary, historical, scientific, etc. – on subjects set by the
local committees. The two principal literary competitions remain
(despite some protest) those for the Crown and the Chair, whose
ceremonies are the most enjoyable and popular of the festival.
The competition for the Crown traditionally calls for the writing
of a long poem in the free metres called *y bryddest*, although in
recent years a poetic sequence or a collection of lyrics has often

been set as a subject. In contrast, the Chair requires an *awdl*, a poem in the alliterative metres, displaying a command of a number of the various poetic measures. To have won at the National still carries great prestige, even though the quality of a crowned or chaired poem may vary from the outstanding to the mediocre. Nevertheless, some of the most lasting, even revered, poems of the last fifty years have been the product of these two competitions.

There are a number of other poetic competitions, for instance a sonnet, a lyric, a satire, an *englyn*, etc. These inspire (or fail to inspire) a large number of poets, who like mayflies go annually through their short-lived lyrical cycle. For these, to write poetry is synonymous with competing, and may even produce a small source of income from their literary prizes. Traditionally, many of these poets, and some outside the eisteddfodic circle, were ministers of religion, or priests of the Church in Wales, and, in one distinguished case, a Catholic priest. The decline of organized religion means that fewer and fewer poets come from this social background and with a specifically Christian viewpoint. In consequence, the eisteddfodic poet – like the poet in general – has migrated to other professions, to teaching, the law, or radio and television. In other cases, however, he remains the rural shopkeeper, or farmer, or craftsman. The eisteddfod, at both local and national level, has also given considerable impetus to women poets; for instance, the 1991 National witnessed the crowning of one of the most promising younger poets, Einir Jones, brought up on an Anglesey farm, but married to a minister in West Glamorgan. It is easy to talk, once again, of the dead hand of the Eisteddfod, and to complain that it nurtures an old-fashioned kind of poetry. Significant examples can be cited in support of this judgement, but in the last few years at least, the Crown has been several times awarded to poets who would be considered modernist or even avant-garde; and the grisly post-mortem investigations after such competitions often reveal that other poets of like tendency have 'come near the top' (to use the eisteddfodic jargon).

5

The emergence of the so-called Modern Poet – our third studio show – can be addressed at this point, since he is a product of the relative collapse of the traditional rural society. Comfortable

with itself, bolstered by its perception of the goodness of rural
values, upheld by its conviction that a Nonconformist God ruled,
OK, it was well placed to condemn the time's evils, and always
from the standpoint of its own religious certainties. That world
of easy virtue had been challenged even as early as the years
following the First World War in Cynan's Eisteddfod *pryddest,
Mab y Bwthyn* ('The Cottager'); but on the eve of the Second
World War, a much deeper anxiety was expressed by Caradoc
Prichard in another *pryddest, Teyrnasoedd Daear* ('The
Kingdoms of the Earth') (1939), which openly advocated suicide
as the only way to avoid '[g]wledd y bleiddiaid' (the banquet of
the wolves). In fact, it took a war and another decade to under-
mine the ingenuous certainties of Welsh society, and the motive
force for change was to be economic and social.

It is generally agreed that T. Glynne Davies's Eisteddfod
pryddest, Adfeilion ('Ruins') (1951), marks the beginning of a
new era in Welsh poetry. Like Cynan's cottager, the unidentified
narrator has returned from war to a society entirely transformed.
The poet took the idealizing cliché of rural life, and made of it a
grotesque cartoon. We see a depopulated countryside, whose
houses stand empty and ruinous. Of the old life only memories
remain, whereas

> Mae'r plant a fagodd Pant y Maes
> Yn furddunod
> Mewn hetiau meddal lliwgar
> Ar strydoedd dinasoedd du.[7]
>
> [The children that Pant y Maes bred
> are ruinous habitations
> in soft, colourful hats
> on the streets of blackened cities.]

In a European context this was not a new theme – for instance,
we find it expressed with great feeling in the novels of Miguel
Delibes, that describe the changes which have come to the
peasant economy of northern Castile. What intensifies the
theme's importance in Wales is that the severe and increasing
decline in the rural economy and the consequent exodus to the
cities have principally affected those regions in which the Welsh
language had remained strong, with the result that the traditional
culture has thereby also been undermined.

Glynne Davies's poetry is significant in other ways. Firstly, he expressed openly a religious scepticism that had only very slowly percolated into a culture in which the Christian faith had been regarded as an almost essential ingredient. With a time-lag longer even than usual, certain deep changes that had affected European culture at the beginning of the century – and which gave rise, for example, in Spain to the *Modernista* movement – were at last being felt in Wales. I refer to the loss of religion leading to a sense of emptiness and lack of purpose, on the one hand; and on the other, the discovery of a new sensibility and a different kind of poetic language. It is important to emphasize, nevertheless, that a number of poets, among them some of the best, have continued to be inspired by their Christian convictions.

Secondly, Glynne Davies, like others in that generation, found their inspiration in everyday subjects that older poets would have judged 'unpoetic'. Also, the very notion of there being a 'poetic language' was cast to one side. The preference for the *vers libre* over rhyme and count of syllable was a further expression of this new freedom. It was at this time that the divide and conflict between the Traditional and the Modern poet were most acutely felt. Older critics protested, saying that the poets had created a gap between themselves and their audience, or that this was no way to save the Welsh language! A modernist of an older generation, Alun Llywelyn-Williams, countered by accusing the typical Welsh reader of not knowing how to read poetry, and of being ignorant of what went on in the poetry of other literatures.

In the perceptive lecture I quoted earlier, Dafydd Glyn Jones reflected on some of the consequences of the break-up of the traditional culture. There would come in its place 'a culture less democratic and less cohesive, and at the same time more diversified, more tolerant perhaps, of genuine art and genuine trash'.[8] The epithets seem well chosen, though a general tolerance has yet to break out. The gap between the new art and the old is measured in the charge of 'élitist' and 'academic' from the one side, and 'outmoded' from the other. Certainly, educational opportunities have taken the new-style poet into a different social and cultural sphere; and often his reading reflects a knowledge of other literatures. In addition, with the disappearance of any clear notion of what is poetic, the poets have declared open season: the result has been a poetry that is extremely varied and adventurous, though not necessarily of high quality always.

The most striking feature of the new poetry has been its political commitment. This was characteristic of certain older poetry too, in which socialist ideas, or more commonly the call for a Free Wales, were heard. But now with the growing realization that the demise of the Welsh language seemed increasingly probable even in the short run, the poets began to take an active role in the movement to bring about conditions more favourable to the survival of our tongue. This has included the fight for civil rights for Welsh-speakers, and for measures to ensure that there is proper provision of homes for the native people of the Welsh countryside. Attention has been drawn also to the devastating effect on cultural life of the influx of settlers from the English cities into the Welsh heartland. Over the last twenty years the actions of Cymdeithas yr Iaith (The Welsh-Language Society), which believes in the use of non-violent illegal action where persuasion has failed, have led to numerous members being sent to gaol, among them Welsh writers. The poets have marked with deep sincerity what they regard as the sacrifices made by their fellow Welsh men and women.

One or two poets, however, have expressed the feeling that this obsession with the language has caused them to overlook the greater injustices elsewhere in the world. The poetry, in fact, seems not to bear out this charge. Iwan Llwyd in his 'Plant y Chwedegau' ('The Children of the Sixties') remarked on the contrast between two generations, his parents' and his own. The latter has suffered unemployment, which alienates a man, and bows him down; they are

> cenhedlaeth terfysg a helynt,
> blodau rhyfel ydynt,
> yn gwywo'n grwm yn y gwynt.[9]

> [the generation of protest and riot,
> they are the flowers of war,
> withering, head held low, in the wind.]

That conviction has certainly led several poets to identify not only with the Welsh cause, but with Africa, and Nicaragua, and Northern Ireland.

Women poets gravitate towards the modern movement, and prefer to use the *vers libre*. The reason is difficult to find, though it may be simply historical; namely, that only in the last twenty years or so have women had the confidence to venture into what remains in many ways a male preserve. There are at least a half dozen women who have published their verse, to which must be added the considerable eisteddfodic detritus – the leftovers of poetic competitions – that should some day occupy critical attention. These poets are not to be identified as necessarily feminist: indeed, I suspect that one or two of them would reject that epithet. The best-known, Menna Elfyn, is certainly a feminist, however, aware of herself as wife and mother, and declaring her solidarity with other women as, for example, in her poem on the unemployed:

> I bob dyn sy'n ddi-waith
> mae dwy wraig adre
> ar faliwm yn y falen.[10]

> [to every man out of work
> there are two women at home,
> on Valium in their depression.]

Her interests are again reflected in her choice of theme for a recent venture, a dramatic presentation of Simone Weil.

Two other, to my mind more accomplished, poets are Nesta Wyn Jones and Einir Jones. They explore those inward recesses of experience that have become the province of many women poets, but both are aware also of their commitment to the tragedy and struggle of others, both at home and abroad. Both observe and record the natural world with a scientist's intentness, and with a poet's ability to see surprising similarities; thus for Nesta Wyn, the dead larches are 'like fish-bones';[11] for Einir, the sunset is a woman putting on make-up. In 'Creu' ('Creating') Einir Jones sees her function as making other people see. Her poem ends with an injunction to the imagined observer, or reader:

> 'sbiwch';
> ac mi welan'
> heb gen ar eu ll'gada;
> a'u dysgu nhwtha
> i glywed y
> dim,
> cyn diddymdra.[12]

['Look!';
and they'll see
without scales on their eyes;
and teach them
to hear the
nothing,
before nothingness.]

In this respect both poets reflect the wider interest in description that marks much recent poetry, and which is partly inspired by the medieval tradition of *dyfalu*, the use of highly imaginative lyrical hyperbole to evoke the natural world.

Other women poets use a deliberately colloquial, 'unpoetical' language. Their landscapes are sometimes urban, at other times seem rooted to the kitchen sink. What gives them particular value is their openness in dealing with sexual experience, with no desire to shock, or strike a pose. In this they have rediscovered an older Welsh tradition, which Nonconformity fortunately had not quite managed to suffocate. It is no coincidence that the titles of two volumes by these women poets are taken from the poetry of the Cardiff poet and pop musician Geraint Jarman. He is a product of the city, from which he often draws his inspiration. He is also a *dysgwr* (a learner of the Welsh language) – as are an increasing number of the younger poets – and his idiom is simpler, less literary than that of many other modern poets; inevitably, he is less able to draw on the wealth of idiom of the countryside. He also represents the bridge between poetry and pop, as well as that between poetry and public performance. He marks, therefore – perhaps surprisingly – the desire for a return to poetry's medieval roots in public celebration.

6

One of the most interesting – and ultimately influential – developments in the last fifteen years has been *Cyfres y Beirdd Answyddogol* ('Series of the Unofficial Poets'), published by Lolfa Press. Initially it was a kind of *Salon des Refusés*, representing poets whose work had been turned down for a grant by the literary panel of the Arts Council, or the Welsh Books Council. More recently, it has simply become a different tradition within Welsh poetry, and as Gerwyn Williams has shown in a recent article in a volume of critical essays *Sglefrio ar Eiriau* ('Skating on Words') (1992), there has been a tendency recently for them to be accepted as a strand of the more official tradition, without serious sacrifice of principle or practice on their part. Indeed, the most able among them, Iwan Llwyd, was given the accolade – or if you prefer, the poisoned chalice – of winning the Crown in the National Eisteddfod in 1990. What distinguishes them as a tendency – group is not the appropriate word – is obvious in the work of some of the women poets already discussed. Their idiom is easy, direct, their work is not aimed at the typical reader of Welsh poetry, their subject-matter is the experience of everyday. For the most part, they speak for the secularized society that Wales has largely become. One of them has commented on how he found that the more traditional Welsh poetry had nothing to say to him, and that he had turned else-where, to find an affinity in the Merseyside poets.

Iwan Llwyd in particular has referred to a dual problem. Firstly, secularization and the increasing tendency for people's social sphere to be bilingual and culturally homogenized have largely removed the referential language on which the poet depends. He expressed it thus in a poem entitled 'Y Drws Clo' ('The Locked Door') in his volume *Dan Anesthetig* ('Under Anaesthetic') (1987):

> Gynt yr oedd geiriau'n allweddi,
> ond eisoes aeth eu crefft yn fregus
> a'u ffynhonnau'n hesb.[13]

> [Before words were keys,
> but already their craft has become brittle,
> their sources dried up.]

In an introduction to this poet's earlier volume *Sonedau Bore Sadwrn* ('Saturday Morning Sonnets') (1983) the novelist William Roberts suggested that the older-style poetry, especially that in the alliterative metres, placed the poet in danger of 'becoming alienated from his audience, and the act of writing poetry turning into a dilettante and pointless exercise'.[14] The second problem which Iwan Llwyd has specifically addressed is that of winning back the audience. In an article in *Barddas* (1985) he noted that the basis for everyday conversation was football, last night's television, a film or radio programme:

Unemployment is the new norm; the television screen is the Bible; records of rock music are the accompaniment to a dinner or a celebration. You cannot ignore this. The poet's language must encompass the language of this new *cyfarwydd* [storyteller, entertainer in medieval times], or else he will become meaningless to his audience.[15]

In a recent editorial in *Barddas*, Alan Llwyd has challenged the implication of this point of view. If the audience is alienated by the old-style (and particularly the alliterative) poetry, he asks, how does one explain that it is the poetry of Alan Llwyd that sells best, and not the poetry of the Unofficial Poets? It is a fair line of argument, but misses the point. Iwan Llwyd and the others are aiming at the increasingly large potential audience which has to be wooed, even seduced, into accepting that poetry is something for them. This explains the interest which associates of this group have in public performance. They are intent – in public halls, in schools, in pubs, in any place where people meet – to bring poetry to people's attention. The link with pop music is shown by Steve Eaves who performs his poems to the guitar, or by Jina who writes and performs her own jazz songs, or by Gareth Siôn whose surrealist lyrics for the Jecsyn Ffeif group are made up of literary fragments. This tendency, I suspect, will become more marked, but its effectiveness in reaching an audience is directly linked to an improvement in recording standards, and to the widespread availability of hi-fi equipment of a high standard.

7

In this chapter I have been more concerned with following general trends than with writing an appreciation of individual poets. I should not conclude, however, without stating my opinion that Wales, despite its small population, has produced over the last forty years a number of poets of true stature. Waldo Williams, to whom an essay in this volume is dedicated, produced in *Dail Pren* ('The Leaves of the Tree') (1956) a collection of his most mature verse. Saunders Lewis and Gwenallt – both religious and nationalist poets of great power and conviction who had been at their peak in the thirties and forties – were still active, as was Williams Parry to whom I have already referred. The fifties witnessed the early lyrical challenges of a Cardiff-born *dysgwr* and *enfant terrible*, Bobi Jones, who remains prolific as both poet and critic, and whose verse is available to a larger audience in English translation. Rhydwen Williams, a poet-novelist now in his eighties, has celebrated the grandeur and decline of the Rhondda Valley, where coal has finally ceased to be mined. Euros Bowen, another Cwm Rhondda man, was initially considered the obscure poet *par excellence*, but survived into a period that had learned how to read his often difficult verse. Gwyn Thomas, whose evocative, always forward-moving and experimental poetry has often anticipated later trends, demonstrates how excellent poems can come out of everyday occurrences, and be expressed in simple language. Finally, Alan Llwyd, an accomplished lyricist in both the traditional alliterative idiom and in the modern style, not only expresses the pessimism of a whole generation, but has the breadth of imagination, depth of feeling, and mastery of technique that are the hallmarks of the great poet.

I suspect that the multi-screen shows to which I referred earlier will continue, and that we shall be richer for it. After all, there is no reason why one show should cease in order to please another, different audience. Furthermore, as we have seen, there is an occasional tendency for one stream of poetry to mingle with another, thereby enriching it. One thing is certain: people will go on doing their own thing. Furthermore, they will go on doing so within a consciously Welsh frame of reference. In that sense talk of a periphery is meaningless. The Anglo-Welsh writer is almost necessarily aware of the dominance of a metropolitan culture to which he or she remains subservient; the Welsh writer is free of this constrictive feeling, even though in the world of everyday he or she cannot escape the encroachment of a much more powerful culture. In the attempt at a more satisfactory self-definition many Welsh people (like the Scots) prefer to see themselves in relation to Europe, rather than to London. It is a point of view that has a long and respected tradition within the Welsh nationalist movement, but the concept has gained wider currency as a result of the development of the European Community (now Union). It is highly ironic that the British government, having clutched at the principle of subsidiarity as if they had invented it, in order to guard what they regard as their sovereign interest, should nevertheless be very unwilling to acknowledge that principle when it comes to the various countries that make up Great Britain. In contrast, many Welsh writers would be happy to think of themselves as citizens of a *Europe des régions*.

Notes

1 Pennar Davies, *Llef: Casgliad o Gerddi* (Llandybïe, Cyhoeddiadau Barddas, 1987), 19–20: 'Cofiaf y bardd-ysgolhaig / a bontiffigiai yn ein diweddar Ddadeni / ac a efelychai Heine /mewn telyneg felys-brudd/ a sôn am y gwynt yn wylo / wrth ei ffenestr fach ac esgus clywed / ei alar actol ei hun / yng nghwynfan y gwynt.' . . . 'am fod y fath agendor / yn ymestyn rhwng gobaith a gwobr.' . . . 'Chwerthin rhag wylo mae ton ac ewyn,/ wylo am fod pob daion-i'n/ esgor ar ddinistr.'

2 R. Williams Parry, *Cerddi'r Gaeaf* (Dinbych, Gwasg Gee, 1952), 4. The first volume of his poetry, *Yr Haf a Cherddi Eraill* ('The Summer and Other Poems') appeared in 1924.

3 Aneirin Talfan Davies, 'Y Gelfyddyd Lenyddol yng Nghymru', in *Astudio Byd* (Llandybïe, Llyfrau'r Dryw, 1967), 17–21, and 1958 quotation on p. 23.

4 Bedwyr Lewis Jones, 'Llenydda yn Gymraeg' ('Writing in Welsh'), in *Y Chwedegau*, no editor's name given (Caerdydd, Avalon Books, 1970), 23–32, quotation on p. 24.

5 Dafydd Glyn Jones, 'Some Recent Trends in Welsh Literature', in *Literature in Celtic Countries*, Taliesin Congress Lectures, edited by J. E. Caerwyn Williams (Cardiff, University of Wales Press, 1971), lecture 8 (177–207), quotations on p. 177.

6 Alan Llwyd, *Barddoniaeth y Chwedegau; Astudiaeth Lenyddol-Lanesyddol* (Caernarfon, cyhoeddiadau Barddas, 1986), 32.

7 'Adfeilion' in *Cerddi T. Glynne Davies* (Llandybïe, Cyhoeddiadau Barddas, 1987), 180–9, quotation on p. 187.

8 Ibid., 177.

9 Iwan Llwyd, *Dan Anesthetig: Cerddi* (Caerdydd, Gwasg Taf, 1987), 12.

10 Menna Elfyn, *Aderyn Bach mewn Llaw: Cerddi 1976–90* (Llandysul, Gwasg Gomer, 1990), 69.

11 Nesta Wyn Jones, *Cannwyll yn Olau* (Llandysul, Gwasg Gomer, 1969), 40 ['Fel esgyrn pysgod'].

12 Einir Jones, *Pigo Crachan* (Llandybïe, Christopher Davies, 1972), 34.

13 Iwan Llwyd, *Dan Anesthetig*, op. cit., 10.

14 William Roberts, in the Introduction to Iwan Llwyd, *Sonedau Bore Sadwrn*, (Talybont, Y Lolfa, 1983)

15 Iwan Llwyd, 'Cyfarwydd Newydd' ('A New Entertainer'), in
    Barddas, 99–100 (1985), 24.

Further Reading

Clancy, Joseph P. (trans.), *Twentieth Century Welsh Poems* (Llandysul, Gomer Press, 1982).

ap Gwilym, Gwynn and Llwyd, Alan (eds.), *Blodeugerdd o Farddoniaeth Gymraeg yr Ugeinfed Ganrif* (Llandysul, Gwasg Gomer/Cyhoeddiadau Barddas, 1987) – an anthology of twentieth-century poetry.

Bobi Jones, *Selected Poems*, translated by Joseph P. Clancy (Swansea, Christopher Davies Publishers Ltd., 1987) – a selection of verse (in English translation) by the best-known of contemporary Welsh poets.

Jones, Dafydd Glyn, Some Recent Trends in Welsh Literature, in Williams, J. E. Caerwyn (ed.), *Literature in Celtic Countries*, Taliesin Congress Lectures, lecture 8 (Cardiff, University of Wales Press, 1971), pp. 177-207 – a brilliant and thought-provoking study.

Jones, Gwyn (ed.), *The Oxford Book of Welsh Verse in English* (Oxford, OUP, 1977) – this includes translations of some Welsh poems from the recent period.

Jones, R. Gerallt (ed.), *Poetry of Wales 1930–1970* (Llandysul, Gwasg Gomer, 1974) – a selection of Welsh poems in English translation.

Rowlands, John (ed.), *Sglefrio ar Eiriau: Erthyglau ar Lenyddiaeth a Beirniadaeth* (Llandysul, Gwasg Gomer, 1992) – a series of critical essays, including Gerwyn Williams's 'Darlunio'r Tirlun Cyflawn: amlinellu cyd-destun ar gyfer cyfres Beirdd Answyddogol y Lolfa' (pp. 115–50) – a very interesting analysis of the present state of Welsh poetry-writing, and the various groupings represented.

Stephens, Meic (ed.), *The Arts in Wales 1950–75* (Cardiff, Welsh Arts Council, 1979) – good on general background, and containing an article by John Rowlands, 'Literature in Welsh' (pp. 167–206).

7

Beyond the Caledonian Antisyzygy: Contemporary Scottish poetry in between cultures

URSULA KIMPEL

1

Recent literary and cultural theory has come to perceive multi-culturality or cross-culturality as the inevitable condition of modern societies world-wide – the result of colonial and imperial expansion and of labour migration – and, what is more, as the inevitable condition of creativity. Thus, in their important study of *Theory and Practice in Post-colonial Literatures* (1989), Bill Ashcroft, Gareth Griffiths and Helen Tiffin write:

> Both literary theorists and cultural historians are beginning to recognize cross-culturality as the potential termination point of an apparently endless human history of conquest and annihilation justified by the myth of group 'purity', and as the basis on which the post-colonial world can be creatively stabilized.[1]

According to Ashcroft, Griffiths and Tiffin,

> impetus towards decentering and pluralism has always been present in the history of European thought and has reached its latest development in post-structuralism. But the situation of marginalized societies and cultures enabled them to come to this position much earlier and more directly.[2]

But in any case, such a position had to be hard won against a dominant discourse which privileged homogeneity rather than heterogeneity as the basis of cultural identity. 'The problem is that we have been taught to see culture in terms of unity and completeness', the Scottish critic Cairns Craig writes in the official programme of a Commonwealth Writers Conference which took place in Edinburgh in July 1986. Speaking not only for Scottish literature, but also for the experience of the writers from all over the English-speaking world assembled at the conference, Craig spells out the condition of what he calls 'Being Between':

> Most of us inhabit a fractured culture, a bi-culturalism of language, nation, tradition or class, whose effects we expect to be destructive because we assume that the self-division of our language and our culture cannot help but be reflected as a fissure in the organisation of our poetry. We do not live, however, within a language or a tradition, but between languages and traditions. It is those poets who have lived 'in between' who have made the most powerful contributions to the literatures of English in the twentieth century.

Craig goes on to maintain that in 'Scotland the dialectic between Scots and English and between Gaelic and English has generated an immense amount of linguistic experiment which may act as a kind of map for the possibilities of such biculturalism'.[3] But the history of Scottish literature in this century also provides a kind of map of the powerful obstacles inherent in the process of coming to terms with the experience of cultural heterogeneity when confronted with the strong pressure of inherited homogenizing ideologies.

A tension between the experience of cultural heterogeneity on the one hand and a strong pressure for cultural homogeneity on the other hand may be said to be the main driving force behind the development of Scottish literature throughout the twentieth century. From this tension the process of cultural self-determination which was started by the Scottish Literary Renaissance at the beginning of this century derived its momentum. It was perpetuated by a key term of the Scottish Renaissance: G. Gregory Smith's self-consciously apologetic conception of the 'Caledonian antisyzygy' (or combination of opposites) as formulated in his history of Scottish literature of 1919.[4]

In modern Scotland a number of factors make for a patchwork of the most heterogeneous cultural fields, such as Scotland's history between independence and the United Kingdom of Great Britain; its three language communities – the Gaelic, the Scots, and the English – often overlapping, more often mutually indifferent or even hostile; and its long history of being involved in different waves of pre-industrial and industrial migrations. Yet the model of a homogeneous national culture inherited from the nineteenth-century United Kingdom has exerted a very strong pressure throughout the present century. As a result, for the greater part of the century the dominant discourse in which Scottish writers have located themselves tends to view the multiplicity of Scotland's cultural inheritance as an embarrassment and a major predicament for creative work. And ever since the Scottish Literary Renaissance, considerable effort has been spent on an attempt to construct a homogeneous unity out of the disparate elements of Scottish culture.

Most notably the challenge was taken up by two major Scottish poets in this century, Edwin Muir and Hugh MacDiarmid. Their work in the late thirties, in particular – criticism and poetry – was wholly dominated by a colossal effort of 'Seeing Scotland Whole', as MacDiarmid put it in his autobiography *Lucky Poet*.[5] They both took their cue from Gregory Smith's conception of the 'Caledonian antisyzygy'. Between them, Muir and MacDiarmid succeeded in inflating this problematic conception to such proportions that for decades to come it almost paralyzed any debate on what modern Scottish culture might be. Contemporary Scottish culture has been persistently haunted by the spectre of the 'antisyzygy'. Its favourite hunting ground seems to be sweeping statements on the state of Scottish culture of the more maudlin kind. But as a close second comes 'serious' criticism. Indeed, many critics, poets among them, have gone out of their way to provide an ample, and seemingly inexhaustible, supply of blood for the ghosts.[6] Yet contemporary Scottish poetry and criticism have also provided spaces beyond the 'antisyzygy' in which a new attitude towards the heterogeneous experience of Scotland could be developed.

2

The 'Caledonian antisyzygy' is the problematic offspring of a discourse commonly known as 'Eng. Lit.'. The discourse of 'Eng. Lit.', as developed in the late nineteenth century, is based on a conception of English national literature as expressing the spirit of English national life, its history mirroring the growth of the national mind. It was largely developed by writers from the peripheries of Britain, mainly Scottish and Irish intellectuals (drawing on continental, mainly German models), as part of a strategy by which they wrote themselves into English culture.[7]

In this century, the discourse of 'Eng. Lit.' turned out to be much more tenacious than the United Kingdom itself. Originally developed as a strategy supporting integration into the United Kingdom by writers from the peripheries themselves, it proved to be hard to get rid of when, at the beginning of the century, Scottish and Irish writers began to reassert their own cultural traditions. Their acts of reassertion typically took the form of an attempt to establish an *Irish* or *Scottish* national identity independent of the English. Yet this is precisely the point where trouble started for Scottish writers: in their attempts to construct a national literature of their own, these writers, often trained within the discourse of 'Eng. Lit.', inevitably came up against the standards set by English literature. Compared with the 'Great tradition' of English literature, Scottish literature to their embarrassment looked a very patchy affair. Nowhere is this clearer than in a history of Scottish literature written at the beginning of the century by a Scottish lecturer in English at Edinburgh University: G. Gregory Smith's *Scottish Literature: Character and Influence* (1919). It was a passage of this book which provided the Scottish Literary Renaissance with its famous phrase, the 'Caledonian antisyzygy'. In reflecting on the course of Scottish literature, Gregory Smith here notes 'two considerations of contrary bearing':

> One is of encouragement; that the literature is a literature of a small country, that it runs a shorter course than others, and that there is no linguistic divorce between its earlier and its later stages, as in southern English. In this shortness and cohesion the most favourable conditions seem to be offered for the making of a general estimate. But, on the other hand, we find at closer scanning that this cohesion, at least in formal expression and in choice of material, is only apparent, that the literature is remarkably varied, and that it becomes, under the stress of foreign influence and native division and reaction, almost a zigzag of contradictions. The antithesis need not, however, disconcert us. Perhaps in the very combination of opposites – what either of the two Sir Thomases, of Norwich and Cromarty, might have been willing to call 'the Caledonian antisyzygy' – we have the reflection of the contrasts which the Scot shows at every turn, in his political and ecclesiastical history, in his polemical restlessness, in his adaptability, which is another way of saying that he has made allowance for new conditions, in his practical judgement, which is the admission that two sides of the matter have been considered. If there-

fore Scottish history and life are, as an old northern writer said of something else, 'varied with a clean contrair spirit,' we need not be surprised to find that in his literature the Scot presents two aspects which appear contradictory. Oxymoron has ever been the bravest figure, and we must not forget that disorderly order is order after all. We can be indifferent to the disciples of De Quincey who will suspect us of making 'ambitious paradoxes' and 'false distinctions'. We may dwell on these incongruities, the better to explain their remarkable synthesis in Scottish literature; as we may, in a later chapter, on the breaks and thwarts, the better to show the continuity of a literary tradition.[8]

Gregory Smith here is at pains to prove that Scottish literature is a true expression of the Scottish mind. The idea of an organic national literary tradition, as exemplified in the discourse of 'Eng. Lit.', is clearly present in the background as the standard of comparison and it provides the framework in which the passage is enclosed. Thus the passage begins and ends by naming the most important aspects of the standard: 'cohesion' and 'continuity'. This framework at the same time reveals what Gregory Smith perceives as the chief characteristic of Scottish literature, namely its *lack* of coherence and continuity, and it contains the discontinuity it has revealed in a semblance of coherence and continuity. Working from within the interpretative framework of 'Eng. Lit.', Gregory Smith clearly perceives Scottish literature as deficient (hence his all too frequent assurances to the effect that nobody needs to be worried by the worrying state of affairs he describes). He therefore adapts the framework in such a way that it fits Scottish literature.

Of crucial importance here is the paradoxical term around which the whole passage is set. 'Antisyzygy' means a combination of opposites. With the help of this term, Gregory Smith performs a conjuring trick of admirable, if doubtful, ingenuity: he locates the phenomenon which he is describing in a tradition which embraces both English and Scottish literature. The trick works by tentatively ascribing the freakishly quasi-humanist term to two seventeenth-century authors, both well-known for their idiosyncratic style and masters of 'ambitious paradoxes', one from Scotland: Sir Thomas Urquhart of Cromarty, author of *The Jewel* and translator of Rabelais, and one from England: Sir Thomas Browne of Norwich, author of *Religio Medici*,

Pseudodoxia Epidemica, Hydriotaphia and *The Garden of Cyrus*. These two 'Sir Thomases' might well have coined a phrase like 'Caledonian antisyzygy' and, more importantly, like seventeenth-century literature in general,[9] they both took great delight in any 'zigzag of contradictions'. By naming them as possible authors of his term, then, Gregory Smith indicates a tradition comprising both Scotland and England, in which the embarrassing lack of coherence and continuity displayed by Scottish literature might look more normal than otherwise. Despite the ingenious conjuring trick, however, the idea of the 'Caledonian antisyzygy' clearly bears the traces of its origin in some deeply troubled thinking about Scottish literature, the trouble arising mainly from Gregory Smith's desperate need to make sense of Scottish literature in terms of the discourse of 'Eng. Lit.' within which he was working. In the final analysis the 'Caledonian antisyzygy' is an expression of a sense of inferiority induced by the uneasy existence of Scottish literature in between conflicting cultural fields.

3

In 1936 the poet Edwin Muir published a famous book of criticism, *Scott and Scotland. The Predicament of the Scottish Writer*,[10] in which he spells out the implications of the 'Caledonian antisyzygy' as formulated by Gregory Smith and takes it to its logical extreme. The argument offered in *Scott and Scotland* could be summarized as follows: if one accepts the notion that a homogeneous culture reflected in a homogeneous body of literature is the highest aim to be achieved, then no amount of clever reasoning and no 'ambitious paradoxes' can explain away the fact that a fragmented cultural inheritance must be ultimately harmful. The only solution, then, would be to join the one cultural tradition available which does seem to fulfil the norm.

For Muir, as for Gregory Smith, this meant English culture. Throughout his book, English culture as the standard of comparison applied stands for completeness, Scottish culture for fragmentation. The whole book is pervaded by a juxtaposition of images of completeness and fragmentation: England possesses an organic society, a homogeneous language, a rich and continuous literary tradition; Scotland's society is fragmented, it does not possess a homogeneous language, its literary history is nothing but a series of disconnected figures. Through this set of juxta-positions Muir re-enacts a fable of loss. In the particular story of *Scott and Scotland* this loss is identified as 'the lack of a whole mind' (p.9) brought about by a 'far-reaching dissociation' (p.72). This dissociation had set in as a result of the loss of Scots as an autonomous language and the concomitant introduction of English into Scotland. Both were brought about by a complex interaction of historical and religious events (the Reformation had introduced the English Bible; the Unions of Crowns and Parliaments in 1603 and 1707 meant that Scots was replaced by English as the official language of all Scotland). According to Muir, this meant 'that Scotsmen feel in one language and think in another; that their emotions turn to the Scottish tongue with all its associations of local sentiment, and their minds to a standard English which for them is almost bare of associations other than of the classroom' (p.8). It also meant the loss of a common language, capable of expressing the full range of modern experi-ence on all levels of discourse and in all literary genres and it finally led to a fragmentation of Scottish culture as a whole. Muir maintains that 'Scotland will remain a mere collection of districts' unless Scottish literature finds an 'adequate language' in which to recreate a sense of a full national life (p.112). This, according to Muir, could only be achieved by an 'act of faith' (p.113) similar to that performed by Yeats in Irish literature, an act of faith by which Scottish writers would take full advantage of English as the only language capable of full expression still available to them (Scots being disqualified by its fragmentation into numerous local dialects and its impoverished literary tradi-tion, and Gaelic by its minority status). This would still involve a loss, be only a partial solution to the 'Predicament of the Scottish writer', since English could never be invested with those 'associations of local sentiment' which belong to the vernacular. Writing in English, then, in Muir's view could only be an approx-imation to the ideal of wholeness, but certainly the closest approximation possible. Indeed, it is only in the dreamlike vision of his poetry, written in the classical blank verse of Shakespeare, Milton, and Wordsworth (the great tradition of English poetry which Muir chose to join), that Muir can finally perceive fragmented Scotland as 'a difficult country, and our home' ('The Difficult Land'),[11] in which the violence and waste of its history is bound into a mythical pattern, the scene fixed in the timelessness of myth, the speaker's voice gathered into the collective 'we' of a national community.

4

Whereas Muir, facing what he perceived as Scotland's fragmentation, opted for the English language and the English tradition in literature as a cultural field in which to root his poetry, MacDiarmid, at about the same time, firmly opted for the indigenous Gaelic tradition. By the 1930s, MacDiarmid, partly in a furious reaction against Muir, had come to see the Gaelic as the only genuinely Scottish tradition. Given his own background in Lowland Scots culture and given that Gaelic culture is only a minority culture in modern Scotland (and a much beleaguered one at that), this decision was fraught with obvious difficulties. It was a decision, in fact, which may seem even more problematic than Muir's decision for the English tradition. But, interestingly, MacDiarmid's understanding of the Gaelic tradition offered him a way of dealing positively with Scotland's fragmentation, a way which may be described as love of the land itself in all its diversity. In Gaelic nature poetry he found a praise of place and the minutest detail of nature which delights in diversity rather than homogeneity. This attitude to place gave MacDiarmid not only a precedent for his own tendency to value equally each and every patch of Scottish soil, irrespective of the different histories and traditions encoded in them. It also gave new resonance to his favourite notion of the 'Caledonian antisyzygy' which he increasingly came to associate with the value system of Gaelic nature poetry:

> In the wonderful diversity and innumerable
> Sharp transitions of the Scottish scene,
> The source of our Scottish antisyzygy,
> I . . . See now the reconciliation of all opposites.[12]
>
> ('Dìreadh I')

Thus the notion of the 'Caledonian antisyzygy' undergoes an important transformation in the work of the later MacDiarmid (cf. particularly the travel-book *The Islands of Scotland* and the 'Dìreadh' sequence of poems with its three bird's-eye views of Scotland[13]). It is no longer rooted in a supposed common English/Scottish tradition, going back to the seventeenth century, as it was in Gregory Smith's text, but in the utterly un-English, much older, indigenous Gaelic tradition. And whereas Muir, faced with Scotland's linguistic diversity, mournfully opted for English as the lesser evil, MacDiarmid energetically embraced the vision of a future 'world language'[14] which would thrive precisely on a diversity of languages such as Scotland had inherited. Although this 'world language' would not be identical with any of Scotland's three languages, its roots would be in Gaelic, not in English.

This shift of perspective made it possible for MacDiarmid, firstly, to prove that contemporary Scottish culture could be explained in terms of an indigenous tradition, in other words, that against all appearances contemporary Scottish culture was based on a continuous tradition and, secondly, to attach positive value to Scotland's fragmentation, which had proved so troublesome to Gregory Smith and Muir. In fact, 'fragmentation' increasingly comes to be replaced by 'diversity', a term with much more positive connotations, in MacDiarmid's writing of the thirties, prose and poetry. MacDiarmid thus prepared the way for a view of Scottish culture which no longer needed to be apologetic about its fragmentation. Indeed, the 'Caledonian antisyzygy' in his hands came close to meaning a diversity *no longer in need of* the reconciliation of opposites indicated in the term 'antisyzygy'. Nevertheless, in the final analysis both Muir *and* MacDiarmid still share Gregory Smith's basic assumption that a country's culture is valid only in so far as it can be shown that it is based on a common national identity. Hence their attempts to link Scottish culture to a single line of tradition, the English in Muir's case, the Gaelic in MacDiarmid's case. Yet the enormous 'act of faith' involved in *both* attempts indicates that the idea of a common national identity has finally arrived at breaking point. This is true for both Muir and MacDiarmid, regardless of the fact that their respective 'acts of faith' take very different forms. It is difficult, indeed, to imagine how Scots from all backgrounds could rally round either Muir's vision of 'The Difficult Land' or MacDiarmid's Gaelic 'Vision of a World language'.

5

With Muir and MacDiarmid the project of 'Seeing Scotland Whole' arrived at a point where it could hardly be continued. A witty epitaph to the whole project may be found in Edwin Morgan's concrete poem 'A Chaffinch Map of Scotland' (1965)[15] which teasingly takes up Muir's and MacDiarmid's triple concern with the diversity of Scotland, a focus on the country as a whole, and a language to express its true tradition. The 'Chaffinch Map of Scotland' consists of an accurate inventory of the local variations of the bird-names as they occur in Scotland, typographically arranged on the page in such a way that it resembles the outlines of the map of Scotland. Read aloud, this map of Scotland is onomatopoeically transformed into a chorus of birdsong (rhythmically patterned by different line lengths, the line breaks and gaps in the lines shaping the contours of Scotland on the page) which takes the sound shape of the word 'chaffinch' through a series of variations: 'chaffinch / chaffinchaffinch / . . . / chaffie chye chaffiechaffie / . . . / shillyshelly / . . . / shilfyshelfyshelly / shellyfaw / shielyshellyfaw / . . . / shilfyshelfyshelfy chaffiechaffie / . . . / shilfy / shilfyshelfy', and then laconically breaks off with the *one* term in the whole list – located in the southernmost corner of Scotland – which is *not* phonetically related to 'chaffinch': 'brichtie'. This 'Chaffinch Map of Scotland' (a pun on 'half-inch map', of course) wittily and playfully satirizes any attempt at charting 'Scotland Whole'.[16] It totally lacks the searching seriousness of either Muir's or MacDiarmid's visions (Scotland a birdsong: 'syzygy, 'syzygy, 'syzygy . . .). At the same time it demonstrates at a very 'concrete' level how effectively the linguistic variety of Scotland may be used for poetic purposes, thus at one sweep brushing aside both Muir's argument for English as the only possible language for Scottish literature and MacDiarmid's heady metaphysical construction of a Gaelic 'world language'.

Indeed, many contemporary Scottish poets after Muir and MacDiarmid seem to be tired of the subject of Scotland altogether. Iain Crichton Smith has spoken of his feeling that 'there is nothing real in Scotland that you can actually operate on to make real poetry', that there is 'just talking about what has gone on in the past' and he compares the case of Scotland with the very different case of contemporary Ireland where the pressure of

everyday violence *does* create a powerful commitment to the
question of Ireland: 'I think the Irish poets are very lucky, in a
sense, because they have to deal with real things.'[17] Norman
MacCaig, asked about his Scottish loyalties, gave a scornfully
polemical answer which betrays his extreme exasperation with a
nationalism locked into mournful contemplation of Scotland's
past and his refusal to deal with any generalizations about
national character as against a concern with the individual:

> I don't like the Scots, and I don't like their history. Liars, murderers,
> traitors, not only in the Highlands, the Borders as well. I think the
> Scots are awful . . . I think everybody's awful, except when you meet
> a particular instance, and some of them are so wonderful and marvel-
> lous . . . and don't tell me they came from their filthy history.[18]

Whereas Crichton Smith in a way regrets the absence of a cause
which might generate commitment to the idea of Scotland,
MacCaig utterly refuses to join any such cause, even if it would
present itself. The jibe against the Scots' 'filthy history' is a refusal
to consider at all seriously Muir's contention that Scotland's
history must be a 'predicament of the Scottish writer'. MacCaig's
insistence on the individual instance would allow neither general-
izations about the collective identity of '*the* Scottish writer' nor
about the meaning of Scottish history as a whole.

6

In contemporary Scottish poetry there is still a powerful commit-
ment to the experience of Scotland. But the attempt to imagine a
common national identity seems to have been abandoned for
good. Instead, poets tend to express their sense of Scotland
through an exploration of the landscapes, the history, the tradi-
tions, the languages of those Scottish regions and places which
more immediately belong to their own personal background. In
the attitude to place in contemporary Scottish poetry we thus
observe a phenomenon which – adapting Tom Nairn's famous
phrase of 'The Break-Up of Britain'[19] – we may call 'The Break-
Up of Scotland': a shift from a predominantly national to a
predominantly regional concern. This is certainly a shift towards
places more clearly recognizable and closer to the actual experi-
ence of Scotland than Muir's and MacDiarmid's Scotlands of the

mind. But the regional places of contemporary Scottish poetry are by no means less resistant to attempts to imagine them in a single vision, encoded securely in a single unbroken line of tradition or a single perspective. They tend to be precarious inter-spaces between landscape, history, and the traditions and languages involved in Scottish culture. Three examples from the work of Sorley MacLean, Norman MacCaig, and Edwin Morgan may serve to illustrate the point.

Sorley MacLean's 'Hallaig' (1954)[20] is perhaps the most famous poem of place in contemporary Scottish poetry and has become a touchstone for any concern with the difficult regional places of Scotland. It is a meditation on the changes worked by time on the place where the poet's family lived for centuries ('Time, the deer, is in the wood of Hallaig'), written in Gaelic and translated into English by the poet himself. Hallaig is seen as a place of desolation where the old vegetation has taken over from the people driven away in the clearances; yet in the speaker's vision the desolation seems alive with the people who once lived there:

> Na fir 'nan laighe air an lianaig
> aig ceann gach taighe a bh' ann,
> na h-igheanan 'nan coille bheithe,
> dìreach an druim, crom an ceann.

> The men lying on the green
> at the end of every house that was,
> the girls a wood of birches,
> straight their backs, bent their heads.

The place of Hallaig in this poem is an inter-space, encoded in the *difference* between past and present and in the *difference* between two languages. In fact, the poem itself has ceased to be monolingual: MacLean's English translation from his Gaelic is not only an expendable concession to the multilingual publishing situation in Scotland, but an essential part of the poem, reflecting the fact that the speaker's perspective on Hallaig no longer allows for a space in which Gaelic would *not* have to compete/coexist with English. The inter-space from which Hallaig emerges is frozen in time by the speaker's loving vision:

and when the sun goes down behind Dun Cana
a vehement bullet will come from the gun of Love;

and will strike the deer that goes dizzily
. . .
his eye will freeze in the wood,
his blood will not be traced while I live.

Yet the speaker sees himself as a poacher illegally hunting time, his prey, at nightfall. Thus his vision is an extremely precarious one which has to be guarded in secrecy as long as he lives.

Norman MacCaig's poem 'A Man in Assynt' (1967)[21] is also concerned with a difficult place in Gaelic Scotland. But its speaker – in not belonging to the Gaelic language community himself – is yet further exiled from the place than MacLean's poacher in the country of his ancestors. The landscape of Assynt, scene of the notorious Sutherland Clearances which left it as desolate as MacLean's Hallaig, is seen with the eye of a visitor from Edinburgh who loves it but does not belong to it:

Up there, the scraping light
whittles the cloud edges till, like thin bone,
they're bright with their own opaque selves. Down here,
a skinny rosebush is an eccentric jug
of air. They make me,
somewhere between them,
a visiting eye,
an unrequited passion,
watching the tide glittering backward and making
its huge withdrawal from beaches
and kilted rocks. And the mind
behind the eye, within the passion,
remembers with certainty that the tide will return
and thinks, with hope, that that other ebb,
the sad withdrawal of people, may, too,
reverse itself and flood
the bays and the sheltered glens
with new generations replenishing the land
with its richest of riches and coming, at last,
into their own again.

The Assynt of MacCaig's poem is neither just primordial landscape, nor just a place defined by its history of loss. At the beginning of the paragraph quoted here it seems completely governed by the mind of the observer which gives it a structure between 'Up there' and 'Down here' and encodes it in striking conceits ('a skinny rosebush is an eccentric jug/of air'). Yet the observing mind, oscillating between memory and hope, is itself governed by the cyclical rhythms of nature, ebb tide and flood tide. The place of Assynt thus is at the intersection between the landscape, its history, and the mind of the outside observer.

Even more than Assynt, the urban wasteland of Edwin Morgan's 'Glasgow Green' (1968)[22] resists the attempt to be defined by a single voice. Glasgow Green in this poem is encoded between different voices, harshly set against each other. The scene is set by a strictly conventional, somewhat melodramatic, poetic evocation of mood: 'Clammy midnight, moonless mist . . . Meth-men mutter on benches,/pawed by river fog . . .' Into this scene, the immediacy of direct speech intrudes violently, a Glasgow dialect voice enacting a homosexual rape:

> 'What d'ye mean see me again?
> D'ye think I came here jist for that?
> I'm no finished with you yet.
> I can get the boys t'ye, they're no that faur away.
> You wouldny like that eh? Look there's no two ways aboot it.
> Christ but I'm gaun to have you Mac
> if it takes all night, turn over you bastard
> turn over, I'll –'

And here a different voice interrupts with a sharp 'Cut the scene'. This voice insists on the brutal reality of the scene, not to be defused and made acceptable by any conventions of horror fiction: 'the sweat/is real, the wrestling under a bush/is real, the dirty starless river/is the real Clyde'. Yet this voice also notes an aspect of the place very different from the violent nocturnal incident, coming to another break in the poem with the first naming of the place:

>   . . . washing blows
>   where the women watch
>   by day,
>   and children run,
>   on Glasgow Green.

By the time the place is named for the first time, then, the poem
has moved through a number of different voices and aspects all
belonging to the place, thus constituting it as a multidimensional
reality. At this point, another voice breaks in, the passionately
insistent voice of popular pulpit oratory, searching for a meaning
between the violence and the peacefulness, culminating in a
prophetic appeal to reinvent the place:

> Water the wilderness, walk there, reclaim it!
> Reclaim, regain, renew! Fill the barns and the vats!
>
> Longing,
> longing
> shall find its wine.

Yet this vision of renewal is denied its fulfilment in the poem. In
the last paragraph an altogether more sceptical voice takes over
from the passionately prophetical voice and encodes the place in
a metaphor defining it as a place in which the universal principle
of desire acts itself out perpetually:

> Let the women sit in the Green
> and rock their prams as the sheets
> blow and whip in the sunlight.
> But the beds of married love
> are islands in a sea of desire.
> Its waves break here, in this park,
> splashing the flesh as it trembles
> like driftwood through the dark.

The place of Glasgow Green thus remains suspended in a space
of never-fulfilled desire between the violence and the peaceful-
ness, between acceptance and the hope for renewal. None of the
voices in this poem is ultimately allowed to gain control over the
others.

These three examples all testify to a continuing process of rein-
venting Scotland. They all take Muir's and MacDiarmid's
investigations one important step further: having abandoned the
attempt to construct a common national identity out of a diver-
sity of elements in favour of a commitment to places which have
a more immediately personal significance for them, MacLean,
MacCaig, and Morgan discover the experience of heterogeneity
within the very place they have singled out for closer inspection.

The important point, however, is that they do not attempt to reconcile this heterogeneity in one single vision but let their places exist, precariously and changeably, in the spaces between conflicting influences. Thus they do justice to the experience of Scotland in all its diversity – and they do so without recourse to a concept like the 'Caledonian antisyzygy'.

7

Yet critical concepts, once established, tend to acquire a life of their own which lasts long after their usefulness has been exhausted. Contemporary criticism, at any rate, was rather slower in discarding the 'Caledonian antisyzygy' than poetry. Thus the discourse of the 'Caledonian antisyzygy' and the 'Predicament of the Scottish Writer' resurfaced with a vengeance when, in 1979, the referendum on the 'Scotland and Wales Act' failed to produce enough support for even a modest degree of Scottish independence. Initially writers, in an attempt to make sense of their cultural situation, responded to this failure by reviving the debate Muir and MacDiarmid between them had already thoroughly exhausted. Muir's *Scott and Scotland* was reissued in 1982. The publisher's blurb announced it as still 'one of the most important and provocative criticisms of Scottish literature to be written in this century' and made it the subject of a conference which was to discuss the implications of Muir's analysis for contemporary writers. This proved to be the 'Cultural Non Event of the Year', as Joy Hendry noted at the time.[23] Any number of mournful clichés about 'the Scottish Writer' were freely bandied about, the claims of Gaelic and Scots to the true inheritance of Scotland were discussed with more or less conviction, and where Muir's book was confronted at all it was indiscriminately dismissed without even the attempt to place it in a broader perspective. The question of what the 'Predicament' of Scottish writers might be and how it could be overcome was lost beyond recovery in this debate.

In fact, apparently unnoticed by the prophets of doom, the question itself was becoming obsolete. Against all expectations, the 1979 débâcle proved to be far from detrimental to Scottish culture. On the contrary, the 1980s saw an upsurge of creativity which amounted to something like a new Scottish Renaissance.

Among the signs of the times was the appearance of an important new magazine, started by young writers and intellectuals directly in the wake of 1979. *Cencrastus*, which in its subtitle self-confidently links Scottish to 'International Literature, Arts and Affairs', offered a forum for a lively and fiercely intellectual debate on Scottish culture – certainly not a cosy hunting ground for the ghosts. At about the same time Tessa Ransford and Tom Hubbard began building up quite literally a 'room of their own' for Scottish poets, the Scottish Poetry Library in Edinburgh, which made it possible for the first time for a wider public to become acquainted with a wide range of poetry published in all three of Scotland's languages. Thus it became possible to acquire a knowledge of Scottish poetry which was no longer dependent on what the institutions of 'Eng. Lit.' might or might not provide.

This process was continued in the eighties with the appearance of several new histories of Scottish literature, notably Roderick Watson's *The Literature of Scotland*, which paved the way by giving 'a straightforward account of the lives, times and major works of Scotland's writers',[24] and the four-volume *History of Scottish Literature* edited by Cairns Craig,[25] which charts the terrain more closely through individual essays by a wide range of specialists focusing on particular aspects of Scotland's literary inheritance. Watson still paid cautious tribute to 'the presence of such factors as the 'Caledonian antisyzygy' . . . without proposing these as necessary, or exclusive proofs of Scottishness'.[26] In the volumes edited by Craig, any such considerations are notably absent. And it was Craig who formulated, in his introduction to the volume on the twentieth-century, the critical dogma which seems to be beginning to supplant that of the 'Predicament of the Scottish Writer':

> In defiance of critical theories that assert otherwise, the apparent lack of a coherent tradition, the lack of a coherent national culture, far from impeding development have been major stimuli to creativity. Scottish writers have been inspired by the condition of being between cultures rather than within a culture . . .[27]

This statement appears somewhat too purposefully optimistic when applied retrospectively to the whole story of Scottish literature in this century. Muir and MacDiarmid clearly aspired to 'the condition of being . . . *within* a culture'. If this has certainly not prevented them from writing very fine poetry, it has not exactly helped them either. And by no stretch of the imagination could it be said that the discourse of the 'Caledonian antisyzygy' which they bequeathed to contemporary Scottish culture did anything at all towards creating a lively intellectual climate which might prove a positive stimulus to creativity. On the contrary, this discourse proved positively stifling, as becomes painfully obvious when reading the documents of the 1982 debate on the 'Predicament of the Scottish Writer'. And even in 1992 Douglas Dunn still senses a 'skeleton' rattling in the 'Caledonian cupboard'.[28] But Craig's statement does indeed summarize the new spirit of the Scottish cultural renaissance of the eighties. This renaissance took its intellectual stimulus certainly not from the outworn discourse of the 'Caledonian anti-syzygy' but rather from the new international discourse of the multicultural society which became prevalent throughout the eighties and provided a fresh perspective on Scottish culture, too. With regard to the most recent Scottish poetry Douglas Dunn notes: 'If anything explains the unclenched nationalism, or refusal of any kind of nationalism on a poem's surface, it is the eclectic reading and wider range of influences to which younger writers have exposed themselves.'[29] The national perspective on Scottish culture was beginning to give way to a comparative perspective. This new comparative perspective was evident in the programme for the Edinburgh Commonwealth Writers Conference in July 1986. It was perhaps best summarized by Seamus Heaney, speaking at the 'International Conference on the Literature of Region and Nation' which took place one month later, in August 1986, at the University of Aberdeen. 'I have a sense that nowadays the writers on the outskirts know more about one another than ever before and have begun to take cognisance of each other in ways that are fortifying and illumi-nating',[30] Heaney said, and he concluded his 'regional forecast' by maintaining that

> poets in these various regional, post-colonial or off-center situations have long ago been freed to throw away the cracked looking-glass of the servant and to scan the world instead through the cunningly arranged and easily manoeuverable periscope of their submerged sensibility.[31]

As Craig points out, the 'fragmentation and division which made Scotland seem abnormal to an earlier part of the twentieth century came to be the norm for much of the world's population'[32] – as it is, indeed, for the disintegrating English society of our days. Which means, of course, that the standards of 'Eng. Lit.' have become obsolete even in England. Consequently, there is no longer any reason why Scottish writers should apologize for not conforming to these standards.

8

Diversity in itself is hardly a meaningful concept. In order to be experienced as meaningful, the 'situation between cultures rather than within a culture' requires the continuing effort of defining places in between from which speaking and writing becomes possible. Such places will have to be scrupulously exact as to the details of landscape, history, and language; but above all, inevitably, changeable and eminently precarious. In fact, places such as Edwin Morgan's 'On the Needle's Point': 'Of course it is not a point at all./ We live here, and we should know.'[33] The place on the needle's point may eventually even turn out to be something like a precarious paradise:

> But I like it on the point, good
> is the dark cavern, good the craggy walks,
> good the vertiginous bare brightness,
> good the music, good the dance
> when sometimes we join wings and drift
> in interlinking circles, how many thousands
> I could never tell, silent ourselves,
> almost melting into light.[34]

At any rate, 'On the Needle's Point' is probably as good a place as any from which to develop a poetics of the truly multicultural society.

Notes

1 Bill Ashcroft, Gareth Griffiths, Helen Tiffin, *The Empire Writes Back. Theory and Practice in Post-colonial Literatures* (London, 1989), 36.
2 Ibid., 12.

3   Cairns Craig, 'Being Between', official programme of the Commonwealth Writers Conference, Edinburgh, 17–21 July 1986, 7. Craig's argument here is based on several previous publications, in particular his important essay 'Peripheries' in *Cencrastus*, 9 (1982), 3–9.

4   G. Gregory Smith, *Scottish Literature. Character and Influence* (London, 1919).

5   'Seeing Scotland Whole' is the title of a chapter in MacDiarmid's *Lucky Poet* (1943) (reprinted London, 1972).

6   Witness, most recently, Robin Bell's relentlessly facetious introduction to his otherwise useful anthology of contemporary Scottish poetry, *The Best of Scottish Poetry. An Anthology of Contemporary Scottish Verse* (Edinburgh, 1989).

7   Important contributions were made, for example, by the Scottish writer Thomas Carlyle and the Irish critic Edward Dowden. This is not sufficiently realized in recent English accounts of 'The rise of English' (Eagleton) which tend to over-emphasize the role played by Matthew Arnold. Cf. Terry Eagleton, 'The rise of English', in his *Literary Theory* (Oxford, 1983), 17–53; Chris Baldick, *The Social Mission of English Criticism, 1848–1932* (Oxford, 1987).

8   *Scottish Literature: Character and Influence*, op. cit., 3–5.

9   For complex reasons, seventeenth-century English literature proved to be a useful point of contact with 'mainstream' English literature for poets from the 'peripheries' throughout this century. Cf. T. S. Eliot's 'Metaphysicals' essay of 1921 and, more recently, Seamus Heaney's praise of George Herbert in *The Redress of Poetry. An Inaugural Lecture Delivered Before the University of Oxford on 24 October 1989* (Oxford, 1990).

10 Rpt. Edinburgh, 1982. Subsequently, page numbers in brackets refer to this reprint.

11 Edwin Muir, *Collected Poems* (London, 1984), 238.

12 Muir's and MacDiarmid's contributions to the discourse of the 'Caledonian antisyzygy' are discussed in more detail in a previous version of this essay: Ursula Kimpel, 'Modern Scottish Poetry. Beyond the "Caledonian antisyzygy"', in Lothar Fietz, Paul Hoffmann, Hans-Werner Ludwig (eds.), *Regionalität, Nationalität und Internationalität in der zeitgenössischen Lyrik* (Tübingen, 1992), 284–302.

13 *The Complete Poems of Hugh MacDiarmid*, ed. Michael Grieve and W. R. Aitken (Hardmondsworth, 1985), vol.II, 1170.

14 Extracts from *The Islands of Scotland* (1939) are reprinted in Alan Bold (ed.), *The Thistle Rises. An Anthology of Poetry and Prose by Hugh MacDiarmid* (London, 1984); the 'Dìreadh' sequence, written as part of MacDiarmid's 'Mature Art' project submitted to Faber and Faber in 1938, although it was not published independently

before 1974, is reprinted in *The Complete Poems of Hugh MacDiarmid*, vol.II, 1163–93.

15 'A Vision of World Language' was to be the title of a long poem which MacDiarmid began writing in 1939. The only part of this project which was ever completed is 'In Memoriam James Joyce' (*Complete Poems*, vol.II, 737–889). This poem develops the idea of and itself acts out the movement towards a 'world language'.

16 'A Chaffinch Map of Scotland' was one of Morgan's contributions to Emmett Williams's famous *Anthology of Concrete Poetry* (New York, 1967).

17 Christopher Carrell (ed.), *Seven Poets* (Glasgow, Third Eye Centre, 1981), 47. The seven poets presented in this attractive publication (with portraits by the Scottish painter Alexander Moffat, photographs by Jessie Ann Matthews, interviews, selections of their poetry, biographical and bibliographical material) are Hugh MacDiarmid, Norman MacCaig, Iain Crichton Smith, George Mackay Brown, Robert Garioch, Sorley MacLean and Edwin Morgan.

18 Ibid., 38.

19 Tom Nairn, *The Break-Up of Britain* (2nd edn. London, 1981).

20 Reprinted in Sorley MacLean, *Spring Tide and Neap Tide. Selected Poems 1932–72/Reothairt is Contraigh. Taghadh de Dhàin 1932–72* (Edinburgh, 1981), 142–5.

21 'A Man in Assynt' was commissioned by the BBC and broadcast in 1967. It was printed in MacCaig's collection *A Man in My Position* (1969) and reprinted in his *Collected Poems* (London, 1985), 214–20.

22 'Glasgow Green' appeared in Morgan's collection *The Second Life* (1968) and was reprinted in his *Selected Poems* (Manchester, 1985), 30–3.

23 In her editorial to the special issue of *Chapman* devoted to the question 'The State of Scotland – A Predicament for the Scottish Writer?' *Chapman*, 35–26 (1983), 1.

24 Roderick Watson, *The Literature of Scotland* (London, 1984), Macmillan History of Literature series), 4.

25 *The History of Scottish Literature*, general ed. Cairns Craig, 4 vols. (Aberdeen, 1987–8). Watson and Craig provide the best general introduction to Scottish literature. The individual essays in Craig's *Aberdeen History of Scottish Literature* also provide suggestions for further reading.

26 Roderick Watson *The Literature of Scotland*, op. cit. 4.

27 Cairns Craig (ed.) *The History of Scottish Literature*, vol.IV,, (Aberdeen, 1987), 3.

28 In his introduction to the *Faber Book of Twentieth-Century Scottish Poetry* (London, 1992), xlv.

29 Ibid.
30 Seamus Heaney, 'The Regional Forecast', in R. P. Draper (ed.), *The Literature of Region and Nation* (London, 1989), 22.
31 Ibid., 23.
32 *The History of Scottish Literature*, vol.IV, op. cit., 7.
33 Edwin Morgan, *Selected Poems*, op. cit., 105–6.
34 Ibid., 106.

Anthologies of modern Scottish poetry:

Bell, Robin (ed.), *The Best of Scottish Poetry. An Anthology of Contemporary Scottish Verse* (Edinburgh, 1989).

Dunn, Douglas (ed.), *The Faber Book of Twentieth-Century Scottish Poetry,* (London, 1992) (with an introductory essay by Douglas Dunn: 'Language and Liberty', xvii–xlv).

Kerrigan, Catherine (ed.), *An Anthology of Scottish Women Poets* (Edinburgh, 1991).

King, Charles (ed.), *Twelve Modern Scottish Poets,* (London, 1971).

King, Charles and Smith, Iain Crichton (eds.), *Twelve More Modern Scottish Poets* (London, 1986).

MacAulay, Donald (ed.), *Nua-Bhardachd Gailidhlig/ Modern Scottish Gaelic Poems* (1976) (rpt. Edinburgh, 1980).

For a comparative perspective on modern Scottish poetry see also:

France, Peter and Glen, Duncan (eds.), *European Poetry in Scotland. An Anthology of Translations* (Edinburgh, 1990).

Hulse, Michael; Kennedy, David and Morley, David (eds.), *The New Poetry* (Newcastle upon Tyne, 1993).

8

Poetry in Scottish Gaelic, 1945–1992

DERICK S. THOMSON

This chapter should begin with a gentle warning. Its author has been writing poetry throughout the whole period under review, has edited the periodical which has published most of the periodical poetry of the time (*Gairm*), and has acted as publisher for most of the books of Gaelic poetry which appeared. That experience and involvement cannot easily be excluded from discussion of the topic.

The post-war period is probably one of the most interesting and vital in the whole history of Scottish Gaelic poetry, both in the quality of work produced and in the range of tensions and options that have arisen. We can usefully discuss the social and linguistic and intellectual background to the poetry before confronting it in detail.

1

The Gaelic-speaking population of Scotland is small, in the region of 80,000 to 90,000 for our period, and about half of that total is dispersed throughout the country, as small minorities in English- or Scots-speaking communities. The overall percentage of Gaelic-speakers in Scotland's population was 1.6 per cent in 1981, much smaller in many towns, and as high as 80–90 per cent in a few island communities. In the immediate post-war period, though the overall total of Gaelic-speakers was scarcely larger, the concentrations were different, with more island communities reaching percentages in the nineties, and with larger urban concentrations, at least in Glasgow. These were almost entirely *native* speakers, whereas now the number of *learner* speakers has grown significantly, while the linguistic integrity of formerly strong Gaelic communities has been seriously under-mined.

Economic considerations have, throughout the period and for long before its start, dictated that English gives a passport to employment. The consequent emphasis on English in the educational system was often overdone, so that many native Gaelic-speakers left school basically illiterate in Gaelic. They would, however, have some access to oral Gaelic culture, and, depending on geographical location and general cultural background, this would either be on a narrow, parochial level or have an additional historical depth in certain areas or families. It was common to find Gaelic-speakers who were familiar with English literature, but not with Gaelic literature. The background to this situation is complex, and here there is room only to list some of the relevant factors: economic need to migrate or emigrate, the attractions of employment in army, navy, merchant navy or colonial service, the linguistic assumptions imposed by Empire or UK citizenship.

As a result of these tensions and necessities, the Gaelic population could be roughly categorized as follows (in respect of possible reaction to Gaelic poetry): *a* illiterate in Gaelic, *b* illiterate in Gaelic but sympathetic to oral literature, *c* largely illiterate in Gaelic but familiar with English, or French, or Classical literature, *d* literate in Gaelic, *e* highly literate in Gaelic. That range of potentials was of course subject to the restriction that only a few people in any group are strongly attracted to poetry, but probably the percentage in Gaelic society was somewhat higher than usual because of the great historical prominence of song and poetry in the culture. Those in categories *d* and *e* above, the most literate in Gaelic, have a range of attitudes to poetry or verse, with their interests lying at various points in a scale that might be roughly designated as follows: local traditional verse, oral song and poetry more generally, *cèilidh* song (much of this being popular nine-teenth- and twentieth-century song), modern 'pop'-style song, traditional poetry including eighteenth- and seventeenth-century poetry, non-traditional poetry of the present. These categories are not mutually exclusive, but there are prejudices that come into play, so that some aficionados of pop would not tolerate eighteenth-century verse, and some admirers of eighteenth-century verse would not tolerate modern non-traditional verse.

At the most literate end of the scale some people become attracted to modernist developments in other literatures, principally English, Anglo-Irish and American, but also French and Spanish and German and Russian. This was a natural consequence of involvement in literary studies in an educational or career environment. A number of our Gaelic poets of the last fifty years have been professionally involved in teaching literature at either school or university level, and innovation in poetic method and style has come from these. On a different level there is apt to be tension between persons operating in a localized Gaelic area and those in an urban colony or in some sort of detached 'national' situation. There is a stance from which it is proclaimed that only by living in a strong Gaelic community can a poet be a spokesman of the Gaelic community. This is palpable nonsense, but it exists. Again, there is a wide range of possible stances, from the cosy community one to the most esoteric, avant-garde ones. Poetry has become much more cosmopolitan in the course of the twentieth century, but some smaller language communities may have had to move further in a shorter time: this has been the case with Scottish Gaelic.

Some of the community and individual tensions referred to became very clear to me in the early 1950s, in the opening years of the periodical *Gairm*, which began to appear in 1952. Some of these were based on local loyalties, so that the magazine could lose subscribers from Luing or Jura because these islands did not feature sufficiently in its pages. Sometimes the prejudices were more dialectal, and there are still Gaelic writers who push their own dialectal features. But the most vocal complaint was against non-traditional verse, then at the stage of challenging the long-accepted traditional forms. Sometimes this was mainly a protest by the old against innovation by the young. More commonly it was a defence of traditional metrics and poem construction, for Gaelic has a long history of fairly elaborate and strict metrics, and a rich tradition of assonantal music in its verse. Many other stylistic motifs and clichés had become woven into this poetic fabric, for example, a love of compilation, runs of near-synonyms, place-name litanies, clichés of nostalgia or protest. To some extent it was this somewhat hidebound character of traditional verse that the young poets of the time were impelled to jettison, so that there was a direct confrontation. It is true that the traditional system had already changed considerably in the nineteenth century, losing some of its metrical complexity, and often substituting nostalgia or cosiness or triviality for an older militancy or confidence. Thus there was felt to be a need to break with tradition on a number of fronts, and to make poetic state-ments that were more relevant to the time. The break also involved, very importantly, new concepts (not specifically of a metrical nature) of poem structure.

It was in these areas that a wider experience of other litera-tures, and especially of twentieth-century literature, made its impact. The world of poetry was clearly not to be confined to Uist or Skye, to battle-warriors or evicted crofters or homesick sailors; its metrics did not have to be regular and repetitive; a poem's plot could take a wide variety of forms. Whitman and Eliot were part of the metrical landscape, Yeats and Pound and the French Symbolists had further opened up the conceptual repertory, MacDiarmid's 'A Drunk Man looks at the Thistle' had provided a new model for a Scottish poem sequence.

In addition, the concept of a Scottish literary Renaissance, an expression used by the French critic Denis Saurat, and much elaborated by Hugh MacDiarmid, had the effect of attracting Gaelic writing to a wider context, ending its political isolation and defensive stance, and encouraging more positive and cosmopolitan initiatives. The earlier moves in Ireland towards political independence and literary assertion were admired, although Gaelic writing there was somewhat slower in coming into prominence. The nationalist movement in Scotland, despite a long history of 'home rule' attitudes, had a more strongly cultural impetus in the 1920s and 1930s, and a relatively weak political one, and this may have allowed interest in Gaelic to grow gradually, rather than flare up in a militant way. In the first two decades of the century, Ruaraidh Erskine of Mar had estab-lished strong links between political nationalism and Gaelic resurgence, through his various periodicals, especially *Guth na Bliadhna* ('The Year's Voice'), which ran from 1904 to 1925. He strongly emphasized the Irish connection too, and after the Russian Revolution developed Communist leanings. Probably to a greater extent than is commonly realized he may have influ-enced MacDiarmid's attitudes in the early post-1918 years. In any case, that combination of political and cultural burgeonings

was influential in liberating Gaelic writers, consciously or uncon-
sciously, bringing them into the larger Scottish stream, and
extending their horizons to Ireland, England, France and Russia,
for example. We can see some of these influences appearing in
Gaelic writing, particularly in poetry, from the First World War
years, again in the 1930s and 1940s, and in the quarter century
after the Second World War, creating what can be described as a
new norm in Gaelic poetry.

2

All the modern Gaelic poets show these influences to one extent
or another, while some were particularly influenced by individual
writers – Sorley MacLean by MacDiarmid, Donald MacAulay by
Pound – and several of the writers (including the author of this
Chapter) by Yeats.

Naturally, many of the central themes of earlier Gaelic poetry
survive in the post-war period, but with different emphases and
presentations. The theme of place or homeland is prominent,
sometimes with place-name litanies, but the treatment is less
sentimental or romanticized. It is also more oblique. Donald
MacAulay's 'Ceartaigh' refers to a little island off his native
island of Bernera (Lewis): he has a boy's memory of it as a 'Land
of multiple dances, of cotton-grass, wrens and bees', but also of
giants and heroes and fairies; it is also 'lagan còmhnaidh Ariel 's
Chaliban' ('the nook in which Ariel and Caliban dwell'), a refer-
ence that immediately distances the poem from the traditional
model, though it is followed directly by a run of place-names,
'Taigh-an-Talla 's Am Port Cam 's A' Chreag Mhòr'.[1] Poetry
about the historical clearances of tenants by landlords concerned
to develop profitable sheep-farming or to reserve land for game-
hunting still occurs in our period, but the landlord may now be
an incoming hotelier as in Catriona Montgomery's poem 'I see
you going the rounds of the tables',[2] and she thinks for a moment
that Catherine the Great of Russia has come to visit. Strathnaver
in Sutherland was the location of one of the most notorious
clearances of the early nineteenth century, but the burning of
houses is recalled as though it were a personal reminiscence at
the start of my poem 'Strathnaver':

In that blue-black sky,
as high above us as eternity,
a star was winking at us,
answering the leaping flames of fire
in the rafters of my father's house,
that year we thatched the house with snowflakes.[3]

Love poetry in the period is more confessional and certainly less stereotyped than the romantic set-pieces that were popular earlier, though here we need to recall an earlier Gaelic tradition of direct confessional song. The youngest of our poets to achieve a published profile, 25-year-old Anne Frater, gives expression to frustrated love using the imagery of glass (molten sand) through which she sees (perhaps) her loved one: she ends the poem with darting images of hope and doubt:

. . . Saying there is nothing
on the other side of the glass
but the mercury of my hope,
and that it isn't a window at all in front of me
but a cold mocking mirror.[4]

Probably frustration in love is more productive of poetry than is fulfilment: one of Iain Crichton Smith's early poems 'Tha thu air aigeann m' inntinn' ('You are at the bottom of my mind') uses the image of a diver on the sea-floor and his mate in the surface craft losing contact with each other, so that

. . . I do not rightly know your appearance or your manner
after five years of showers
of time pouring between me and you.

['S chan aithne dhomh ceart d' fhiamh no do dhòigh
an dèidh còig bliadhna shiantan
tìme dòrtadh eadar mise 's tù][5]

Change in society is an insistent theme in the poetry of this period, and the Second World War made a decisive watershed, reinforcing and almost completing the process, started by the First World War, of isolating the ancient Gaelic world and putting it into a museum showcase. Some of the post-war poets experienced aspects of that ancient world, and recall it lovingly. Sorley MacLean had written most of his significant poetry before 1943 (though various editions of his collected poems have appeared since 1977), but one of his best poems falls into our period: in 'Hallaig' he recalls a vanished society,

> . . . the girls a wood of birches,
> straight their backs, bent their heads.
> . . .
> and their beauty a film on my heart
> before the dimness comes on the kyles . . .[6]

My poem 'An Dàrna Eilean' ('The Second Island') suggests the impossibility of recovering lost experience:

> . . . [we] saw a loch in the island,
> and an island in the loch,
> and we recognised
> that the dream had moved away from us again.
>
> The stepping-stones are chancy
> to the second island,
> the stone totters
> that guards the berries,
> the rowan withers,
> we have lost now the scent of the honeysuckle.[7]

Mary Montgomery, further removed by her youth from the old world, wants to salvage some of it, though it has become a museum piece:

> . . . I must go to the museum
> . . . to see my history's artefacts
> before the half-vision I have
> of the half-story
> gets lost
> swept away by the brush at my heel.[8]

There was a strong tradition of religious verse in Gaelic, latterly confined largely to hymnody and elegy, especially for clergymen (both Catholic and Protestant). The great majority of post-war Gaelic poets appear to be agnostic, though they vary greatly in the explicitness of their attitudes. By contrast, Fearghas MacFhionnlaigh takes up a committed Christian stance, and brings his expertise in art and music into play in his complex and delicate distillation of experience, especially in his two long poems *A' Mheanbhchuileag*[9] ('The Midge') and *Iolair, Brù-dhearg, Giuthas*[10] ('Eagle, Red-breast, Pine'). The second of these, a glowing appreciation of his late mother, was published in 1991.

MacFhionnlaigh is also explicitly a Scottish Nationalist, as are several of the poets, particularly Hay, Thomson, Crichton Smith, William Neill, Maoilios Caimbeul, Mary Montgomery and Anne Frater. George Campbell Hay has several effective nationalist poems in his early collections *Fuaran Slèibh* ('Mountain Spring') (1947) and *O na Ceithir Airdean* ('From the Four Airts') (1952).[11] He wrote a good number of frankly propagandist political poems in later decades, but for various reasons was not able to add much to his innovative and exciting output of the 1940s. A highly significant part of that output did not appear in print until 1982, and we will return to that later. Thomson's nationalism surfaces in poems from the early 1940s also, becoming most explicit in a collection of 1977, *Saorsa agus an Iolaire* ('Freedom and the Eagle'), and continuing in his most recent collection *Smeur an Dòchais* ('Bramble of Hope') in 1992.[12] Smith was a later convert, and his poetry distances itself from politics, at least in any party sense. William Neill's nationalism is unequivocal. His first publication of scale is in the anthology *Four Points of a Saltire*[13] (1970), which includes two of his Gaelic poems, much evidence of his interest in Celtic topics, and work in Scots and English. His later work confirms this profile, as in *Making Tracks* (1988), but with an increasing Gaelic ingredient. *Cnù a Mogaill* (1983) is an all-Gaelic collection.[14] Maoilios Caimbeul, author of *Bailtean* ('Villages') (1987) and *A' Càradh an Rathaid*[15] ('Mending the Road') (1988) is a committed nationalist among other things. Mary Montgomery and Frater are also very openly committed. This tradition of political nationalism is an old one in Gaelic, surfacing notably in the work of William Livingston during the last century, and discernible in Alasdair Mac Mhaighstir Alasdair in the mid-eighteenth century. It was reinforced by the renaissance movement of the 1920s and 1930s. Other poets have had different political backgrounds: James Thomson, author of *Fasgnadh*[16] ('Winnowing') (1953) had a Liberal allegiance, though his poetry is mainly on religious and philosophical themes; MacLean was a Communist sympathizer in the 1930s, and has a strong left-wing lobby still; Aonghas MacNeacail and Catriona Montgomery have similar sympathies. Poets' press in Scotland is strongly influenced by such considerations.

The political area is one in which the widening of geographical horizons shows most clearly in recent Gaelic poetry. European, and to some extent world politics have entered most people's living-rooms, and the poetry reflects this regularly. MacLean had brought the Spanish Civil War into his poetry in the later 1930s, one of Hay's finest poems 'Bizerta' describes battle conditions in North Africa, while his 'Truaighe na h-Eòrpa' ('Europe's piteous plight') laments the destruction of European cities, Thomson comments on the Hungarian repression of 1956 and on the Chernobyl disaster of the 1980s, MacAulay, Smith and Caimbeul reflect on nuclear disaster, and MacNeacail writes about the plight of American Indians. Angus Campbell wrote vividly, in both prose and verse, about his experiences in a Polish prison camp during the war. Involvement with the world outwith Gaelic boundaries shows in other ways also. MacAulay has a short series of poems inspired by his brief tour of duty in Turkey in the mid-1950s, where some of the poorer people's conditions remind him of his home island, and he comments sardonically on both societies in 'Amasra 1957':

> . . . In the evening an old man will come riding
> on an ass,
> barefoot, sitting erect
> like the righteousness of his goad –
> the strict discipline of Allah . . .
>
> In Lewis they would mock him![17]

A number of Christopher Whyte's poems are set in Italy, where he taught from 1977 to 1985. In 'Fontana Maggiore' he gives us the designer of the fountain, built in the main square of Perugia in 1272–3, reflecting on his work. Other poems of his are set in Yugoslavia, or include translations from German and Russian poetry. Whyte learnt Gaelic, at first in Italy, and has achieved a notable fluency in his writing of it. The deepest poetic exploration of a very different culture was made by George Campbell Hay. His *Mochtàr is Dùghall*[18] ('Mokhtar and Dougall') was not published until 1982, and its existence was known only to a handful of people, although it was mainly written in Italy, during the latter part of the Second World War, with additions made in Macedonia and Tarbert Loch Fyne in

1946 and 1947. It was intended to be a detailed juxtapositioning of the Arab and the Gaelic ways of life. The Arab part was largely completed, but Hay's psychiatric illness disrupted his plans for the Gaelic section which is fragmentary and undeveloped. The Arab section is a brilliant, imaginative recreation of the old Arab world which Hay had got to know from direct experience and from his reading. He describes four generations of Arabs, showing their way of life and ways of thinking, and including a brilliantly racy account of Mochtàr's grandfather Omar, and especially of his meeting in the desert with the strange tribe of the Touaregs. A shorter, well-known poem of Hay's, 'Atman', had featured an Arab, but left readers unprepared for the depth and range of this long poem, which must be regarded as Hay's supreme achievement.

Different kinds of contemporary issues surface in recent poetry, especially by women poets. Feminism and greenness break through the heather, especially in the work of the two Montgomeries, Mary and Catriona, of Meg Bateman, and of Frater, and Frater has a striking poem about conception by implant, *Clann a-màireach* ('Children of tomorrow') in *Gairm* 160.[19]

Another area in which connections have been made with the world at large is that of translation. Hay was a keen translator (from Italian, Modern Greek, Croatian and Arabic in particular). Roderick MacDonald has translated the body of Robert Burns's poetry. A recent anthology of translations from European verse includes 108 poems translated from some twenty languages over the last forty years. It appeared in 1990, entitled *Bàrdachd na Roinn-Eòrpa an Gàidhlig / European Poetry in Gaelic*.[20]

Several of the poets write regularly in more than one language. George Campbell Hay and William Neill use Gaelic, Scots and English, and Iain Crichton Smith has written poetry in English and Gaelic since the early 1950s. Smith also observes ironically, in *An t-Eilean agus an Cànan* ('The Island and the Language') the code-switching between Gaelic and English that is common in parts of Gaelic society.[21] Most of the poets provide English versions of their Gaelic poems when they publish in periodicals (other than *Gairm*), and frequently in their published collections also, and in general Scottish anthologies. This practice was largely set in place in William Maclellan's periodicals of the mid-

1940s (*Poetry Scotland* and *Scottish Art and Letters*). Recently there have been instances of Irish versions of Scottish Gaelic collections, for example by Maoilios Caimbeul and Màiri NicGumaraid. A considerable amount of recent Gaelic verse has appeared in Welsh translation by John Stoddart.[22]

3

Many of the developments of theme and emphasis to which I have referred do not appeal to the public for traditional verse. For the most part this is not surprising. As Gaelic verse has moved towards a more cosmopolitan perspective its appeal has to some extent been defined by the move. In traditional verse itself there were various levels of acceptability, and in some ways the new verse added a further layer that was less accessible. But we have to take account also of the widespread interest in verse in Gaelic society, and the continuing existence of local or 'village' verse, which was topical and entertaining, gossipy, witty or satirical, and above all accessible to its natural community. There is a long tradition of such verse in Gaelic, and it was still flourishing in the immediate post-war period. Donald Macintyre of South Uist and Paisley is a very good example of this, with his *Sporan Dhòmhnaill*[23] of 1968. Donald Morrison of Scalpay Harris is another. The move from carts and spring-carts to rudimentary cars and lorries had been celebrated in verse in the early decades of the century, and later innovations such as artificial insemination of cattle, or the setting up of a Western Isles Council in the mid-1970s, got the traditional verse treatment, as did the famous removal of the Stone of Destiny from Westminster Abbey in late 1951 (this is one of Macintyre's best-known songs). To switch from that to discussions of classical music or art, or to the political complexities of Neruda's poetry is to leap into another world. There were some who voiced objections to the new arcane verse (as they saw it), but for the majority there was no encounter. But it is fair to say that a modern Gaelic poet can also enjoy the local verse: the shut-off valve seems to work in one direction only.

The traditional verse had a strong metrical and linguistic character. It used a variety of rhythmical, rhyming and assonantal techniques, often with a dense level of metrical ornament consisting of end-rhymes, internal rhymes, rhyme between stanzas, and alliteration. It had lexical richness too, though this did not necessarily go with conceptual richness or intellectual depth. These technical characteristics gave it a strong persona, and on a superficial view at least any verse that lacked these was deficient. There were hearty, and sometimes bitter arguments on these lines in the 1950s, and they surface occasionally still, in a less partisan form.

This brings us to a consideration of the forms the new verse cultivated. The innovations were partly metrical, but more importantly conceptual and structural. There was a wide variation in the degree to which the first wave of new poets moved away from regular metrical structure. Two of the group kept their loyalty to the regular stanzaic structure, with MacLean in the main using quatrains and couplets, and Hay a wider range of traditional metres. Both were suspicious of free verse, and when one of them tried it he was uneasy with it. Thomson, Smith and MacAulay all used traditional forms, but increasingly wrote in freer forms. These forms begin to appear perhaps as early as the very late 1930s (with an earlier, isolated instance from the First World War), but their growth in use is a feature of the later 1940s and the 1950s. From these beginnings free verse moves towards becoming the norm rather than the exception for a series of younger poets. Of the eight poets in Whyte's anthology of 1991, only one, Catrìona NicGumaraid, seems attracted to regular rhyming stanzas.

Perhaps the revolution has gone too far, as revolutions often do. The earlier free verse, and to some extent the current free verse of the older poets, continues to use rhyme, but not in a regular patterning: rather to achieve an emphasis, or make an echo, but also with an ear to internal music. The structure of Gaelic, especially its vowel repertory, lends itself to such music-making. The early practitioners of free verse clearly felt that the traditional structures were too ossified, and were impinging on, even impeding, the poetic statements they wanted to make. That was probably the main incentive to move towards free verse, though the existing examples in other literatures were a powerful attraction too. But the musical possibilities still offered their own attractions.

In a paper published in Dublin in 1974, *The New Verse in*

Scottish Gaelic: a structural analysis,[24] I analysed the structures of a body of new Gaelic verse by five poets, consisting of 420 poems running to slightly over 9,500 lines, showing that by then *vers libre* was chosen in 42.9 per cent of poems, four-line rhymed stanza in 26.9 per cent, eight-line rhymed stanza in 10.1 per cent, and other stanzaic forms in smaller numbers still. Since this total includes the main work of both MacLean and Hay, both biased towards the regular stanzaic forms, it can be seen that free verse had made considerable inroads by the early 1970s, and that trend has been further confirmed since then.

Equally important, if not more so, are the developments in the structuring of poems which characterize the new verse in Gaelic. There are some links and correspondences between metrical and structural innovation, but the two do not necessarily go hand in hand. Older traditional Gaelic verse often tended to concentrate structural development on the stanza, especially on longer stanzas, and poems often dealt with a succession of aspects of their themes in successive verses. This linear development of a poem's theme is to be contrasted with an organic development which achieves an overall entity for the poem, rather than a series of paragraphs or vignettes. In Gaelic poetry of the modern period, some poets show a strong preference for organic structure, often building the poem round a dominant image, though that image may make its appearance early or late in the poem. In extreme cases of organic structuring every element in the poem can be seen to relate to the central image. I may quote again an example used in that Dublin lecture of 1974 to illustrate the last point. It is a poem by Donald MacAulay, entitled 'For Pasternak, for example . . .', and it goes as follows:

> You winnow in a contrary wind
> living seed out of beard and chaff
> since you have understood that those who hated you
> did not recognise
> your love:
> you prepare seed for planting
> since you have understood their disability –
> they consign all seed to the mill.[25]

The poem is ostensibly about agricultural activity, in this case on a croft, and contrasts the attitude of living for the day only, with that of preparing for next season's crop. All the elements of the poem tie in with that central image, except for the reference to love and hate, which seem too strong for the literal situation. The title, which was added later, makes the love and hate references easier to accommodate. But the poem is not about any of these matters, and it is probably about MacAulay's uneasy situation in his home community, where people were not concerned about new poetry, or the life or death of their language, simply taking that language for granted. He brings Pasternak in to soften his 'criticism'. This organic method of constructing a poem can lead to ambiguity, but it can be powerfully effective too. It often depends on the use of extended metaphor. John Killick, in a review[26] of *Creachadh na Clàrsaich*, refers to the influence of the Symbolist movement in twentieth-century Gaelic poetry, but suggests that the discoveries have been domesticated 'to such an extent that [they can be used] in a variety of contexts with a sensual immediacy that strikes the reader as inevitable. The near-colloquialism of the diction employed is the secret of [the] taming of a potentially disruptive technique.'

In my 1974 analysis of structure, a fairly high correlation showed up between organic structure and free verse, and a low correlation between organic structure and the various forms of regular verse. Organic structure was also shown to coexist with certain stanzaic structures, but the chances of some distortion of that organic drive seemed clearly greater in these cases. I have not extended that analysis over the last eighteen years, but have the impression that the organic technique is less widespread in the work of poets using free verse now, and may be more specifically linked with two or three poets of the period 1950–80.

The post-war period has clearly been one of movement and experiment in Gaelic poetry. One remarkable feature of the period has been the appearance of a number of poets who are not native Gaelic-speakers: William Neill, Fearghas MacFhionnlaigh, Christopher Whyte and Meg Bateman fall into this category, as do more occasional poets such as Victor Price and Julian Ronay. In some cases these new poets seem more secure in English, and they do not fully inherit the nuances of language or tradition, bringing instead to the poetic tradition other interests and sensibilities. This is a scenario which has been much more deeply explored in Ireland. It is a contributory source of the alienation

from the new poetry felt by many native Gaels. As the Irish expe-
rience seems to show, it is possible to weather such a transitional
period and to reach a new consensus.

Clearly the great majority of committed writers of poetry in
Gaelic have responded positively to the mid-century 'revolution',
in one or more of its aspects, and in addition to bringing a new
kind of life to the tradition have extended the poetic experience
for the Scottish public and to a modest degree for a wider public.

Notes

1　For these poems by MacAulay, see Dòmhnall MacAmhlaigh,
   Seòbhrach as a' Chlaich (Glasgow, Gairm Publications, 1967).
2　*Gairm* No. 74, (Glasgow, Gairm Publications, 1971, 162).
3　Ruaraidh MacThòmais/Derick Thomson, *Creachadh na Clàrsaich/
   Plundering the Harp* (Edinburgh, Macdonald, 1982), 94–6.
4　*Gairm* No. 153 (1990), 34.
5　Iain Crichton Smith, *Nua-bhàrdachd Ghàidhlig/Modern Scottish
   Gaelic Poems* (Edinburgh, Southside, 1976; later Edinburgh,
   Canongate), 68–70.
6　Ibid., 86–8.
7　Derick Thomson, *Creachadh na Clàrsaich*, op. cit., 220–21.
8　Original poem in Christopher Whyte (ed.), *An Aghaidh na
   Sìorraidheachd* (Edinburgh, Polygon, 1991), 174–7.
9　Fearghas MacFhionnlaigh, *A' Mheanbhchuileag* (Glasgow, Gairm,
   1980).
10　*Iolair, Brù-dhearg, Giuthas* (Dept. of Celtic, University of Glasgow,
   1991).
11　George Campbell Hay, *Fuaran Slèibh* (Glasgow, Maclellan, 1948)
   and *O na Ceithir Airdean* (Edinburgh, Oliver and Boyd, 1952).
12　Derick Thomson, *Saorsa agus an Iolaire* (Glasgow, Gairm, 1977)
   and *Smeur an Dòchais / Bramble of Hope* (Edinburgh, Cannongate,
   1992).
13　William Neill, *Four Points of a Saltire* (Edinburgh, Reprographia,
   1970).
14　William Neill, *Making Tracks* (Edinburgh, Gordon Wright, 1988)
   and *Cnù a Mogaill* (Dept. of Celtic, University of Glasgow, 1983).
15　Maoilios Caimbeul, *Bailtean* (Glasgow, Gairm, 1987) and *A'
   Càradh an Rathaid* (Dublin, Coiscéim, 1988).
16　James Thomson, *Fasgnadh* (Stirling, Learmonth, 1953).
17　Dòmhnall MacAmhlaigh, *Seòbhrach as a' Chlaich*, op. cit., 93.
18　George Campbell Hay, *Mochtàr is Dùghall* (Dept. of Celtic,
   University of Glasgow, 1982).
19　*Gairm* No. 160 (1992), 311.

172   DERICK S. THOMSON

20 MacThòmais, Ruaraidh (ed.), *Bàrdachd na Roinn-Eòrpa an Gàidhlig/European Poetry in Gaelic* (Glasgow, Gairm, 1990).
21 Iain Mac a' Ghobhainn, *An t-Eilean agus an Cànan* (Dept. of Celtic, University of Glasgow, 1987). See especially pp.40–43.
22 See especially John Stoddart, *Cerddi Gaeleg Cyfoes* (Cardiff, University of Wales Press, 1986).
23 Donald Macintyre, *Sporan Dhòmhnaill* (Edinburgh, Scottish Gaelic Texts Society, 1968).
24 Derick Thomson, *The New Verse in Scottish Gaelic: a structural analysis* (University College Dublin, 1974).
25 Dòmhnall MacAmhlaigh, *Seòbhrach as a' Chlaich*, op. cit., 87.
26 *PN Review*, No. 34, (Manchester, 1983), 38–40.

Further reading

Black, Ronald, 'Thunder, Renaissance and Flowers: Gaelic Poetry in the Twentieth Century', in Craig Cairns (ed.), *The History of Scottish Literature*, Vol. IV, (Aberdeen University Press, 1987), 195–215.

Blackburn, John (ed.), *Hardy to Heaney* (Edinburgh, Oliver and Boyd, 1986).

Dunn, Douglas, *The Faber Book of Twentieth-Century Scottish Poetry* (London, Faber and Faber, 1992).

Lindsay, Maurice (ed.), *Modern Scottish Poetry* (London, Robert Hale, 1986).

Scott, Alexander (ed.), *Voices of our Kind* (Edinburgh, Chambers, 1987).

Thomson, Derick, *An Introduction to Gaelic Poetry* (London, Gollancz, 1974: 2nd ed. Edinburgh University Press, 1990).

Thomson, Derick, *The Companion to Gaelic Scotland* (Oxford, Blackwell, 1983, 1987; new ed., Gairm, Glasgow, 1994).

9

The place of writing and the writing of place in twentieth-century Irish poetry in English

ROBERT F. GARRATT

1

In 1893, the aspiring poet William Butler Yeats delivered a lecture in Dublin on the subject of nationality and literature, arguing for the uniqueness of Irish literature. In the course of this lecture Yeats declared Irish literature separate and independent from English literature because it concerns itself with the local and with what the local represents. English literature, on the other hand, must always seek the literatures of other countries to express itself. Yeats concluded his lecture with the following observation:

> I affirm that we are a young nation with unexhausted material lying within us in our still unexpressed national character, about us in our scenery, and in the clearly marked outlines of our life, and behind us in our multitudes of legends . . . All that is greatest in that literature is based upon legend – upon those tales which are made by no one man, but by the nation itself through a slow process of modification and adaption, to express its loves and hates, its likes and dislikes . . . Our poetry is still a poetry of the people in the main, for it still deals with the tales and the thoughts of the people.[1]

What Yeats pronounced as immediate concerns in 1893 have remained central preoccupations in Irish poetry throughout this century: the importance of landscape, myth and legend to an understanding of the 'Irishness' of Irish literature, the idea of national character, the notion of the 'people' of Ireland, and the paradox that although Ireland is a young nation it has, nonetheless, an ancient history and literary tradition. The young and hopeful poets of the Irish Literary Revival saw much relevance in Yeats's remarks and set about to shape their work according to his national formula. For post-Yeatsian Irish poets, however, suggestions of an Irish Ireland have been worked into poetic clichés and trouble those who seek a more cosmopolitan cultural identity for contemporary Ireland. Indeed, poets like Patrick Kavanagh, Louis MacNeice, John Montague, Seamus Heaney, Derek Mahon, Michael Longley and Paul Muldoon, have attempted, each in his own way, to unwrite the kind of literary nationalism promoted by the youthful Yeats and characterized by the writers of the Revival. Kavanagh, Montague and Heaney present versions of rural experience that treat how people actually live in the country; MacNeice, Mahon, Longley and Muldoon write what might be called an anti-pastoral in which they stress an urban sensibility opposed to the image of Ireland as a land of myth and beauty. These responses, while certainly unique in matters of style and narrative, are nonetheless uniform in this respect, they replace the Revivalist idea of a broad and pervasive national culture with a sense of the local in which each poet portrays the given life of place and time.

To illustrate better the variety and even the contradictions in the treatment of regionalism and the depiction of place in certain contemporary Irish poets, I wish to consider briefly the categories of 'naïve' and 'sentimental' proposed by Friedrich Schiller in his well known essay 'Über naive und sentimentalische Dichtung'.[2] Schiller's notion of the 'naïve' implies a sense of harmony or oneness with nature that allows the poet to write from a perspective of reality and truth. The 'naïve' poet sees from within, as it were, as a part of nature.[3] Schiller's primary example of the 'naïve' are the ancient Greeks who believed in the harmony and order of nature and whose faculties of sense and reason were still coherent and working in concert.[4] By contrast, the modern poet, separated from nature by culture and society, experiences an aggravated sense of loss and psychic fragmentation. He or she thus becomes 'sentimental' toward nature, forced to deal with it as an idea and as a concept ('Idee und Gegenstand') rather than to live with it as an essential part of experience ('Erfahrung').[5] The 'sentimental' poet responds to this predicament by attempting to idealize the lost world of nature or to emphasize the distance between the ideal and the actual.[6]

Schiller developed his categories of the 'naïve' and the 'sentimental' in an effort to distance himself from Goethe and to understand himself aesthetically and intellectually as a post-Enlightenment man in an age that was becoming acutely self-conscious about problems of knowledge. His insight goes far beyond its original reference, however, and has a special relevance for modern and contemporary Irish poetry. The generalized concepts of 'naïve' and 'sentimental' allow us to gauge the treatment of Ireland as place in twentieth-century poetry. The essential task of the Irish Literary Revival was to connect Irish landscape and places with myth and legend and so establish a kind of objective correlative for the various qualities of 'Irishness' connected to the idea of national character. In this phase, Ireland as a place or a region was consciously placed in opposition with England, the seat of industrial and political power. As such, it was conceived as a holy and a sacred ground, a physical embodiment of the ancient religion of nature reflected in myth and legend. This is Celtic Ireland, a pre-Christian and certainly pre-colonial land, whose woods, mountains and seashores are the habitats of the spirits and gods of the otherworld. In this way Ireland as place can gain a distinct integrity and identity, possessing, as Seamus Deane explains, a form of knowledge not subordinate but superior to the rational knowledge produced by the metropolis.[7]

The great movement of cultural nationalism during the Revival required significant effort, however. Yeats's claims about a poetry of the people notwithstanding, the idea of a living tradition of Irish literature and its spiritual connection to the sense of place was lost on a reading public that had been culturally as well as politically colonized by Britain. Moreover, the depiction of Ireland as a place, a region with its own history and culture, was further complicated because the Revivalist poets were themselves products of English culture.[8] Most of them were in a position akin to Schiller's 'sentimental' poet in that they must conjure up and idealize a timeless and legendary Ireland, a land lost to them through political and cultural dispossession.

In this poetic treatment of Ireland, Yeats proves the exception, of course, as he will do throughout most of his great career. As a Revivalist, Yeats was immersed in occultism and arcane studies and believed Ireland to be one of the last places in modern society where the people still lived in harmony with what he called 'the ancient religion of the world, the ancient worship of

Nature . . . that certainty of all beautiful places being haunted'.[9] The young Yeats believed he sensed this when he walked around the Sligo countryside, among the lonely hills or in the dark woods, and he hoped to evoke similar feelings in his poetry that would allow his readers to feel rather than see the natural world. In his early poems, he assumes the role of a 'naïve' poet and stands in relation to nature and to Irish folk material as the ancient Greeks stood to their myths. Similarly, he stands in opposition to what he termed the artificial and what Schiller would term 'sentimental' qualities of the English poetic tradition of his day. 'They look at nature without ecstasy', Yeats wrote of the English poets, 'with the affection a man feels for the garden where he has walked daily and thought pleasant thoughts. They look at nature in the modern way, the way of people who are poetical, but are more interested in one another than in a nature which has faded to be but friendly and pleasant, the way of people who have forgotten the ancient religion.'[10]

Yeats's great 'naïve' achievements are the 1893 book of poems *The Rose* and the contemporary collection of stories *The Celtic Twilight* (1893) and *The Secret Rose* (1897). In all of these books, Sligo provides the background for the poems and stories, not as a regional setting but rather as the sacred places of a living folk tradition. As a 'naïve' poet Yeats evokes the sense of place by surrendering to its mysteries and its natural supernaturalism; he expresses in his early work a harmony between man and nature and a sense that the external world is part of human experience.

One of the central features of Yeats's aesthetic is its fascination with oppositions. His 'naïve' understanding of Ireland grew out of his view of England as an industrial and materialistic society. By the time he was writing the poetry of *Responsibilities* (1914) and *The Wild Swans at Coole* (1919), Yeats characteristically hardened towards his early work. Disillusioned by the cultural politics of the new Irish nation, he rejected the Celticism of the Revival and turned to a new myth of Ireland that celebrates Georgian Ireland and the Protestant Anglo-Irish Ascendancy. In the poetry of *The Tower* (1928) and its companion volume *The Winding Stair and Other Poems* (1933) Yeats shifts from his concentration in the early poems on natural landscapes to man-made objects such as cultivated gardens, grand estates and

houses, planted hills, ancient bridges and especially Thoor
Ballylee, the Norman tower Yeats restored in 1919. Here is a new
Yeats Country, a place of rural aristocratic tradition, called to
mind by the now 'sentimental' poet and presented as an idealized
historical creation to be set against the futility and the anarchy of
modern times. Seamus Heaney notes the tendency in Yeats's later
poetry 'that the poetic imagination . . . imposes its vision upon a
place rather than accepts a vision from it'; the later Yeats is 'one
whose poems have created a country of the mind rather than the
other way round . . . where the country has created the mind
which in turn creates the poems'.[11] In these poems celebrating the
building of physical things and the triumph of the imagination
over the material world, Yeats declares his separation from
modern Ireland and announces his spiritual connection with the
eighteenth century:

> I declare this tower is my symbol; I declare
> This winding, gyring, spiring treadmill of a stair is my ancestral stair;
> That Goldsmith and the Dean, Berkeley and Burke have travelled
>   there.   ('Blood and the Moon')

Place is described by images of physical realities such as towers
and is embellished by the appeal to history, but is empowered
ultimately by the authoritative voice of the poet himself:

> John Synge, I and Augusta Gregory, thought
> All that we did, all that we said or sang
> Must come from contact with the soil, from that
> Contact everything Antaeus-like grew strong.
> We three alone in modern times had brought
> Everything down to that sole test again,
> Dream of the noble and the beggarman.
>   ('The Municipal Gallery Revisited')

2

Once this place of writing was created with such poetic and
rhetorical authority, it naturally provoked a reaction in other
Irish poets to challenge it. The initial direction of post-Yeatsian
Irish poetry, then, is contrapuntal, a movement away from
Yeats's influence by attempting to unwrite the idea of place he
has so effectively written.[12] Among the generation of poets who

immediately followed Yeats, the two who have most effectively unwritten his place of writing are Patrick Kavanagh and Louis MacNeice, although in very different ways.[13] Both Kavanagh and MacNeice criticize the idea of romantic Ireland by presenting realistic portraits of Irish life, Kavanagh from the perspective of rural Ireland, MacNeice from the viewpoint of an urban northerner.

MacNeice's response to romantic Ireland is complicated from the start. Born, as he tells us in his poem 'Carrickfergus', to a Belfast Anglican family, he remained estranged throughout his life to Catholic Ireland. As a result he felt an acute dissociation from Irish matters, caught as he was between British and Irish cultural communities. He could not completely identify with Protestant Northern Ireland, a culture too narrow for his sensibilities:

> . . . the voodoo of the Orange bands
>   Drawing an iron net through darkest Ulster,
> Flailing the limbo lands –
>   The linen mills, the long wet grass, the ragged hawthorn.
>
> ('Autumn Journal', xvi)

Nor could he take solace in a notion of regionalism that his contemporary Ulster poet John Hewitt found so appealing and so essential to his poetry.[14] Hewitt, sounding like a prototype of Schiller's 'sentimental' poet, believes that western man, 'half subdued by a century of increasing standardisation in material things' and 'rapidly losing his individual responses in the hurricanes of propaganda, political, commercial, ideological', can find some measure of meaning and significance only in some smaller unit other than the nation. For Hewitt this meant grounding his art in an Ulster regionalism.[15]

MacNeice is too urbane, sophisticated and modernist, however, to idealize Ulster as his place of writing. He senses no beauty in the industrialized landscape around Belfast, nor can he recall it nostalgically:

> And the North, where I was a boy,
>   Is still the North, veneered with the grime of Glasgow,
> Thousands of men whom nobody will employ
>   Standing at the corners, coughing;
> And the street-children play on the wet

> Pavement – hopscotch or marbles;
> And each rich family boasts a sagging tennis-net
> On a spongy lawn beside a dripping shrubbery.
>   ('Autumn Journal', xvi)

More to the point, he rejects Hewitt's regionalism as he unwrites Yeats's aristocratic Ireland, by stressing the writer's separation from place:

> This is what you have given me
> Indifference and sentimentality
> . . .
> I will acquire an attitude not yours
> And become one of your holiday visitors,
> And however often I may come
> Farewell, my country, and in perpetuum; ('Valediction')

Isolation, alienation, dissociation, these feelings break down the connection between a writer and a region or a place, forcing MacNeice to become a tourist in his own country. Following the peculiarities of his biography, MacNeice's poetry reveals a certain anxiety about the writing of place that contrasts vividly with the conviction of Yeats's tower poems:

> Torn before birth from where my fathers dwelt,
> Schooled from the age of ten to a foreign voice,
> Yet neither western Ireland nor southern England
> Cancels this interlude; what chance misspelt
> May never now be righted by my choice. ('Carrick Revisited')

Patrick Kavanagh, on the other hand, suffers from no such anxieties; the power of his poetic comes from contact with the soil and from a strong attachment to a sense of place. Despite the rootedness of Kavanagh's poetry, he nonetheless stands in opposition to Yeats and to the poets of the Revival in his treatment of place. Almost from the beginning of his career, Kavanagh offered a version of rural life that was brutal in its honesty. Writing from the inside out, he focused on the ordinary, the common and the basic details of country living as a corrective both to the Revivalist fiction and to Yeats's aristocratic myth. His landscapes were the de-romanticized cold, dark hills of a farmer's field –

> My black hills have never seen the sun rising,
> Eternally they look north towards Armagh
> . . .

The sleety winds fondle the rushy beards of Shancoduff
While the cattle-drovers sheltering in the Featherna Bush
Look up and say: 'Who owns them hungry hills
That the water-hen and snipe have forsaken? . . .'

('Shancoduff')

– and his portraits of rural life emphasized the back-breaking realities of farming. In 'The Great Hunger', Kavanagh's celebrated narrative poem about the desperate narrowness of a small farmer's life, the details of routine and labour accumulate to counter effectively the writing of countryside and life by Yeats and the Revivalists. Ploughing, planting, harvesting, repairing, feeding animals, all of this coming round again, year after year, until the protagonist, Paddy Maguire, becomes himself a beast of burden:

Like a goat tethered to the stump of a tree –
He circles around and around wondering why it should be.
No crash,
No drama.
That was how his life happened.
No mad hooves galloping in the sky,
But the weak, washy way of true tragedy –
A sick horse nosing around the meadow for a clean place to die
. . .
He will hardly remember that life happened to him.

('The Great Hunger')

Kavanagh wrote about life in County Monaghan out of real contact with the soil and in opposition to the kind of contact that Yeats claimed for himself, Augusta Gregory and John Synge. Early poems like 'Inniskeen Road: July Evening', 'Art McCooey', and, of course, 'The Great Hunger', can be read as a response to what Kavanagh termed 'the Irish thing', the nationalist movement in literature, 'the Yeats-Synge phoney Ireland . . . eminently suited for export to America'.[16] Kavanagh's poems grow out of a sense of a parochialism, which is linked to the idea of validity. Place for Kavanagh is acceptance of the ordinary and the real, and in the early poems he attempts to reflect rather than invent the life of his parish.

Kavanagh's later poetry, from 1950 until his death in 1967, becomes more preoccupied with the making of poetry and in this sense seems to reflect the anxieties of Schiller's 'sentimental' poet.

During this time Kavanagh was living in Dublin, a peripheral figure in the city's literary world, and his attitude toward his rural subject matter reflects that of an urban consciousness attempting to reclaim a lost innocence. Place in the later Kavanagh is a world invented and restored within the poetic imagination which is its source. 'Kerr's Ass' from the 1960 volume *Come Dance With Kitty Stobling* is characteristic:

> We borrowed the loan of Kerr's big ass
> To go to Dundalk with the Butter,
> Brought him home the evening before the market
> An exile that night in Mucker.
>
> We heeled up the cart before the door,
> We took the harness inside –
> The straw-stuffed straddle, the broken breeching
> With bits of bull-wire tied;
>
> The winkers that had no choke-band,
> The collar and the reins . . .
> In Ealing Broadway, London Town
> I name their several names
>
> Until a world comes to life –
> Morning, the silent bog,
> And the God of imagination waking
> In a Mucker fog.

Here the poetic imagination first recalls some past experience and then becomes itself the true subject of the poem as the power which calls place into being through the act of naming. Specific hardware used in the hitching of the ass – straddle, breeching, winkers, collar and reins – and the details of a market day allow the poet to recall one place while he inhabits another; in London town the poet remembers Irish country life. This practice is not original, of course; many disaffected urban poets from the eighteenth century to the present have conjured up rural locations. Yeats's famous 'Lake Isle of Innisfree' is part of this tradition, the recollection of a tranquil island retreat while standing on the roadway or the 'pavements grey' of a great city. In 'Kerr's Ass', Kavanagh creates a place of writing, to borrow Seamus Heaney's phrase, but one that is far more specific in physical detail than Yeats's abstract Innisfree.

The poetic imagination asserts itself as primary in Kavanagh's later poems, but what it recalls and recreates are the things of a particular world. Moreover, the poet seems to be part of the creation. Unlike Louis MacNeice, Kavanagh exudes the confidence and familiarity of one who belongs to a place of writing. The poem 'Epic' is clear about the deeply felt importance of local politics; the quarrel of two Northern Irish farmers over property lines is contrasted with the coming of the Second World War, described glibly as 'the Munich bother'.

> Which
> Was more important? I inclined
> To lose my faith in Ballyrush and Gortin
> Till Homer's ghost came whispering to my mind
> He said: I made the Iliad from such
> A local row. Gods make their own importance.

It is an audacious moment with the poet basking in the glow of supreme creative power. Not only can he name things into existence and create certain places, but, through the assertion of poetic authority, he also can raise to great proportion the details and the figures of a local argument:

> I have lived in important places, times
> When great events were decided, who owned
> That half a rood of rock, a no-man's land
> Surrounded by our pitchfork-armed claims.
> I heard the Duffys shouting 'Damn your soul'
> And old McCabe stripped to the waist, seen
> Step the plot defying blue cast-steel –
> 'Here is the march among these iron stones'.

In Kavanagh's poetry the parochial and the parish are the centre of the universe; there is no need to go beyond it. The details and the events of this familiar world make possible both the integrity and the authenticity of the poetic voice. But Kavanagh does not simply reproduce the elements of rural life, holding, as it were a mirror up to nature. Rather, he orders and idealizes country life in his role as poet, and, as we have seen in poems like 'Kerr's Ass' and 'Epic', intrudes upon the material. As is the case with most sentimental poets as Schiller has defined them, the matter of place in Kavanagh's poetry exists poetically before it can be found in nature.

3

For a number of contemporary Northern Irish writers Kavanagh and MacNeice are important precursors of a native, that is, non-British voice. Recalling MacNeice's straddling of British and Irish cultures, the Belfast poet Michael Longley claims that Ulster writers have picked up frequencies in MacNeice's poetry that are not heard in London or Dublin.[17] Kavanagh's treatment of his given life has prompted Seamus Heaney to remark: 'Kavanagh gave you permission to dwell without cultural anxiety among the usual landmarks of our life.'[18] In his recent edition of the *Faber Book of Contemporary Irish Poetry*, Paul Muldoon placed Kavanagh and MacNeice conspicuously at the beginning of the volume to indicate their influence upon contemporary poets.

Kavanagh was particularly important to John Montague in the writing of *The Rough Field*,[19] the poetic sequence on Garvaghey, Montague's boyhood farm in County Tyrone. Kavanagh's treatment of the local and the ordinary, especially in the long poem 'The Great Hunger', exerts a special influence upon *The Rough Field*, pushing Montague to another conception of place. Montague seems willing to follow Kavanagh's advice never to doubt the validity of one's own parish, but he adds a special twist. To write Monaghan into being Kavanagh ignored history to concentrate on the particular and the immediate; to write Garvaghey into being, Montague would seek out history better to understand the meaning of place.

The prevailing trope of *The Rough Field* is Wordsworthian: the poet returns to a familiar location known to him as a child and through a series of recollections and meditations recreates a sense of place. Unlike Wordsworth, however, Montague does not rely solely upon personal memory in his attempt to recreate a history of place. He will seek to connect this part of County Tyrone not only with family memories but also with Elizabethan history and the defeat of the Clan O'Neill by the forces of Elizabeth I. In the opening section, 'Home Again', the poet announces his strategy through the narrative of his return. On a bus from Victorian and British Belfast he travels the roads of Ulster, eventually crossing into County Tyrone, the end of the British Pale and the beginning of O'Neill country and Irish Ireland. A change in landscape triggers memories of the Old Gaelic order and Ulster resistance to

English rule and when the bus stops at the crossroads leading to
the old family farm the poet has become nostalgic:

> . . . I assume old ways of walk and work
> So easily, yet feel the sadness of return
> To what seems still, though changing
> . . .
> Harsh landscape, that haunts me
> Well and stone, in the bleak moors of dream.

With such an opening before us, we can read *The Rough Field* as
a triumph of mind over matter. Montague prefers the interior
landscape of imagination and memory to Yeats's solid tower or
Kavanagh's cold, bleak fields. The sense of place that emerges in
The Rough Field comes through the collision of family history
with Irish history as Montague attempts to recreate a lost world:

> All around, my
> Neighbours sleep, but I am
> In possession of their past
> (The pattern history weaves
> From one small backward place)
> Marching through memory magnified:
> Each grassblade bends with
> Translucent beads of moisture
> And the bird of total meaning
> Stirs upon its hidden branch.

Here we see the sentimental poet at his work. To recover 'one
small backward place' the poet must remember what a commu-
nity has forgotten, the history in the landscape and in the local
places contained in the Irish place-names, like the poet's own
farm Garvaghey (the rough field):

> All around, shards of a lost tradition:
> From the Rough Field I went to school
> In the Glen of the Hazels
> . . .
> The whole landscape a manuscript
> We had lost the skill to read
> A part of our past disinherited.

To recall the Irish place-names is to recognize that history and
culture have been preserved in the landscape despite the loss of
the Irish language as the spoken tongue. The poet's task is to

reflect the staying power of the older language, evident in the shaping of the new speech:

> Yet even English in these parts
> Took a lawless turn, as who
> Would not stroll by Bloody Brae
> To Black Lough, or guddle trout
> In a stream called the Routing Burn?

This poetic task is made more difficult by the growth of progress in the area, the rapid industrialization and the separation of contemporary men and women from the old ways. Montague begins with this understanding of loss, but grows to realize that to re-enter and reclaim the Garvaghey of his youth he must remake it poetically.

The unwriting of Yeats's Ireland develops further in the poetry of Seamus Heaney and Derek Mahon who have been influenced, respectively, by Kavanagh and MacNeice. Heaney works, as Kavanagh does, building a sense of place from the inside out; he differs from Kavanagh in that once having established the details of the given life, he seeks a means to transcend it. His early poetry was remarkable for its fidelity to life in rural Derry. *Death of a Naturalist* (1966) and *Door into the Dark* (1969) treat the everyday events of life on a farm, particularly from the perspective of childhood. Labour and recreation are prominent topics and the poet describes turf-cutting, ploughing, bread-baking, roof-thatching, as well as berry-picking, fishing, and frog-catching. In an attempt to go beyond the purely descriptive, Heaney has sought in his recent poetry to break loose from the constraints of the familiar without doing damage to the authenticity of the voice. He writes of this direction in a recent essay on poetry and politics.

> The achievement of a poem . . . is an experience of release . . . A plane is – fleetingly – established where the poet is intensified in his being and freed from his predicaments. The tongue, governed for so long in the social sphere by considerations of tact and fidelity, by nice obeisances to one's origin . . . this tongue is suddenly ungoverned.[20]

The predicaments, considerations of tact and fidelity, the obeisances have grown complex for Heaney since the outbreak of the troubles in 1969 in Northern Ireland. His success at representing what Kavanagh would call the life of his parish has caused some readers to demand from him greater political commitment in his poems. To avoid this pressure and to keep his creative work from becoming the handmaid of politics, Heaney has broadened his aesthetic horizons, particularly in the later books *Sweeney Astray* (1984), *Station Island* (1984) and *The Haw Lantern* (1987). The new direction is implied in 'Making Strange', a poem from *Station Island*. The poem's narrative presents the poet-narrator as a mediator between a visitor, 'one with his travelled intelligence', and the native farmer, 'unshorn and bewildered'. At home with the farmer in his familiar world, the poet nonetheless shares something of the sophisticated tastes and sensibilities of the visitor. Troubling over how he will translate the rural experience for the visitor without betraying his integrity, the poet discovers 'a cunning middle voice' that can describe the particularities of the local but also sense its wider, more universal significance. With such a perspective, the poet gains new insight on the world he knows so well:

> I found myself driving the stranger
> through my own country, adept
> at dialect, reciting my pride
> in all that I knew, that began to make strange
> at that same recitation.
>
> ('Making Strange')

These lines suggest a radical change in poetic strategy, one that has a great bearing on Heaney's treatment of place. In the poetry of the 1980s, Heaney grows less interested in pure description and focuses instead upon the evocative and associational aspects of place; nature, place and the given life are presented less for their own sake than for what they trigger in the poet's imagination. In 'Remembering Malibu', for example, the poet measures the real Pacific against the one he imagined:

> The Pacific at your door was wilder and colder
> than my notion of the Pacific . . .

This momentary triumph of the real over the imaginary is short lived however, for, the actual ocean, the Pacific, moves the poet to recollect the stormy and familiar Atlantic off the west of Ireland and the memory dominates the poem.

The later Heaney is more a poet of the mind than one of

nature. One can sense this in very general ways, in the increasing literary and allusive quality of the poetry, in the well-known use of Dante in *Station Island*, for example, in the adaptation of the medieval Irish tale *Buile Suibhne*, and in the growing sophistication of allusion and poetic subject matter. The latter is apparent in Heaney's poetic sequence 'Station Island', where the physical location of St Patrick's Purgatory on Lough Derg becomes only the backdrop for the higher reality of the poem, a series of dream encounters with various ghosts, among them William Carleton, Patrick Kavanagh and James Joyce. These examples indicate the self-conscious and deliberate use of literature and literary tradition as a poetic subject in the later Heaney, something we do not see in Kavanagh, nor in MacNeice.[21]

The interior quality of Heaney's later poetry is apparent in a more particular way in his interest in an interrogation of how a sense of place comes into being. In the Sweeney poems, Heaney utilizes the mask of the legendary mad king of Ulster who sees his environs anew from the heights of various trees and imagines another reality. As the poet-pilgrim in 'Station Island', Heaney undergoes a mortification of the body which produces visions, hallucinations and dreams. In *The Haw Lantern* the poet goes so far as to suggest that our idea of place may only be wishful thinking:

> Once we presumed to found ourselves for good
> Between its blue hills and those sandless shores
> Where we spent our desperate night in prayer and vigil,
>
> Once we had gathered driftwood, made a hearth
> And hung our cauldron like a firmament,
> The island broke beneath us like a wave.
>
> The land sustaining us seemed to hold firm
> Only when we embraced it *in extremis*.
> All I believe that happened there was vision.
>
> ('The Disappearing Island')

Here, in a version of an ancient tale about Irish monks at sea who land on the back of a sea-monster, Heaney posits the idea that what we perceive may be imaginary. Often in Heaney's later poems the poetic voice seeks a substantial fix, a centre, a place, only to find that it remains an idea or a desire. Like the island that gives way under the sea-weary monks, or the void in the landscape when a tree is cut down, or the empty space of silence at the moment of Heaney's mother's death –

> Then she was dead,
> The searching for a pulsebeat was abandoned
> And we all knew one thing by being there.
> The space we stood around had been emptied
> Into us to keep, it penetrated
> Clearances that suddenly stood open.
> High cries were felled and a pure change happened.
>
> ('Clearances, 7')

– these moments of epiphany demonstrate the ultimate in the unwriting of place; they constitute less a corrective of a poet's particular version of locus and more a questioning of aesthetics.

Seamus Deane suggests that Heaney's poetry becomes 'more and more etherialized', that he has moved progressively away from the earthy and substantial world of the early poetry.[22] Deane believes that Heaney has opted for the Herculean intelligence over the Antaean sense of place in order to free himself for the writing of poetry. The emergence of the visionary, or what Deane calls 'ethereal', is also part of an interrogation of the political relevance of aesthetics. The creation of Ireland and of Irishness has been part of the poetic agenda for over one hundred years; the poetic versions of place have been in turn the inspiration or the justification for various political activities during the same period. In his treatment of the fictionalizing of place, Heaney suggests the subjective and perhaps arbitrary nature of contemporary Irish reality.

Unlike Heaney, Derek Mahon has no initial connection to place. He can take no comfort from his native city Belfast, partly because it is war-torn –

> And I step ashore in a fine rain
> To a City so changed
> By five years of war
> I scarcely recognize
> The places I grew up in,
> The faces that try to explain.   ('Afterlives')

– and partly because it is dominated by a Protestantism that Mahon finds narrow and shortsighted.

> Extraordinary people
> We were in our time,
> How we lived in our time
> As if blindfold
> Or not wholly serious,
> Inventing names for things
>
> To propitiate silence.

Cosmopolitan by nature and experience, Mahon conceives of the idea of place from the perspective of an outsider and therefore always feels a stranger in his own land. As an urban Protestant, he cannot identify with the rural west and its associations with Gaelic Ireland:

> Remember the time we drove
> To Donegal and you talked
> For hours to fishermen
> You had worked with, while I,
> Out of my depth in these
> Waters, loafed on the quays?   ('Brighton Beach')

Nor can he admire the Protestant tradition as Yeats did; for Mahon, the contemporary Ulster Protestant has become rigid and hypocritical:

> . . . you could
> wear black, drink water, nourish a fierce zeal
> . . . and not
> feel called upon to understand and forgive
>   but only to speak with a bleak
> afflatus . . .
> . . . this is your
> country, close one eye and be king.   ('Ecclesiastes')

Like MacNeice, with whom he identifies intensely, Mahon is an outsider, what Heaney called in his poem 'Exposure' an 'inner emigré', psychologically separated from community. Mahon's loss is measured against his urbanity and his cosmopolitanism, so that his poetry reflects rootlessness, the inability to connect with place. Physical description of landscapes or city scenes for its own sake almost never appears in Mahon's work; rather, the sense of place exists to reveal an emotional or psychological response from the poet.

5

The preoccupation with place in Irish poetry is understandable when we remember that the idea of a modern poetic tradition in Ireland is a relatively new idea, dating back to the 1880s. It seems only natural in such a self-conscious literary climate that problems of influence and originality would arise. As one poet wrote a version of Irish place into being, a succeeding poet would find it necessary to unwrite that version in an attempt to find a new poetic identity. The writing and unwriting of place are not simply 'naïve' and 'sentimental' responses to a poetic problem, although those terms have a way of clarifying certain aspects of Irish literary history, as I have tried to show. Poetic representation and treatment of place must accept the burden of history, both cultural and political. The search for 'Irishness' means digging back and down to discover pre-Christian Celts, Vikings, Normans, English, Catholics and Protestants in the layers upon which contemporary Ireland is built. Moreover, the contemporary poet must accept the disarming realization that others who have come before have excavated the place.

> Our pioneers kept striking
> Inwards and downwards
>
> Every layer they strip
> Seems camped on before
> . . .
> The wet centre is bottomless.
>
> (Seamus Heaney, 'Bogland')

Notes

1 'Nationality and Literature', *Uncollected Prose of W. B. Yeats*, ed. John P. Fraynes (New York, 1970), 271.
2 The essay is collected in *Schillers Werke*, vol. 20: *Philosophische Schriften*, 1, ed. Benno von Wiese (Weimar, 1962), 413–503. I am grateful to Professor Bernhard Greiner of the Department of German, University of Tübingen, whose conversation with me on parts of this essay helped clarify my application of Schiller's ideas to contemporary Irish poetry.
3 'Wenn man sich der schönen Natur erinnert, welche die alten Griechen umgab, wenn man nachdenkt, wie vertraut dieses Volk unter seinem glücklichen Himmel mit der freyen Natur leben

konnte, wie sehr viel näher seine Vorstellungsart, seine Empfindungsweise, seine Sitten der einfältigen Natur lagen, und welch ein treuer Abdruck derselben seine Dichterwerke sind, so muß die Bemerkung befremden, daß man so wenige Spuren von dem sentimentalischen Interesse, mit welchem wir Neuere an Naturscenen und Naturcharactere hangen können, bey demselben antrifft.' (*Ibid.*, 429). Modern man, however, does not have the same closeness with nature, 'weil Natur bey uns aus der Menschheit verschwunden ist, und wir sie nur außerhalb dieser, in der unbeseelten Welt, in ihrer Wahrheit wieder antreffen . . . Sehr viel anders war es mit den alten Griechen. Bey diesen artete die Kultur nicht so weit aus, daß die Natur darüber verlassen wurde. Der ganze Bau ihres gesellschaftlichen Lebens war auf Empfindungen, nicht auf einem Machwerk der Kunst errichtet; ihre Götterlehre selbst war die Eingebung eines naiven Gefühls, die Geburt einer fröhlichen Einbildungskraft, nicht der grübelnden Vernunft, wie der Kirchenglaube der neuern Nationen . . .' (ibid., 430–31).

4 'So lange der Mensch noch reine, es versteht sich, nicht rohe Natur ist, wirkt er als ungetheilte sinnliche Einheit und als ein harmonierendes Ganzes. Sinne und Vernunft, empfangendes und noch selbstthätiges Vermögen, haben sich in ihrem Geschäfte noch nicht getrennt, vielweniger stehen sie im Widerspruch miteinander' (ibid., 436–7).

5 'So wie nach und nach die Natur anfieng, aus dem menschlichen Leben als Erfahrung und als das (handelnde und empfindende) Subjekt zu verschwinden, so sehen wir sie in der Dichterwelt als Idee und als Gegenstand aufgehen' (ibid., 431).

6 The former condition – the naïve or the real – places primary emphasis upon the external natural world or the objective and mimesis; the latter – the sentimental or the ideal – upon the internal human world (primarily the imagination) or the subjective and epistemology. With the 'sentimental' the concern is with the authenticity and the sincerity of the poetic expression. See Schiller, ibid., 436–41.

7 'Powers of earth and Visions of Air', *Times Literary Supplement*, 16–22 March 1990, 275.

8 Most of the figures of the early days of the Irish Literary Revival were Anglo-Irish Protestants, among them Yeats, John Synge, Lady Gregory, Douglas Hyde, and George Russell.

9 'The Celtic Element in Poetry', *Essays and Introductions* (New York, 1961), 176.

10 Ibid., 178.

11 Seamus Heaney, *The Place of Writing* (Atlanta, Georgia, 1989), 20–1.

12 Seamus Heaney uses the phrase 'unwrite' in his discussion of

.

192   ROBERT F. GARRATT

contemporary Irish poetry (ibid., 20, 47). The idea of post-Yeatsian
poetry challenging Yeats's views and versions of Ireland is consistent
in literary criticism over the past ten years.

13 In his recently edited *Faber Book of Contemporary Irish Poetry*,
Paul Muldoon gives prominent position to Kavanagh and MacNeice
as important sources for contemporary Irish poetry (London, 1986;
rpt. 1989).

14 See Hewitt's 'Regionalism: the Last Chance', in Tom Clyde (ed.),
Ancestral Voices: the Selected Prose of John Hewitt (Belfast, 1987),
122–5.

15 Ibid., 122–3.

16 Letter to Peter Kavanagh, August Bank Holiday, 1947, in Peter
Kavanagh (ed.), *Lapped Furrows* (New York, 1969).

17 Louis MacNeice, Introduction, *Selected Poems* (London, 1988),
xxiii.

18 'The Placeless Heaven: Another Look at Kavanagh', *The
Government of the Tongue* (London, 1988), 9.

19 John Montague, *The Rough Field* (Dublin, 1972).

20 Heaney, *The Government of the Tongue*, op. cit., xxii.

21 We would have to go to Yeats and epecially to Joyce for Heaney's
source. I discuss Joyce's influence on Heaney's notions of poetic
tradition in *Modern Irish Poetry* (Berkeley and London, rev. ed.
1989), 230–58, 280–85.

22 Seamus Deane, 'Powers of Earth and Visions of Air', *op. cit.*, 275–6.

10

And not just for Pharaoh's daughter: Irish-language poetry today

SABINA SHARKEY

Since the Second World War there has been a remarkable and impressive range of poetry written in Irish. This is all the more surprising given the difficulties facing the Irish language. We are now at the stage where one observer of our linguistic state publishes his work under the title *The Death of the Irish Language: A Qualified Obituary.*[1] The title seems apposite; there is a general consensus that if not stone cold yet, the language is *in extremis* and a likely candidate for a grand state funeral. Later in this chapter I would like to offer a caveat to this view of the language and to suggest that there may be a continuity in transformation rather than a simple death, that the evolving bilingual culture may be younger and healthier than is generally credited. But to begin with I would like to pursue the paradox of a blossoming of Irish poetry in a period of language decline.

1

An attempt to formulate a fixed canon of contemporary Irish poetry quickly causes one to revise the image of infirmity. The corpus of poetry is better figured to my mind as a youthful one, caring little for convention, sceptical of tradition and undeniably energetic. Identity, for what it is worth, is emphatically self-contradictory and worth celebrating for that. At least one contemporary poet has viewed this effervescence in more sombre terms. Máire Mhac an tSaoi suggests that the vitality may be of a *fin de siècle* variety: 'Irish – that is Gaelic verse is so intensively conservative that at all times it has taken a major cataclysm to cause it to change. Today it is possible that another crisis, this time the death of a language, is producing another last flowering'.[2] This representation of language as a prime motivating factor in literary production is not unusual. After all both the revival and the nationalist movements of the late nineteenth century prioritized the re-establishment of the Irish language. For literary producers this meant that language was a fundamental determinant not just in the obvious structuralist sense, because it was their *métier*, but additionally because language policy determined the relations of production of literature – the establishment of state patronage and support networks, of a readership, of printing presses, etc. The emphases on the state of the language and language policy as shaping forces within literary production allow for a persuasive dominant narrative and within it one may discern two stages in twentieth-century Irish literary production. In the first the writer is positioned as caretaker of the language and in the second she carries out the more melancholy task of undertaker. So as Mhac an tSaoi's view indicates, however one responds to the richness of contemporary poetry, one still regards it as a bravura graveside performance, its ingenuity a last swansong.

Arguably, however, the interwoven history of language revival and literary production existed alongside other influences in the literary culture, those deriving from an emergent modernism in Ireland, from canons of writing in English and translation and from continental and post-colonial influences. Cultural agency may be done a disservice by being reduced to predominantly caretaking and undertaking responsibilities. And, with regard to the latter, there is a discernible tension between those writers who acquiesced in the projected roles and those who problematized them, giving rise to what Noel McGonagle refers to as two diametrically opposed schools of writing, 'the traditional and the innovative'.[3]

2

The promotion of the Irish language from the 1890s through to the 1930s and the prioritizing of the production of literary texts were part of a romantic nationalist and later of a cultural nativist programme. From the inception of the Free State, language was promoted largely through the Department of Education, where texts were urgently required: 'at the time of the foundation of the

Gaelic League [1893] a mere twenty books were in print in the Gaelic language and these were mostly of a devotional, grammatical or folkloristic nature. There was nothing of contemporary literary nature in existence.'[4] In the light of these unpromising beginnings the speed of Irish literary development was a notable success. The same cannot be said for the first stages of language policy enactments. Between 1881 and 1926 there was a 41 per cent drop in the number of Irish-speakers. Terence Brown has pointed out that this was a result not just of economic and migratory factors but of the ideological demeanour of the Free State. The 'Irish Ireland' movement lost support because it possessed no social programme and expressed its aim in increasingly conservative and authoritarian terms, further distancing itself from a potential following.[5] Throughout the 1930s the state aimed to consolidate a nativist and culturally exclusivist influence in most areas of social life. Myriad forms of communication, from dance-hall culture to literary production, were regulated by increased levels of censorship and restrictive legislation. And where the Irish language was viewed as the badge of a people, a sense of Irish writing was construed accordingly. The written text had a pedagogic purpose. Parochially anchored in subject-matter and form, literature was seen as the repository of the language of ordinary people. It seemed aimed at a reader who, thus accessed to a local idiom and to a social documentation of a community, could extend both his or her vocabulary and his or her understanding of a particular way of life. The question of literary value, if raised at all, was of a secondary importance.[6]

Although we may read the period culminating in the 1930s as one of stasis, if not repression, there is another aspect to the decade which merits attention. For alongside the state advancement of traditionalism, counter-cultures were emerging whose consolidation over the next two decades would open the flood gates for Irish poetry. An urban-based Irish language and cultural movement began to form. In this period a writer's association was founded and an inter-varsity Irish-speaking group, who in turn set up the Irish magazine, *Comhar*. An Irish newspaper, *Inniu*, and a publishing house, Sáirséal agus Dill, were established in the forties, the latter offered an appealing alternative to the state publishing house, An Gúm. Other Irish journals, such as

Feasta, were founded and the formation of An Club Leabhar ('The Book Club'), which guaranteed sales of not less than 3,000 copies. A Dublin-based organization begun in the 1950s, Gaellinn, sponsored Irish productions in the theatre and in new media forms. These efforts increased audiences and readerships which in turn encouraged more innovative Irish writing. But even if we look as far back as 1941 when Myles na gCopaleen published his brilliant satire on 1930s autobiography, *An Beal Bocht* ('The Poor Mouth'), it was clear that the knee-jerk genuflection was no longer an adequate literary response. His irreverent voice was one of the heralds of a more open space in which modern Irish literature, Nualitríocht, was founded.

3

Poets were quick to respond to the challenge of new opportunities in literary representation. Seán Ó Tuama's anthology of *Nuabhéarsaíocht* ('New Poetry') in 1950 provided the evidence of a new departure. Piaras Beaslaí, Liam Gógan and Mícheál Mac Liammóir were among those effecting a transition between the older style and a more modernist and individual-orientated approach. And poets such as Máire Mhac an tSaoi, Máirtín Ó Diréain and Seán Ó Ríordáin came to public attention after the Second World War. Mhac an tSaoi deploys a range of personae drawn from history and mythology. Her poems explore themes of love and its betrayal, 'Ceathrúintí Mháire Ní Ógain' ('Quatrains of Mary Hogan'), of parenting, 'Codladh an Ghaiságh' ('The Hero's Sleep'), and in a poem such as 'Cearca' ('Hens') strands of foreign and personal destiny interwoven in a local history are treasured up in acts of memory and storytelling.[7] Mhac an tSaoi inflects human experience with a gendered voice and may rightly be regarded as the precursor of a strong school of women poets in Irish, including Caitlín Maude, Nuala Ní Dhomhnaill, Áine Ní Ghlinn and Biddy Jenkinson.[8]

Ó Diréain and Ó Ríordáin are the other founding figures of contemporary Irish poetry. Between 1942 and 1947 Ó Diréain published four volumes. Ó Ríordáin wrote his influential proto-modernist poem 'Adhlacadh mo Mhathair' ('My Mother's Burial') immediately after the war and titled his first collection *Eireaball Spideoige* ('A Robin's Tail'), published in 1952, from a

line in the poem. That volume and *Brosna* ('Kindling'), published
in 1964, may fairly be regarded as having radically transformed
Irish poetry. Many aspects of Ó Ríordáin's work are condensed
in the early poem 'Adhlacadh mo Mhathair'. At his mother's
graveside, temporal and physical experiences are thrown into
confusion, reminiscence floods the present moment, draining it of
any meaning. A robin hovers over the open grave and the poet
imagines it in communion with the dead woman. He is jealous of
their communication and estranged not just from an emotional
registering of the funeral but from the other people so carelessly
inattentively present. The poem closes with the poet persona in
anguish over his own limitations and desires:

> Ranna beaga bacacha a scríobh agam,
> Ba mhaith liom breith ar eireaball spideoige,
> Ba mhaith liom sprid lucht glanta glún a dhíbirt,
> Ba mhaith liom triall go deireadh lae go brónach.

> [I am writing small, uneven verses,
> I would like to catch a robin's tail,
> I would like to dispel the knee-brushing spirit,
> To journey sadly to the end of the day.]
>   (trans. Gabriel Fitzmaurice)

The interpretation of private and public selves and the poet's
alienation from both, and his dissatisfaction with social and spir-
itual representatives (neighbours and priest), are explored in the
poem. His urge for a transcendentalism, for initiation into mysti-
cal rites and communions, balances against a heightened, almost
existential awareness of sensory and material phenomena. Many
of his subsequent poems are poised between the ascetic and the
sensory while adopting religious and philosophic discourses to
voice the individual quest. The poet persona often vacillates
between a wished-for retreat, religious or secular, from social
groupings and a desire for immersion in a local community.
Freedom may be lonely and the group a benign solace. Yet it is
only the frightening limitlessness of an individual's liberty that
makes this community palatable. Ó Ríordáin disparages the mass
and even while purporting to embrace it, in a poem like 'Saoirse'
('Freedom') the tone is more denigratory and patronizing than
emphatic. It is a posturing identification at best:

Is loirgeod comluadar daoine
Nár chleacht riamh saoirse,
Ná uaigneas:

. . . Ó fanfad libh de ló is d'oíche,
Is beidh mé íseal,
Is beidh mé dílis
D'bhur snabsmaointe . . .

[And I will seek the company of people
who never practised freedom
or solitude:

. . . Oh, I will stay morning and evening
And I'll be humble,
Faithful, obedient
To your stub-thoughts.]   (trans. Gabriel Fitzmaurice)

Philosophical and religious quests do not feature prominently in
Ó Díreáin's writing. But his too is an isolated voice in the city
and he shares with Ó Ríordáin a distaste for many aspects of
mass culture and materialism. His earlier experience on Aran is
frequently contrasted with contemporary urban life in the poems.
The island is represented either as an idyllic pre-lapsarian space
or as a contemporary ethical alternative, a community offering a
retreat from the excesses of the metropolis. Poems such as
'Blianta an Chogaidh' ('War Years'), 'Faoiseamh a Gheobhadsa'
('I will find solace') and 'Ár Ré Dhearóil' ('Our Wretched Era')
juxtapose stale uprooted city life with the unspoilt natural land-
scape of Aran and the innocent toil of its islanders. Ó Ríordáin
and Ó Díreáin's innovative formal techniques and their focus on
probing individual subjectivity position them both as modernists
in style and subject matter. Ó Ríordáin has been likened to T. S.
Eliot where a poetry shares the fragments of a culture and
reaches for a revitalizing ethical credo. These Irish poets also
exhibit the mass civilization and minority culture views propa-
gated by English writers such as Eliot and Leavis. Finally, it is
notable that in both poets a sense of disease, disorder or spiritual
malaise is often represented in sexual terms. In the first poem of
his collection, *Brosna* ('Kindling'), the poet determines to break
from English, here personified as a 'striapach allúrach' ('foreign
whore') and his agency will be to offer to the Irish language or

muse thoughts stolen from her store – 'Is sínim chugat smaointe /
A ghoideas-sa uaithi . . .' ('and I shall offer you thoughts stolen
from her').⁹ Ó Díreáin's critique of unnatural city practices
invokes a series of implicit norms regarding, in this instance,
sexual love, courtship and women's reproductive functions:

> . . .
> Na hainmhithe is na héin
> Nuair a fhaighid a gcuid dá chéile,
> Ní gach ceann is luaithe chucu
> A ghlacaid in aon chor.
>
> I gcúiteamh an tsíl
> Nach ndeachaigh ina gcré,
> I gcúiteamh na gine
> Nár fhás faoina mbroinn
> Nár iompar rí ráithe
> Faoina gcom,
> Séard is lú mar dhuais acu
> Seal le teanga iascachta
> Seal leis an ealaín . . .

> [Birds and beasts
> When they couple together,
> . . . The firstcomer's not always the one
> They decide to take.
>
> To compensate for the seed
> That did not enter their flesh,
> To compensate for the child
> That did not grow in their womb
> That they didn't carry nine months
> In the hollow of their bodies,
> The least they'd accept as doing
> Was a spell at foreign languages,
> A spell at the arts . . .]

> (from 'Ár Ré Dhearóil' ('Our Wretched Era'),
> trans. Tomás Mac Síomóin and Douglas Sealy)

Perhaps Patrick Kavanagh is the nearest equivalent of an Irish
poet writing in English expressing uncertainty through a misogy-
nist discourse. Ó Díreáin's projections are echoed in Kavanagh's
snide jibes at women with 'hips too heavy for thinking'. Both
poets also share similar treatment of the country–city divide.

Declan Kyberd has posed the question as to whether
Ó Ríordáin is an Anglo-Irish writer, building his argument not

primarily on linguistic but on psychic factors.[10] The harnessing of an innovative energy to new styles and subject-matters, which is the hallmark of both poets, is accompanied by a new hybrid consciousness. Whether selecting or, as Ó Ríordáin would phrase it, thieving, from another culture's resources, the hybridity of their poetic psyche and the hyphenated condition of their linguistic and cultural contexts seems irrefutable.

4

By the 1960s this semi-permeation of writing in Ireland by the two languages was to become more established. Poets such as Críostóir Ó Floinn, Eithne Strong, Pearse Hutchinson and Mícheál Ó Siadhail worked across both media, gaining a wider audience for their work and enriching their poetry through this crossing of subject and linguistic boundaries. A collection such as Eoghan Ó Tuairisc's *Lux Aeterna* (1964) indicates how this process may have added a resilience to Irish poetry. His poem 'Aifreann Na Marbh' ('Mass of the Dead') is one of the finest long poems in the twentieth century, by a writer who has been consistently committed to a practice in both Irish and English. Translations by Ó Siadhail and Hartnett of their own poems have been deservedly highly respected; Hartnett's journey between the two languages is a case of the contemporary poets wrestling with and affecting provisional pacts between them.

The poem which titles and closes Hartnett's 1975 collection, *A Farewell to English*, teases out some of the issues. The 'gentle mechanism of [his] verse' is released and with hands 'sunk . . . into tradition' he sifts the centuries for words to describe his sensations. Irish words come, clichés at first, but their force and flight suggests a whole untapped potential, the release of a repressed source:

> The clichés came
> at first, like matchsticks snapping from the world
> of work: mánla, séimh, dubhfholtain, álainn, caoin:
> they came like grey slabs of slate breaking from
> an ancient quarry, mánla, séimh, dubhfholtach,
> álainn, caoin, slowly vaulting down the dark
> unused escarpments, mánla, séimh . . .

> . . . Then Pegasus
> pulled up, the girth broke and I was flung back
> on the gravel of Anglo-Saxon.
> What was I doing with these foreign words?[11]

The ironic ambiguity of the last line is surely that the winged Pegasus was carried by the fusion of both languages in rhythmic sequence, the issue of which now are the 'foreign words' is not easily settled by a reader. Hartnett's poem is critical of a failure to do right by 'great men' who 'walked in rags / from town to town / finding English a necessary sin / the perfect language to sell pigs in'. Those implicated include our new literati who dine on the 'celebrated Anglo-Irish stew' and the general populace who traded on 'Irish dreams' for a state 'of files and paper-clips . . .' [and] 'forms in triplicate'. Bidding 'farewell to English verse / to those I found in English nets', the poet announces his decision to write in Irish forthwith:

> I have made my choice
> and leave with little weeping:
> I have come with meagre voice
> to court the language of my people.

His next collection, published by the same Gallery Press, *Adharca Broic* ('Badger Horns') (1978), would suggest that this linguistic choice is an invigorating, enabling one: 'Uaisle mé ná tír ar bith: / Teanga mise, an líon a bhailíonn gach iasc', ('Nobler than any country am I, / I am language, the net that gathers all fish').

But the difficulty of maintaining a writing practice solely in Irish begins to burden the poet and by 1984 he unloads some of that weight in a poem mockingly titled 'Féin trua' ('Self Pity'):

> . . .
> gan suim ionam ag criticí
> gan chuntas ó mo chairde
> fear dearúdta ag an litríocht,
> im bhastard, im aonarán
> tá na Gael amhrasach romham
> 'ceapann ne Gaill gur
> as mo mheabhair atáim
> Siúlaim sleibhte iar-Luimní
> breac-Ghalltacht mo dhúchais:

do thréig mé an Béarla --
ar dhein mé tuaiplis?

[Critics ignore me
friends neglect me
literature has forgotten me
I'm a bastard, all alone.
The Gael distrusts me
The Gall thinks me insane.
I walk the hills of west Limerick,
my native half-English speaking district;
I have deserted the English tongue
have I made a mistake?][12]

After a decade of maintaining an allegiance to one language, Hartnett's hard-won consciousness of his own literary integrity moves him to engage of necessity in both languages. His subsequent work includes 'A Necklace of Wrens' (1987), wherein he presents a selection of his Irish poems alongside his own translations, two volumes in English, *Poems to Younger Women* (1988), *The Killing of Dreams* (1992), and an Irish volume, *Haicéad* (forthcoming). In addition, his translations of classical and of other contemporary poets confirm his generosity of imagination and his exceptional poetic skills.

5

The 1970s also saw the emergence of a group of poets around University College, Cork, first introduced to a reading public via the new literary journal, *Innti*. This younger generation included Michael Davitt, Gabriel Rosenstock, Liam Ó Muirthile and Nuala Ní Dhomhnaill. It is difficult to generalize about their work. I would stress again that the exuberance of post-1960s poetry resists easy canonical pronouncements. Their voices are refreshingly varied and their styles range from Rosenstock's sparse Irish haiku to the long-lined storytellings of Ní Dhomhnaill. Through the circulations of their work, particularly in *Innti*, a new audience became attuned to these different lyrical and modern epic talents and subjects. The old country-city, nature-alienation dualities were superseded by a poetry which found and sung itself in urban and migrant locations, as in Davitt's somnambulist poem 'Cuairt ar Thigh M'Aintíní an

Nollaig sarar Rugadh mé' ('A Visit to my Aunt's house the
Christmas before I was born'). Technologies of modernity are no
longer anathema to poetic discourse. Rosenstock's poem 'Teilifís'
('Television'), subtitled 'faoi m'iníon Saffron' ('for my daughter
Saffron'), is occasioned by television but far from contained by
it:

> Ar a cúig a chlog ar maidin
> Theastaigh an teilifís uaithi.
> An féidir argóint le beainín
> Dhá bhliain go leith?
> Síos linn le chéile . . .
> Stánamer le hiantas ar scáileán bán.
> *Anois! Sásta?*
> Ach chonaic sise sneachta
> Is sioraf trid an sneachta
> Is ulchabhán Artach
> Ag faoileáil
> Os a cionn.

> [At five o'clock in the morning
> She wanted television.
> Who can argue with a little woman
> Two and a half years old?
> Down we went together . . .
> We stared in wonder at the white screen.
> *Happy Now?*
> But she saw snow
> And a giraffe through it
> And an arctic owl
> Wheeling
> Above it.]   (trans. Gabriel Fitzmaurice)

Arguably there is a major psychological shift in poems of this
newer generation. Where the poet persona was previously seen as
a lone and solitary figure, often pitted against an indifferent or
hostile crowd, the poet's exploration of subjectivity now seems
more relational both in personal and in social terms. Davitt's
political poems centre around themes of terrorism, consensus and
dissent, his cause 'Ach ceart ag cách / Croílar a mhianaigh féin c
aimsiú' ('a person's right to crank the centre of his own being').
His poems attempt to respond to the dehumanizing effects
of political violence, whether in Palestine, 'Ó Mo Bheirt

Phailistíneach' ('O my two Palestinians') or in Northern Ireland, 'Do Bhobby Sands An lá Sular Éag Sé' ('For Bobby Sands on the Day Before he Died'), and in the latter poem when he speaks of a 'voice of your people' it is without simplification or cant:

> Fanaimid, ag stánadh,
> inár lachain i gclúmh sóch,
> ar na cearca sa lathach
> is an coileach ag máirseáil thart
> go bagarthach ar a ál féin,
> ar ál a chomharsan,
> is i ngurth na poimpe glaonn:
> 'coir is ea coir is ea coir'.
> Thit suan roimh bhás inniu ort.
> Cloisimid ar an radió
> glór do mhuintire faoi chiach,
> an chumha ag sarú ar an bhfuath:
> is é ár ngiú duit
> go mbuafaidh.

> [We wait, staring,
> like ducks in cosy plumage,
> at the hens in the mire
> while the cock struts
> threateningly around his own brood
> and his neighbours'
> pompously crowing:
> 'A crime is a crime is a crime'.
> You fell into a death-sleep today.
> We heard on the radio
> the catch in the voice of your people,
> sorrow overwhelming hate:
> our prayer for you
> is that it will.]   (trans. Gabriel Fitzmaurice)

On the subject of more personal relations, to compare Davitt's poem on the death of his father, 'An Scáthán, i gcuimhne m'athar' ('The Mirror, in memory of my father'), with Ó Ríordáin's 'Adhlacadh mo Mhathair' ('My Mother's Burial') is to register both a generational distance and a shift in sensibility which is not attributable merely to individual poetic treatment or temperament.

6

Nuala Ní Dhomhnaill is perhaps the best-known poet writing in Irish today, and as Mhac an tSaoi comments in her introduction to the *Rogha Dánta* ('*Selected Poems*'), 'it is almost impossible to do justice aesthetically to this poet's production'.[13] Her earlier published volumes in 1981 and 1984 confirmed her as a major poet and the two recent volumes of selected and new Irish poems accompanied by translations, *Rogha Dánta* and *Pharaoh's Daughter*, have accessed her work to a more general audience.[14] The poems in *Pharaoh's Daughter* have been translated by thirteen Irish poets, including Ciaran Carson, Seamus Heaney, Medbh McGuckian, John Montague and Michael Longley, while the selected poems are all translated by Michael Hartnett or the author herself. Ní Dhomhnaill's poetic range is so wide that many contemporary poets find in her work a thread that weaves delicately into English and into their own diverse poetic idioms. Reworkings of Irish or classical mythological materials, epic accounts of local adventures, anarchic, humorous or unabashedly frank celebration of erotic pleasure are all embraced by her pen. Poems such as 'An Bhabóg Bhriste' ('The Broken Doll'), 'An Bhean Mhídhilis' ('The Unfaithful Wife'), 'Fear'('Looking at a Man'), 'Ceann' ('Head') and 'Aubade' should not be missed by those who wish to read her poems in Irish alongside the excellent translations provided in *Pharaoh's Daughter*. Ní Dhomhnaill's poem for her daughter, 'Dán do Mhelissa' ('Poem for Melissa'), is in my view equal in grace to Yeats' 'A Prayer for my Daughter', and a less suspect treatment of the theme; it is translated by Hartnett in *Rogha Dánta*. The last poem in *Pharaoh's Daughter* is 'Ceist ne Teangan' ('The Language Question'), translated by Paul Muldoon:

> Cuirim mo dhóchas ar snámh
> i mbáidín teangan
> faoi mar a leagfá naíonán
> i gcliabhán . . .
>
> . . .
> féachaint n'fheadaraís
> cá dtabharfaidh an sruth é,
> féachaint, dála Mhaoise,
> an bhfóirfidh iníon Fharoinn?

[I place my hope on the water
in this little boat
of the language, the way a body might put
an infant . . .
. . . only to have it borne hither and thither,
not knowing where it might end up;
in the lap, perhaps,
of some Pharaoh's daughter.]

With this poem we have returned to the question of language and the agency of the poet writing in Irish. Ní Dhomhnaill has cast the poet persona as a carer, though hardly a caretaker. Hope and faith are also acts of abandonment, the willingness to let 'ceist na teangan' sink or swim, founder or find favour, and this suggests a quite different relation between language and literature than those indicated at the start of this chapter. In an interview in 1987 Ní Dhomhnaill said of Irish poets working in the English or Irish language: 'We're both talking to ourselves about the things that concern us, without having to look over our shoulders and tell others out there what they want to hear.'[15] Ní Dhomhnaill identifies this liberated voice as that of an Irish- or English-speaking 'aborigine'. I would be more inclined to term it post-colonial. The older sentiments which associated modernization with Anglicization, demonizing both and defining Irish and Irishness by contrast, have now died. The promotion of Irish has shifted from compulsory and authoritarian approaches to a more consensual model, aiming at bilingualism. Government support and programmes have been redirected accordingly, for once basing their policies on national surveys which confirm strong majority support for bilingual objectives. The tremendous activity and energy invested in translation (of Heaney's and other contemporary poets' works into Irish as well) is perhaps an acknowledgement that with the old model of language exchange, where Irish would simply replace English, gone, Irish texts can relocate within an international literary culture. There is a plurality of translation strategies to negotiate. The poet, Biddy Jenkinson, for example, chooses to be translated from Irish to French rather than English.[16] The emergence of dual format texts is the corollary of our bilingual orientation and the success of these texts from the 1980s onwards is encouraging. I have drawn appreciatively on Kyberd and Fitzmaurice's anthology of contemporary Irish poetry, *An Crann Faoi bhláth* ('The Flowering Tree'), relying on Fitzmaurice's translations at points throughout this essay. Both it and Dermot Bolger's earlier anthology, *An Tonn Gheal* 'The Bright Wave' (1986), are other proofs positive, if proof be needed, that the language today is dancing on the pace.[17] Ní Dhomhnaill in hope and abandonment cast the language out to sea. Irish poetry too seems to be in full sail, but neither to Aran nor to Byzantium, nor to a kindly Pharaoh's daughter only. Its nets and its orientation are cast wider now than at any time over the last 300 years. We wish it good fortune, *bon voyage, slán abhaile.*

Notes

1 Reg Hindley, *The Death of the Irish Language, A Qualified Obituary* (London, Routledge, 1991).

2 See Tim Pat Coogan (ed.), *Ireland and the Arts* (London, Namara Press, no date given), 143.

3 Noel McGonagle, 'Writing in Gaelic since 1880', in T. Bartlett *et al.* (ed.), *Irish Studies, A General Introduction* (Dublin, Gill and Macmillan, 1988), 102.

4 Ibid., 101.

5 Terence Brown, *A Social and Cultural History 1922–1985* (London, Fontana, 1985), 67–9.

6 For a brief summary of the reception of Gaeltacht autobiography throughout the 1920s and 1930s see Gearóid Mac Eoin, 'Twentieth Century Irish Literature', in Brian Ó Cuív (ed.), *A View of the Irish Language* (Dublin, Stationery Office, 1969), 61.

7 These first two poems may be read in dual format (Irish alongside English translation) in Declan Kyberd's and Gabriel Fitzmaurice's (eds.) very fine anthology, *An Crann Faoi Bhláth (The Flowering Tree. Contemporary Irish Poetry with Verse Translations)* (Dublin, Wolfhound, 1991), 80–5, 88–91. Where I draw on translations from Fitzmaurice I acknowledge this gratefully at relevant points throughout this chapter. Mhac an tSaoi's poem 'Cearca' is reproduced in Irish and translation in that excellent collection of women's writing, Ailbh Smyth (ed.), *Wildish Things, An Anthology of Women's Writing* (Dublin, Attic, 1989), 61–4.

8 See Máire Mhac an tSaoi, *Margadh ne Saoire* (1956), *A Heart full of Thought* (1959), *Codladh an Ghaiscígh agus dánta eile* (1973), *An Galen Dubhach* (1980), *An Cion Go Dtí Seo* (1987), all published by Sáirséal Ó Marcaigh; Caitlín Maude, *Dánta* (Coiscéim, 1984); Nuala Ní Dhomhnaill, *An Dealg Droighinn* (Cló

Mercier, 1981), *Féar Suaithinseach* (An Sagart, 1984), *Pharaoh's Daughter* (Meath, Gallery Press, 1990), *Rogha Dánta / Selected Poems* (Dublin, Raven Arts, 1991); Aíne Ní Ghlinn, *An Chéim Bhriste* (Coiscéim, 1984), *Gairdín Pharthais agus Dánta eile* (Coiscéim, 1988); Biddy Jenkinson, *Baisteach Gintli* (Coiscéim, 1986), *Uisce Beatha* (Coiscéim, 1988).

9   Seán Ó Ríordáin, 'A Ghaeilge im Pheannsa', in *Brosna* (Dublin, Sáirséal agu Dill, 1964), 10.

10 See Declan Kyberd, 'Seán Ó Ríordáin: File Angla-Éireannach?' ('Seán Ó Ríordáin: An Anglo-Irish Poet?') in Eoghan Ó hAnluain *An Duine is Dual: Aistí ar Sheán Ó Ríordáin* (The Natural Person: Essays on Seán Ó Ríordáin (Dublin, An Clóchomhar, 1980), 111.

11 Michael Hartnett, *A Farewell to English* (Meath, Gallery Press, 1975), 78–84.

12 Michael Hartnett, *Do Nuala: Foighne Chrainn (For Nuala: The Patience of a Tree)* (Dublin, Coiscéim, 1984), 22. This poem and translation are reproduced in McGonagle's essay, op. cit., 114.

13 See introduction to Nuala Ní Dhomhnaill's *Rogha Dánta / Selected Poems*, op. cit., 10.

14 For details, see note 8.

15 See Nuala Ní Dhomhnaill's interview with Lucy MacDiarmid and Michael Durcan, 'Q & A: Nuala Ní Dhomhnaill', *Irish Literary Supplement*, 6, 2 (Fall, 1987), 42.

16 See Jenkinson's 'Belvedere (An Grá Cuntraphointeach)' ('Belvédère (Amour en Contrepoint)'), 'Don chrann Ginko . . .' ('A Ginko la femelle . . .'), 'Ogham', in *Wildish Things*, op. cit., 119–25.

17 Dermot Bolger, *An Tonn Gheal / The Bright Wave: Poetry in Irish Now* (Dublin, Raven Art, 1986).

III
FIVE POETS

Charles Tomlinson

Tony Harrison

Waldo Williams

Gillian Clarke

George Mackay Brown

11

Charles Tomlinson:
An Eden in Arden

RAINER LENGELER

This chapter is concerned with place in a more mythic sense than is usually implied in the discourse of region and metropolis, centre and periphery, which assumes a pattern of action and reaction. But it may be a strength that the poetry of place can transcend that pattern and tap the secret springs of vision, a kind of ultimate autonomy.

My argument falls into four parts. I shall begin by outlining man's predicament, as Tomlinson characterizes it, 'between an Eden lost and promised paradise',[1] and then focus, in the main part, on the concepts of plenitude and origin, both of them crucial to an understanding of his Eden myth. To elucidate what is meant by plenitude a number of chance meetings with Eden are analysed first. Characteristically in all of these a holistic viewpoint is held up against the 'perspective avenue'.[2] Moving on to plenitude as infinite space, Tomlinson's reinterpretation of that term is discussed, in particular his approach to reality as 'space made articulate'.[3] A third facet to deal with is that of perfection. Here I shall concentrate on one poem, 'Departure', and bring in the poet's own distinction of a linguistic as opposed to a physical place. After this enquiry into plenitude part three examines Tomlinson's presentation of Eden in terms of origin, while the whole is rounded up by a running commentary on 'In Arden', the poem to which I am indebted for my title.

'Between an Eden lost and promised paradise'

To call Eden Tomlinson's favourite and most important myth is no exaggeration. Time and again he mentions, or alludes to, the biblical garden man once possessed and dreams of regaining. I hasten, however, to add, that his understanding of the myth is not that of orthodox Christianity, say of Milton's *Paradise Lost* and *Paradise Regained*, but is basically concerned with man's outlook on the world, on nature and life. When, under the impression of the ravages of industrialization, the poet left his native Midlands as a young man and came under the spell of Cézanne's paintings and writings, he wanted, in his own words, to earn the right to use the artistic ethic of Cézanne as a basis for his poetry:

> It seemed to me a sort of religion, a bringing of things to stand in the light of origin, a way, even, of measuring the tragic fall from plenitude in our urban universe.[4]

Eden, then, means two things: plenitude and a way of looking at things in the light of origin. I take it that 'this light of origin' is meant as a metaphor for a prelapsarian outlook that, potentially at least, may be regained. In any case, if, in a number of poems, Eden is called 'cruel' (236), 'unenterable' (271), 'inaccessible' (365), a greater number of references are confident of 'The perpetuity of Eden' (160) and even hint at the possibility of it 'coming round again' (26), of a 'lingering at the gate' (382), of 'regaining the gate' (365), of an 'Eden ungated' (290) or of 'Eden rescinding its own loss' (248).

Since Tomlinson himself has linked up his concept of plenitude with epistemology I have turned for further elucidation to some of his so-called prose poems. This is how two of the aphorisms in 'Tout entouré de mon regard' depict man's predicament

> Surrounded by your glance, you are the pivot of that scale half of which balances in darkness behind you . . .
> To see, is to feel at your back this domain of a circle whose power consists in evading and refusing to be completed by you. (190)

Epistemologically the fall from plenitude means that in spite of the astonishing range of the glance, or some of the other senses for that matter, man's capacities of perception and knowledge remain woefully limited. The poems mention at least four obstacles to a total picture of reality. Owing to the limited radius of the eye man does not see what lies at his back or beyond his horizon. Then, there is the darkness of night acting as a barrier and refusing to be penetrated. Third comes the 'perspective avenue',[5] i.e. our penchant for approaching the whole of a thing, a view, a situation, by a single viewpoint. Finally, our grasp of reality falls short of totality because of the time factor:

> We cannot pitch
> our paradise in such a changeful
> nameless place and our encounters
> with it.   (77)

Things appear to us only in an unending flux of time. The total number of facets being endless, the circle refuses to be completed by us. However, if there is no denying these restrictions, there is no need to despair either. In 'In the Borghese Gardens' man's situation appears nicely balanced 'Between an Eden lost and promised paradise'.[6] But, of course, since Eden has essentially to do with an outlook on life and things, belief in it is as much a prerequisite to regain it as 'the will to wish back Eden'.[7]

That it is actually possible to come into Eden's presence is confidently affirmed at the beginning of the poem with that title:

> I have seen Eden. It is a light of place
>   As much as the place itself; not a face
> Only, but the expression on that face: the gift
>   Of forms constellates cliff and stones: (159)

The implication seems to be that there are at least two ways of coming across Eden. If the first is due to chance, with the light contributing to the epiphany, the other apparently results from a talent for forms that is pre-eminently the prerogative of the artist and the poet, whose gift for forms and shapes extends to circumstances and constellations. Could it be that this gift for making out constellations is somehow related to Tomlinson's concept of plenitude? That the Edenic vision is not atomistic but holistic may also be inferred from the description of the wind and the clouds in the same poem:

> The wind is hurrying the clouds past,
>   And the clouds as they flee, ravelling-out
> Shadow a salute where the thorn's barb
>   Catches the tossed, unroving sack
> That echoes their flight. And the same
>   Wind stirs in the thicket of the lines
> In Eden's wood the radial avenues

> Of light there, copious enough
> To draft a city from.   (159)

By breaking up the scene into successive perceptions, the poet consents to time and completes 'segment to circle, chance into event'.[8] The scene, moreover, constitutes one whole inasmuch as the fleeing clouds, the tossed sack and the stirrings in the thicket demonstrate all of them the influence of the same wind. However, since further evidence is needed before we draw conclusions, I suggest that we examine a wider range of these chance meetings with Eden or comparable revelation scenes.

Plenitude as a point of view

'Hyphens' is a serio-comic poem in which the speaker alleges that a listing like 'lawns, gardens, houses, / the encircling trees' (255) is left vague and unloved by the caption 'The country's love- / liness', but is restored to a whole by the misreading 'the country's love-lines'. I skip the ironies and other formal subtleties of the text but should like to point out the holism in 'but what I saw / was a whole scene / restored', in the 'drawing together' and in 'the encircling trees' as integration motif. In 'The Greeting', more serious in tone, someone casts a glance 'idly, half blindly / into the depths of distance', and is rebuked by the speaker:

> space and its Eden
> of green and blue
> warranted more watching
> than such gazing through: (260)

For once, however, the roofs answer man's negligence 'with an unlooked-for greeting'. Again, the holism is overtly voiced in the last stanza:

> one instant of morning
> rendered him time
> and opened him space,
> one whole without seam.   (260)

A new element is brought in by the opening up of space, which appears also in 'Night Transfigured' where it is treated in greater detail. At the beginning the night shuts out space and prevents the speaker from seeing more in and behind it than a black wall.

Then, by mere accident, a torch-beam falls into a clump of towering nettles, and the wall becomes transparent:

> An immense, shifting crystal
>   latticed by shadow, it swayed from the dark,
> Each leaf, lodged blade above blade
>   In serrated, dazzling divisions.   (160)

However impressive the appearance of the nettles, what concerns us here is 'the night / In its reaches and its nearnesses'. To quote yet a third poem, 'Fireflies', the dark itself 'is spaces / . . . Discovered depths' (338). In this poem the close world of a rose is discovered by the pulsing light of the firefly in it; turning upwards, the speaker realizes how 'cosmos grows' out of the circlings of tiny stars on darkness with the result that the whole of darkness becomes 'a forming rose'. Once again the opening up of space, here as darkness seen through, combines with a holistic viewpoint. Before we go on to the discussion of space itself it may now be affirmed that signs of a holistic ideal are ubiquitous, whether explicit as in 'The Greeting' or subtly penetrating and shaping the poetical vision and structure as in 'Fireflies'.

Plenitude as infinite space

As Tomlinson's reinterpretation of space is 'revolutionary', a warning should be sounded from the beginning against the fallacy that equates space with emptiness, thus degrading it to a boundary or, in the language of painters, to a mere frame. Questioning the division between space and substance in 'The Miracle of the Bottle and the Fishes', the speaker quotes Braque, the cubist, saying: 'I begin . . . with the background that supports the picture / like the foundation of a house'.[9] By way of illustration the beginning of the poem, as it were, transforms the piled-up table top of Braque's still life into a cliff-side:

> One might even take it for
> a cliff-side, sky high
> accumulation opening door on door
>
> of space.

By breaking down the frontier between substance and space, new space, the infinity of space is brought in. Braque achieves this by his layers and the segmentation of space:

> We do not know
> with precision or at a glance
> which is space and which is substance,
>
> nor should we yet: the eye must stitch
> each half-seen, separate
> identity together
>
> in a mind delighted and disordered by
> a freshness of the world's own weather.

This echoes one of Tomlinson's early poems, 'Aesthetic' from *The Necklace* (1955), notably the conviction that 'Reality is to be sought, not in concrete, / But in space made articulate' (3). The same creed underlies numerous other poems, nature poems as well as poems that turn inward, and it is to one of the last category that I shall turn next. In 'The Dream' (252) a sleeper in a modern city is troubled by

> some constricted hope
> That asked a place in which it might pursue
> Its fulness, and so grew away from him,
> Swayed into palpability like a wall:

Thus a hope for fulness or plenitude, as I should like to vary the term, grows away from the dreamer like a wall. All of a sudden, however, the wall ceases to function as a 'confine' and becomes a way out to freedom instead:

> His hand
> Still feeling for that flank of stone,
> The space that opened round him might have grown there
> For the resurrection of a being buried
> By the reality that too much defined it:

If the burial motif links the need for fulness with the well-known death-in-life theme of Romantic and modern poetry, 'the reality that too much defined it' specifies the constriction that is also equated with the merely given and threatening inertia in the following lines:

> now
> The transitions of the dream, the steps and streets,
> The passageways that branched beneath
> Haphazard accumulation of moon on moon,

> Spurned at each turn a reality
> Merely given – in inert threat
> To be met with and accommodated.

Against the merely given, human nature or, to be more precise, the mind sets possibility.[10] The mind remedies the constrictions of modern actuality by bringing to light 'The dream of a city under the city's dream'. Being dictated by blind greed the latter functions as a kind of daydreaming, while the dream of a city, 'proportioned to the man whom sleep replenishes', is presented as 'reading with opened eyes' in contrast. The streets and passageways in the dream are both adequate and salutary to the sleeper inasmuch as they point out and satisfy vital psychic needs, in our case the pursuit of fulness. In fact, the replenishments of sleep in our text tie up with this pursuit of fulness as they link with the 'variants on a theme' in line 29:

> The ways
> He walked seemed variants on a theme
> Shaped by a need that was greed no longer,
> The dream of a city under the city's dream,
> Proportioned to the man whom sleep replenishes
> To stand reading with opened eyes
> The intricacies of the imagined spaces there
> Strange and familiar as the lines that map a hand.

From *The Necklace* onwards Tomlinson has shown a special liking for the theme-variation motif implying as his belief that the totality of the theme is only brought about, if at all, in an endless string of variations. It comes, therefore, not as a surprise that the ways the dreamer walked are presented as inroads into 'imagined spaces' and are called 'variants on a theme / Shaped by a need' for fulness. Now, although the relationship between space and potentiality has been touched on in the foregoing I think it should be dwelt on for a moment. In one of his meditations on the skull Tomlinson is hardly interested in the traditional death symbolism but sees it above all as an emblem of potentiality:

> If the skull is a memento mori, it is also a room, whose contained space is wordlessly resonant with the steps that might cross it, to command the vista out of its empty eyes. (189)

In another of these aphorisms the skull of art is directly defined as a skull of possibility (191). This I find particularly striking in poems where opposites evoke each other. The delightful 'Juliet's Garden' is built on that principle. The little girl, leaving the garden because she wants to find out what it is like when she has left, cannot stand the idea of it being there when she is not, so she rushes back, 'her new-found lack / the measure of all Eden' (230). Other poems that come to mind in connection with opposites are 'The Door' ('For doors / are both frame and monument', 112) and 'A Given Grace'. In the latter, two cups 'afloat and white / on the mahogany pool / of table' 'challenge and replenish' the eye by their emptiness (115). In a number of instances the dialectic of opposites even leads to the transformation of possibility into actuality. The reader cannot help smiling when in 'Mushrooms' the gatherer is first deceived by false appearances, but soon led 'through illusion to a rind / That's true – flint, fleck or feather' (293). A more serious case is that of 'The Marl Pits', where the utopia comes true when the landscape of disembowellings is reclaimed and the pits become sheeted with 'lakes that wink and shine / Between tips and steeples, . . . As if kindling Eden rescinded its own loss' (248). To give a third example, in 'Ode to Arnold Schoenberg' the Jewish composer takes highest credit for transforming the possible into the real:

> But to redeem
>> both the idiom and the instrument
>>> was reserved
>> to this exiled Jew – to bring
>>> by fiat
>>>> certainty from possibility.   (104)

After this praise the poem ends with a sort of Edenic vision, evoking the wintered tree of the unfolded word 'creating, cradling space / and then / filling it with verdure'.

Summing up what has been said about space we should bear in mind that Tomlinson's redefinition of the term is the outcome of his view on reality as plenitude. By turning space from a limit into an integration factor new inroads into infinity are made, whether outwards, inwards, or into the realm of possibility. Thus it becomes the founding ground 'that gives place to Atlantis' (164) or Eden, for that matter.

Plenitude as perfection

In a whole series of poems plenitude appears in yet a different guise, that of perfection. Among these 'Departure' is of special interest to us in that it presents the image of perfection most characteristically, as 'a place of perpetual threshold'.

Departure

You were to leave and being all but gone,
   Turned on your selves, to see that stream
Which bestows a flowing benediction and a name
   On our house of stone. Late, you had time
For a glance, no more, to renew your sense
   Of how the brook – in spate now –
Entered the garden, pooling, then pushing
   Over a fall, to sidle a rock or two
Before it was through the confine. Today,
   The trail of your jet is scoring the zenith
Somewhere, and I, by the brink once more,
   Can tell you now what I had to say
But didn't then: it is here
   That I like best, where the waters disappear
Under the bridge-arch, shelving through coolness,
   Thought, halted at an image of perfection
Between gloom and gold, in momentary
   Stay, place of perpetual threshold,
Before all flashes out again and on
   Tasseling and torn, reflecting nothing but sun.   (289)

Descriptions of a running water shown in a succession of aspects, flushing, being hemmed in, pooling, pushing, spilling over, figure as a favourite motif in Tomlinson's poetry.[11] There is, however, something particular about 'Departure' in so far as the subject is part of a poem of farewell and culminates in an epiphany. Before disappearing under the bridge-arch the waters of the brook are halted, as it were, for the fraction of a moment and become an image of perfection in the thought of the onlooker. The poet himself kindly has pointed out to me that the departing guests of the poem were Octavio Paz and his wife and that the topography is that of his own home, Brook Cottage in Ozleworth, Gloucestershire, owing its very name to the brook described. The poem is thus grounded in actuality, but for all that background knowledge the reader who has never seen Brook Cottage is thrown back on the linguistic place, to use the poet's own distinction between the physical and the linguistic place. Linguistic place means the line ordering and syntax, pauses, enjambment, the meshing of rhyme and assonance, rhythm, tempo, and last but not least, it means the words, their phonetic modulations no less than their shadings in meaning. To come straight to the lines 13–20, I think that certain details such as the line ending after 'disappear' (l.14), enacting, so to speak, the disappearance of the waters, or the separation of adjective and noun by the line ending in 'momentary / Stay' (ll.17f.) are too spectacular to be overlooked by any reader. In fact the repeated enjambments do not speed up the tempo but rather seem to slow it down. There is, however, a problem there in the central lines 16–18. While terms like 'halted', 'momentary stay', 'place' denote a complete standstill, other linguistic elements suggest a slow progress in time. Thus in the oxymoron 'in momentary / Stay' the four syllables of the adjective, read or pronounced one after another and in conjunction with the enjambment, distinctly connote movement, possibly a slowing down to a final stop, while the denotation of both words points to the opposite, a standstill. And the same paradox holds good for other aspects of the still moment, the 'neighbouring'[12] of time and place in the two oxymorons ('in momentary / Stay, place of perpetual threshold'), or the marriage between darkness, light and colour in terms like 'gloom' or 'gold' or, for that matter, of feelings and the outer world in both terms. I do not want to lengthen the list, but then, I think that an inquiry into linguistic place in 'Departure' can hardly exclude one of its glories, the sound orchestration in it. And, although I shall limit myself to the vowel patterns and concentrate on the epiphany proper, certain inroads into other parts of the poem will be inevitable.

To start with the largest group, some forty-odd i-phonemes crowd the poem, half of which are packed in the epiphany (ll.13–20), where they set off scattered clusters of u-, ou-, and e,- æ, ɛə-, ei-phonemes, to name only the major ones. I have subdivided the i-cluster further into four groups, the first of which is made up of words that denote, or evoke at least, a state or image of transience: 'leave', 'being all but gone', 'disappear', 'stream', 'brink', 'bridge'. Here one could also include the progressive ing-forms, seven in number, like 'flowing', 'pooling', 'pushing'. The second group, small in number, actually only the two words 'to see' and 'image', refers to visual perception. Group three consists entirely of 'particles': pronouns, prepositions, conjunctions, adverbs like 'it', 'which', 'in', 'between', 'before', 'here'; group four, similarly, of endings, pre- and suffixes with i-phonemes: 'be(stows)', 're(new)', 'dis(appear)', '(cool)ness', '(halt)ed', '(flash)es', '(moment)ary', '(be)ing', '(reflect)ing'. The last two groups, in particular, demonstrate that in sound symbolism denotation is less important than evocation. What is evoked is suggested by a cumulation of similar sounds but not necessarily by the meaning of the single word, let alone syllable. In ll. 13–14: 'it is here . . . where the waters disappear' the i-symbolism does not derive its meaning from the denotation of any one of the three words 'it is here' but from the overall situation, which is that of the disappearing waters under the bridge-arch and which the cumulative i-sounds help to colour acoustically. This is different in the case of the word 'disappear' because it actually denotes the overriding issue and can therefore function as a key to our understanding of the sound symbolism. As the example shows, sound symbolism works on holistic principles, and one wonders whether our findings concerning the i-symbolism hold good for the rest of the poem, for instance, whether they may be applied to the first part of the poem. Here the situation is characterized by the leave-taking glance on the brook. To be more precise, the leaving guests turn 'to see that stream / Which bestows a flowing benediction . . .', and 'to renew' their sense of how the brook enters and overcomes the garden as a sort of confine. Undoubtedly the correspondence between 'to leave' and 'to see that stream' with the later 'image' of the disappearing waters is corroborated strikingly by the cumulative i-phoneme in both passages, but I think it has to be admitted that the i-cluster, at the beginning, is less numerous owing to a considerable number of u-sounds and a few glowing ou-phonemes. Now, whether we like it or not, we must contrast the i-cluster with at least a few other phonemes to catch a glimpse of the whole. As I pointed out already, there is a marked alternation of i- and u-sounds from the first line onwards. Just to list some of the obvious instances: 'to leave' (l.1), 'to see' (l.2), 'to renew your' (l.5), 'brook in spate' (l.6), 'pooling . . . pushing' (l.7), 'it through' (l.9), 'your jet is scoring' (l.10). Add to this the fact that the two vowels appear in the terms for the water itself, the one in 'that stream' (l.2), the other in 'the brook' (l.6). Both terms denote the same running water seen from different angles or, if you like, in different episodes. Lines 6–9 describe 'the brook . . . pooling, then pushing . . . sidl[ing] a rock or two / Before it was through the confine'. I think that the reader here comes to associate the u-cluster with the brook's struggle to get past the obstacles and 'through the confine'. In contrast the sixfold i-sound in lines 2–4 ('to see that stream / Which bestows a flowing benediction and a name / On our house of stone') obviously implies an unhindered running that even assumes religious overtones and, under the impact of the glowing ou-sounds, turns into a ceremonial 'flowing benediction'. Now, all of these sound clusters, and some of those I have not gone into like the ɔ:-, ei- and e-, æ-phonemes, reappear in the second part of the poem, and even in the lines 16–18 that make up the still moment proper:

> Thought, halted at an image of perfection
> Between the gloom and gold, in momentary
> Stay, place of perpetual threshold

As has been pointed out earlier, the variety of collocations as well as the complexity of sound patterns have increased, however, by now. Think of the additional shades in meaning, in terms of light, colour and feeling, of the u- and ou-sounds in 'gloom and gold', or the golden glow that the ou-phonemes in 'momentary' or 'threshold' have taken over, being placed in the neighbourhood of the word 'gold', or just register the rich flow of vowels in a line like 'Between gloom and gold, in momentary', that set each other off and, what is more, convey the impression of being present in the place and being 'halted at an image of perfection'. The term, I think, that needs further elucidation here, is the term perfection. In the poem with the title 'Images of Perfection' the speaker, somewhat mysteriously, alludes to a 'complete revelation' (289), but when do we call a revelation complete in space and time? The answer, in the words of the same poem, is 'At the edge of time', the moment, that is, when something is about to end. This is further illustrated in the poem with the title 'The Perfection':

> yet we never know it [sc. perfection]
> until it has been

for the moment it is
and the next has brought in

a lost pitch,
a lack-lustre pause
in the going glow
where the perfection was.   (290f.)

In accordance with this view, so typical of phenomenology, the description in 'Departure' of how the brook enters the garden and overcomes its obstacles is only brought to its completion by 'an image of perfection' lingering at the edge of the bridge-arch under which the waters disappear. So much for the completion in time. But what about place, in what way, for instance, are the stream's 'flowing benediction' and 'name' as well as the brook's 'pooling and pushing' present in the later 'image of perfection'? Now, presence in art is by representation. This is where the linguistic and stylistic correspondences and interactions between the two parts come into play again, not least the vowel patterns with their symbolism. However, it seems to me that the word 'perfection' in the 'image of perfection' carries still a third shade of meaning which is pointedly alluded to in the beginning of the poem 'Rhymes' (290):

Perfect is the word I can never hear
    Without a sensation as of seeing –
As though a place should grow perfectly clear
    . . .

This talk of hearing in terms of seeing or, if you like, this instance of synaesthesia definitely relates our discussion of the concept of perfection with the earlier chapter on plenitude as holism. A place grows 'perfectly clear' and becomes 'complete revelation' (289) when every detail is gathered into a total picture, that is not only perceived in terms of one sense but of all the senses, time, and place, and movement, and colour, and light, all contributing to a sensation of presence.

In my opinion 'Departure' is as much an impressive poem as it is a moving tribute to the Mexican poet-friend. Transfiguring the occasion into art the poem itself has become an 'image of perfection'.

'In the light of origin'

Since what we have heard so far has not much helped us in understanding what is meant by origin, I suggest that we go back once more to 'Night Transfigured'. Commenting the transfiguration of the night the speaker at first sounds almost cryptic: 'To see then speak, is to see with the words / We did not make.' There seems to be a contradiction in the two terms of the equation, triggered off by the synaesthesia 'to see with words'. The dilemma disappears, however, if the seeing and speaking fall together (see the missing comma, the synaesthesia and the ambiguity in 'the words we did not make'). This reading of 'speak' and 'words' as a silent language makes sense and is corroborated by what follows:

> That silence
> Loud with the syllables of the generations, and that sphere
> Centred by a millenial eye . . .
>   . . . we knew that we were sharers,
> Heirs to the commonality of sight . . .
>   The dead had distanced,
> Patterned its [sc. the night's] lineaments, and to them
> The living night was cenotaph and ceaseless requiem. (161)

If I am correct, then, 'To see then speak' means a silent speech in which seeing and speaking fall together. The eye, millenial by phylogenesis and the history of mankind, makes us all sharers of, and heirs to, a common language of perception, the eye representing, as it were, all the senses. But, to be sure, the speech without speech, the words without words carry also the imprint, the patterns of countless dead generations. In Tomlinson's own words from 'Skullshapes': 'The senses, reminded by other seeings, bring to bear on the act of vision their *pattern of images* [my italics]; they give point and place to an otherwise naked and homeless impression. It is the mind sees' (191). The phrase: 'They give point and place . . .' links up with the lines in 'The Dream', in which it is said of the dreamer's hope that it 'asked a place in which it might pursue / Its fulness' (253). This is where the archetypes of humanity's collective memory come into play. If they are readily available to artists and poets that does not imply that they cannot be adapted. On the contrary, to use Tomlinson's own image in 'The Dream', the ways the dreamer walked 'seemed variants on a theme / Shaped by a need . . .' (253). 'Adam' is a case in point. In that poem the biblical myth of Adam's naming the animals is not simply adopted but reinterpreted in several respects. Most important, Eden, existing only in virtuality, is a timeless and perpetual place:

> Adam, on such a morning, named the beasts:
>   It was before the sin. It is again.   (160)

But for all its potentiality Adam, speaking to himself, wants the place to be taken seriously:

> 'When you deny
> The virtue of this place, then you
>   Will blame the wind or the wide air,
>   . . .
>   Mouther or unmaker, madman, Adam.'

What is meant becomes clearer when we go back to the naming itself:

> Flower-maned beasts, beasts of the cloud,
>   Beasts of the unseen, green beasts
> Crowd forwards to be named. Beasts of the qualities
>   Claim them: sinuous, pungent, swift:
> *We* [my italics] tell them over, surround them
>   In a world of sounds, and they are heard
> Not drowned in them;

Two things deserve our attention here: first, the impersonation, which transforms not only flowers and clouds, but also their individualizing qualities into beasts, describes, in the guise of a tale, the way we may experience our natural surroundings any morning, if we care to do so. Second, we should take into account the ambiguity in the phrase 'surround them in a world of sounds'. I take it that this refers first and foremost to a language of perception of which our normal language is, ideally, the exact counterpart. In their mythical names the beasts 'are heard / Not drowned' in their surroundings.

If there were time, the role which the different senses play in our text could be gone into. Instead, I should like to shorten things by quoting Merleau-Ponty on the primacy of perception (it was Tomlinson himself who has praised Merleau-Ponty's *Phénoménologie de la perception* as 'one of our great defenses of poetry'[13]):

By these words, the 'primacy of perception', we mean that the experience of perception is *our presence* at the moment when things, truths, values are constituted for us . . .[14]

This, then, is what Tomlinson implied when he wrote that he wanted to bring things 'to stand in the light of origin'. The idea is taken up in our poem, for in the speaker's words

> We bring
> To a kind of birth all we can name
> And, named, it echoes in us our being.

Since this kind of original perception is theoretically always possible, even modern man may share Adam's belief in 'the perpetuity of Eden' and 'his sense of its continuance / And of its source – beyond the curse of the bitten apple'. To state that Eden is recoverable implies, of course, that modern man has lost it, feels dispossessed and homeless or thinks himself surrounded by the winds of meaninglessness and fortuity. We have come across some of the reasons for this 'despair of Eden': self eclipsing nature and things, the single point of view, modern man's inertia. There are others, but let me finish by confining myself to a brief interpretation of 'In Arden'.

Between an Eden lost and promised paradise

'In Arden' (305) is the enactment of an epiphany, the reader being guided through the forest of Arden to the threshold of Eden. The categoric opening: 'Arden is not Eden . . .' is revoked when and 'Where Adam, Eden, Arden run together' and the impossible has become feasible. As a matter of fact, the surprising turn is prepared for from the very first line, notably in the qualification of the denial: 'Arden is not Eden, but Eden's rhyme', rhyme in Tomlinson's symbolism hinting as much at a hidden consonance as at fortuity, chance. Now, chances or risks belong to the essence of Arden in the first phase of the poem:

> Time spent in Arden is time at risk
> And place, also: for Arden lies under threat:
> Ownership will get what it can for Arden's trees:
> No acreage of green-belt complacencies
> Can keep Macadam out:

Here the threat to the forest of Arden is personified in Ownership and, ingeniously, in that execrable son of Adam, the macadamizer of roads, who holds here the role that in other poems Midas[15] and the anonymous 'this person'[16] are playing. The modern threat to Arden means, on the other hand, that the divide between Arden and Eden is absolute, and that Adam is out:

> Eden lies guarded:
> Pardonable Adam, denied its gate,
>   Walks the grass in a less-than-Eden light
> And whiteness that shines from a stone burns with his fate:

The two terms that need explaining here are the light and the whiteness. In the case of the first it may be helpful to recall an earlier definition: 'I have seen Eden. It is a light of place / As much as the place itself.' As to white, it is pre-eminently the colour of the skull and the bare bone and may also be associated with the glaring light that makes for clear-cut boundaries. As such

> the light is a white lie
> told only to hide the dark
> extent from us
> of a seafloor continent.
> (259)

Both connotations seem to me to be relevant in the passage. Seeing the world in 'a less-than-Eden light', Adam, although 'pardonable', has nothing but the lifelessness of the stone to comfort him. This interpretation is corroborated in the following line with the sunlight even tautening the borderline between the field and the wood. At the same time subtle hints – the line is a shadowline, and the wood lies beyond the field – announce a decisive turn in this middle section of the poem:

> Sun is tautening the field's edge shadowline
> Along the wood beyond: but the contraries
>   Of this place are contrarily unclear:
> A haze beats back the summer sheen
>   Into a chiaroscuro of the heat:

Uniformity of light and colour and the clear-cut divisions give way to a chiaroscuro and a melting of contraries. The statement that 'the contraries / Of this place are contrarily unclear' sounds cryptic, but is in fact quite specific: Neither do they fall together nor do they set each other off, the chiaroscuro, enriched by synaesthesia, being a case in point. For in this particular chiaroscuro light and colour and heat run together. Afterwards the description of the grass is taken up again and, unexpectedly, the scene assumes religious connotations:

> The down on the seeded grass that beards
>   Each rise where it meets with sky,
> Ripples a gentle fume: a fine
>   Incense, smelling of hay smokes by:
> Adam in Arden tastes its replenishings:

Let me begin with the senses. Up to now sight and touch have predominated, for example in the chiaroscuro of the heat. Now comes the turn of smell and taste, while the end of the poem is, strikingly, controlled by hearing. Second, consider the dimensions. With a certain caution one could say that the horizontal line (cf. l.10: 'the shadowline') is being challenged by height in the meeting of rise and sky and in the final section, in addition, by depth (l.20). This completion of line into volume as well as the term 'replenishings' in l.19 may be taken as signs that the process is nearing plenitude. Third, let me draw attention to the religious overtones. In his comment on Cézanne's artistic ethic Tomlinson pointed out that he saw in it 'a sort of religion'. And, indeed, there are numerous references in the poems to baptisms, benedictions, celebrations of rural deities, and incense sacrifices. This religious note links up closely with the poet's concepts of home[17] and humanity and, therefore, his idea of place. The following extract from *The Return* gives at least an approximate idea of what is meant:

> For place is always an embodiment
> And incarnation beyond argument,
> Centre and source where altars, once, would rise
> To celebrate those lesser deities
> We still believe in . . .   (*The Return*, p.9)

One could also refer to Tomlinson's 'Focus' in which Eden is associated with 'a fire's interior palaces' (120), bearing in mind that originally *focus* as 'hearth' and 'fireplace' was closely associated with the cult of the domestic gods and, therefore, with the origins of the family and the place. To return to 'In Arden', it comes as no surprise that the third and final section leads down to the depths of Arden's springs, that is, focuses on the discovery of a real spring. Significantly, we are led to the place itself by a dialectic of opposites, from the 'dense heat' to the cool waters, and, additionally, by echoic 'voices / Of that place that rises through this place / Overflowing'. Let us pause for a moment to consider the succession of 'places' throughout the poem. At the beginning, Arden being not Eden, it was just 'place' that was, like time, at risk. Then, in the middle section, with the contraries running together, the universal anonymous place concretized into 'this place' of line 12. The circle is completed and brought to perfection at the end in the vision 'Of the place that rises through this place', the actual springs being but the outflow or overflow of the archetype. Water brimming and overflowing is one of Tomlinson's favourite images for perfection as a point in time and place. Transformed into runes and rhymes and chords and keys, all of them emblems of consonance, the waters blend with music and become a musical river, in which – for one moment – Adam, Eden, Arden, myth and reality, run together. However, running together does not imply a lasting coincidence. Since everything in our world is subject to time the momentary union is bound to be followed by a dissolution, as the rise of water and music is followed by their fall or cadence:

> Through its dense heats the depths of Arden's springs
> Convey echoic waters – voices
> Of the place that rises through this place
> Overflowing, as it brims its surfaces
> In runes and hidden rhymes, in chords and keys
> Where Adam, Eden, Arden run together
> And time itself must bear to the cadence of this river.

Notes

1   Charles Tomlinson, *The Return* (Oxford, 1987), 1. With the exception of *The Return* and *Annunciations* (Oxford, 1989) Tomlinson's poems are quoted from: Charles Tomlinson, *The Collected Poems* (Oxford, Oxford University Press, 1987).
2   Charles Tomlinson, *The Return*, op. cit., 18.

3 Charles Tomlinson, *Collected Poems*, op. cit. 3.
4 Charles Tomlinson, *Eden. Graphics and Poetry,* Redcliffe Poetry (Bristol, 1985), 14f.
5 Tomlinson, *The Return*, op. cit., 18.
6 Ibid., 1.
7 Tomlinson, *Collected Poems*, op. cit., 159.
8 Ibid., 164.
9 *The Return*, op. cit., 1.
10 Cf. 'Skullshapes', *Collected Poems*, op. cit., 191.
11 Cf. 'Logic' (165), 'The Race' (305), 'Severnside' (349), 'Black Brook' (366), 'Confluence' (371), 'Hearing the Ways' (*The Return*, 45).
12 Cf. 'Images of Perfection' (289).
13 Jed Rasula, Mike Erwin, 'An Interview with Charles Tomlinson', *Contemporary Literature* 16 (1975), 416.
14 J. M. Edie (ed.), *The Primacy of Perception and Other Essays* (Evanston, Ill., 1964), 25.
15 'Legend' (217).
16 'From Porlock', *The Return*, op. cit., 42.
17 Cf. above 'Departure', ll.3–4.

12

Tony Harrison and the poetry of Leeds

RAYMOND HARGREAVES

Tony Harrison's first book of poems, *The Loiners*,[1] begins in Beeston, a working-class area of Leeds, and ends in Newcastle, taking in Nigeria, Prague and Brazil *en route*. The poems move from first, fumbling sexual explorations by the Leeds–Liverpool Canal to Africa where sex is free-and-easy, if not always free. The Leeds poems resist a weight of communal pretence and prohibition. In Africa it is shed, liberating the erotic word-play of 'from *The Zeg-Zeg Postcards*'[2] with their rapt, laconic bisexuality. Returning home brings a sense of loss, the vibrancy of '*négritude*' replaced by a desultory order:

> Leeds City Station, and a black man sweeps
> Cartons and papers into tidy heaps[3]

with rhythm and rhyme converging in a deadening patness and finality. This note of disenchantment is extended to the whole country, though it's only north of Retford that the rot sets in. 'COND' on rusty trucks, caught up in the sound of the train's wheels, makes a refrain which combines 'CONDemned' with deceived, 'conned'.[4] This view need not depend on comparison with another country and another continent, but it arises here with a sense of shock on seeing again, with different eyes, something that was long familiar.

The sense of place in these poems is quite distinctive, milieu and landscape belong to a material world where nature is in retreat. If it is not already clear here, it is clear by the next volume that the significant determinants of region, including the topography of language found there, are social and political. That is the sense of Harrison saying that England made his father 'feel like some dull oaf'.[5] By the same token, the ditches and walls we build around ourselves, though they seem to define our individual sphere, a little island of autonomy, are equally determined from without, which makes the gap that opens between baker father and poet son identical with 'a dreadful schism in the British nation'.[6] That is not to deny there are powerful forces of resistance, strong local characteristics, it is to assert that to operate only with local criteria is inevitably to distort.

On the other hand, if what you value in poetry is precision and sensuality, it is not the choice of theme or location which is decisive. The following lines describe a gargoyle in Prague:

> The last snow of this year's late slow thaw
> dribbles as spring saliva down his jaw.[7]

What matters in terms of precision, etc., is their visual particularity and the Keatsean feel of the rhythm, sensuous, sinuous, with a touch of nausea as a kind of negative equivalent to fluid, palatable 'last oozings hours by hours'.

'Newcastle is Peru' is a gathering together of all these locations, blending visual and historic associations with memory images, a Bacchantic merging of a chair-o-plane over Leeds with a spiral staircase in St Vitus's in Prague, the falling ash in the grate with a remembered scene in Africa. Such links may seem personal and idiosyncratic, yet they are patterned on a deeper sense of connectedness. A Romantic perception of totality[8] is affirmed by some of the identities established – 'you are also Peru'[9] – and qualified by others where the primary links are exploitation and war. As the poem is getting under way, the paper burning in the fireplace shows bombs falling on Onitsha homes, giving an uncanny sense of immediacy, and with this image the regional barriers crumble and fall away. The movement of the poem is indicated by the big wheel at the beginning with its extensive view and rapid movement, so that 'Leeds landmarks blur / to something dark and circular',[10] a movement repeated in a spiral staircase, the whorls of a finger and its print, a hand moving 'with circular dexterity' over another's body, going out and returning, not to form a closed circle, more in the nature of a space probe. This corresponds more or less to a forcefield, except the poem is perhaps too linear, too much like narrative. On the other hand, oneness can only be approached from otherness, it is the only way it can be felt and demonstrated, so there's no avoiding some form of narrative stringing-together. There are other forces at work, however. The transcending, universalizing energy is impeded, this is no joyride, though it has its moments:

> this poor, embattled fortress, this strong-
> hold of love, that can't last long
> against the world's bold cannonade
> of loveless warfare and cold trade.[11]

In principle, any location may open into another, however remote and dissimilar it may seem, which confirms, with an inflection of resignation and despair, an underlying perception of universal interdependence.

Voices, 1

In the copy of *The Loiners* I have borrowed from the University Library, Leeds, I find another reader has had difficulty with a line of 'Newcastle is Peru' and has pencilled alongside 'I faff with paper chips and coal' a query which reads: '? [or 'clips']?'. Evidently 'chips' was read, tentatively, as a misprint, to give 'paper clips', though, as the second question mark indicates, that didn't make much sense either. 'Chips' are what the word says they are, pieces of chopped wood, chips off the old block. The query arose, I imagine, out of an inability to structure the sequence of nouns rather than as adjectival 'paper' plus noun, instigated perhaps by the reader's knowing some other word, like 'sticks' or 'kindling', but not 'chips'. If so, there is a particular irony in this, since the line is domestic, familiar and everyday in content, diction and tone – I'm referring to 'faff', the attention to detail and the omission of a comma to give an even, unemphatic rhythm, the rhythm of routine, and this in its turn characterizes the confessional and demotic drift of *The Loiners*.

Other possibilities of everyday speech are explored in dramatic monologue. The voice speaking in the Brechtian-sounding 'Songs of the PWD Man' is plainly a northern voice, as the obvious 'by heck' and the phrasing, cadence, even alliteration of the following lines show:

> Though I've heard it tell as well it were one of these
> That *white* Police Inspector fancied and forced down.[12]

There's no mistaking this ex-pat's garrulity or his white male complacency or the communal dream he's living out, having it off with 'girls like black Bathshebas' – the phrase sticks – and when he thinks of old men back in Leeds he's exultant, with a dash of virile exhibitionism. There's a blunt energy here, generating a style of aggressive, no-nonsense overstatement, and there's no denying he has a point:

> Yes, better to put the foot down, go fast, accelerate,
> Than shrivel on your arses, mope and squawk and wait
> For Death to drop the darkness over twittering age
> Like a bit of old blanket on a parrot's cage . . .[13]

At the end of the poem he remembers words used by 'old dears' when 'as kids we came croppers', they're the 'same daft words' (I have used them myself): 'look at the hole you've made falling', and he remembers 'that soft tone / Disembodied Yorkshire like my mother's on the phone'.[14] The voice of Leeds/Yorkshire is more audible, in different ways, in *from The School of Eloquence*, and is there inseparable from an exploration of origins, debts and loyalties.

Voices, 2: Ties and mobility

In 'Heredity', placed like a motto at the beginning of the volume, Harrison traces his gift of poetry to two uncles, 'one was a stammerer, the other dumb'.[15] The premise of (his) poetry is thus silence and the struggle for words, both a strong presence in his family during his childhood. The family bond, and its tradition of fighting against inarticulateness, form a double knot, a taut energy capable of generating its own antithesis, a surge of eloquence, and beyond that, possibly, a synthesis in which stammering and silence are integrated, *aufgehoben*, a tongue mobile and sturdy enough to carry the weight of silence and negotiate difficult, rebarbative words. That is both a commitment and a faith, and both are needed, since the going gets so rough the dialectical pattern just suggested begins to look abstract and obtuse. It is complicated, for one thing, by a variant tradition in working-class Leeds which finds an easy talker glib and half-unwittingly acquiesces in limitations imposed by class and education by saying, 'If only I could write what a tale I'd have to tell' and the like. In addition, there's a closeness here, set ways and firm values, a proud and defensive awareness of being, in the words of Harry Lauder's song, 'only a common, old working man', or woman, and a tendency to regard family and home as a stronghold in a world which is, at best, indifferent, with the honourable exception of friends. There is not much room to fit in a member of the family who develops skills and ways for which there is no ready-made place and almost none at all if they go in a direction traditionally beyond the pale. There is a place for sexual, that is, heterosexual candour, though it is rarely the home, and I was about to add it is not in print under your own name, either, but as far as I know there is no such taboo, because there is no such temptation. As a rule, the tale you have to tell is the tale you will never tell, or only anecdotally, to friends and family. Making an exception to that rule puts a fearful strain on family ties, the integrative structure of 'Heredity' falls apart. This is an area where there are extensive affinities with *Tonio Kröger*: the sense of being different, set apart, which is bound up with the gift of poetry, or, more portentously, 'die Macht des Geistes und des Wortes'[16] and the disloyalty latent or potential in being different, then, on the rebound, old allegiances heightened, intensified and expressed in a resolve to depict the lives of ordinary people. Only Mann's theory that artists are produced by middle-class families in decline no longer fits, and there is no ready assumption that the power of the intellect and the word transcends class.[17] Words are embedded in power, they are assertive, combative, prescriptive, coercive and liberating, an integral part of the class struggle.

There is every indication that this is as much a lesson learned from experience as it is a theoretical insight. These poems are preoccupied with language, as the title promises, and chronicle a tough apprenticeship in the craft of words, progressing from the trouble he had finding someone to explain the word 'harlot' to him – '(if only he'd've said it was a pro)' – to a fundamental precariousness, presented here explicitly and mimed in the rapid shift from one register to another:

> Words and wordlessness. Between the two
> the guage went almost gaga. No RI,

> no polysyllables could see me through,
> come glossolalia, dulciloquy.[18]

The wit of this is that the last polysyllabic words are consider-
ably more out of the way than 'harlot'. Their remoteness is a
token of the distance still to go and the scant chance of ever
getting there, while the tongue rises to their liquid sound and
enjoys for a moment a touch of the liberation they signify. The
use of 'come' in the last line is nicely ambiguous, drawing on
Leeds usage, e.g. 'come Christmas' for 'by . . .'[19] to give 'until
glossolalia . . . comes' together with a plea, an invitation: 'Come
glossolalia . . .'

In 'On not being Milton' Leeds speech is equated with an
Enoch, which, as a footnote says, is 'an iron sledge hammer used
by the Luddites to smash the frames which were also made by the
same Enoch Taylor of Marsden'.[20] It 'clangs a forged music on
the frames of Art', which states a counter-position, since that
clanging of 'forged music' evokes an art, though of hunger and
anger, not dulciloquy, and not 'owned language' or 'Art'. Instead
'Articulation is the tongue-tied's fighting', which links this poem
with 'Heredity', and 'Fire-eater' takes up the thread. Father and
uncle 'hauled up grammar / knotted deep down in their gut'
where 'hauled up' is a strenuous action, a work of labour and
labouring men, and 'grammar knotted' takes in 'tongue-tied' and
syntax. The word occurs again:

> Theirs are tongues of fire I'm forced to swallow
> then bring back knotted, one continuous string
> igniting long-pent silences . . .

'Forced to swallow' relates ambivalently to an inheritance which,
in the nature of things, is not chosen and to a response of accep-
tance and commitment, as in 'I'm forced to admit', where the
coercion comes from within oneself. This is a birthright that has
to be borne, and is consciously received and affirmed, their
tongues swallowed and brought back on the tongue, knotted,
held together, coherent, the poet as entertainer/magician emerg-
ing from a tradition of struggle the poem traces back to Adam
and finally presents as a triumphant rising out of torment:

> And though my vocal chords get scorched and black
> there'll be a constant singing from the flames.[21]

'Constant' contains a promise of constancy and loyalty, even if the torment is never-ending, and the last phrase not only reads 'out of the flames', flames themselves sing, and pentecostal 'tongues of fire' are heard singing in them.

In 'A Good Read' the double knot is given another twist. The son is here as sceptical about art as his father, but 'put[s] it down in poems, that's the bind'. That is a deceptively casual-seeming phrase; 'bind' is another tie, a knot that holds, cohering like syntax, a being bound by and bound to metre, rhyme, stanza, structure, a bond/bind stronger than the arguments against it.

The bind of poetry pulls against family and class loyalties, creating a tension out of which emerge these and other poems, a tension of forces held together by their opposition, in pulling against one another pulling together, making for coherence, structure and direction:

> Their aggro towards me, my need of them's
> what keeps my would-be mobile tongue still tied.[22]

Once more the syntax is tightly knotted: 'would-be mobile tongue' relates to the shared struggle for words and to a counter-tendency, separatist in effect, if not in intention, pinpointed with wry wit in 'Social Mobility'[23] – in becoming articulate he outclasses himself –, whilst 'tied' picks up knots and (family) ties and echoes 'tongue-tied', which is there in the sound of the poem – 'would-be mobile tongue still tied' –, overriding the syntax, denoting a nexus of crossed allegiances. The sequence 'tongue-tied' – 'mobile' – 'tongue tied' corresponds to the dialectical pattern outlined earlier, though if all is well it should sound less pat by now. Each poem is a fragment of confession, with its own structure, a specific degree of balance and imbalance, a particular poise, but not a position.

Voices, 3: Loiner

In the poems under *from The School of Eloquence*, both in the volume with that title and in *Selected Verse*, Loiner[24] appears in a form of duologue and, within the limits of the printed word, is reproduced with remarkable fidelity. This could be vindicated along the lines of the naturalist argument that local idiom evokes milieu. You cannot puff out flat vowels, add 't's and 'h's (by way of minding your 'p's and 'q's), straighten out the syntax, drop bits of local idiom – 'wobbly on mi pins' – or if you do, you produce something anonymous, pale, more than half dead, and you miss the point, which, by definition, is a precise, unique location. This line of argument could be applied to the use of Loiner, say, in *The Big H*,[25] which is not otherwise a naturalist play, but it only goes some way towards accounting for its use in these intensely personal and dramatic poems haunted, as they are, by the voices of a vivid and precise aural memory. The words quoted often have the full weight of words never to be forgotten, words that have gone home, sunk in, and, preserved in the silt of memory, are ready to be dug up again, looking like new. I feel sure this is exactly what was said and imagine a voice, a gesture, a person, a particular way of living and looking at things, with its strengths and bias and its roots in environment and tradition. This applies generally, and not only to the devastated and devastating words recorded.

There's a peculiar clarity, for instance, about the image of the father and his words in 'Currants':

> I saw him poise above the currants and then spit:
> *Next Sunday you can stay 'ome wi' yer mother!*[26]

That has the distinct light of a moment of shocked recognition that leaves a deep imprint. Young Harrison may have realized intuitively, but too late, what he had done to offend his father, or he may have needed some time to work it out. Either way the impact is immediate and lasting, and the offence is grounded in the rites and values, the unwritten code, of working men. There's a ring of finality, last words, here, a sudden, peremptory 'right-that's-it' tone that brooks no contradiction, a ring and tenor that give the poem its shape, and in return his words receive the emphasis due to them at the end of the poem, as its last word.

The way Harrison and his mates used to talk in his grammar-school days is epitomized in 'Me Tarzan':

> *Off laikin', then to t'fish 'oil* all the boys,
> *off tartin', off to t'flicks* but on, on, on.[27]

That, like the Tarzan call and *Twelfth Street Rag* as a signature tune, is not so clearly anchored in a particular occasion, it is typical of their energetic, elliptical style with its automatic down-

grading and in-built wariness ('tartin' for 'chasing girls', 'fish 'oil'
for 'fish-and-chip shop'), and, of course, they are adolescents.
Likewise, when he shouts down from the attic window: 'Ah
bloody can't. Ah've gorra Latin prose', that immediately estab-
lishes his community with them and sounds just right, authentic
Leeds expression of frustration and disgust, with a weight of
despondency on the long, clear 'o' – not a diphthong – at the end
of the line. To Poe's ear, this was the 'most sonorous' and poten-
tially the most melancholy and beautiful vowel in English and 'r'
the 'most producible' consonant.[28] Here the 'o' is followed by a
sibilant hiss, repeated in the marvellously compact 'Cissy-bleed-
ing-ro's':

> His bodiless head that's poking out's
> like patriarchal Cissy-bleeding-ro's.

Working with the possibilities of popular speech, Harrison hits
on that aggressive tearing-apart – cf. 'Margaret-bloody-Thatcher'
(an entirely random example) – which generates 'Cissy', his own,
perhaps his mates', judgement on his stay-at-home, grammar-
school self, savaging this figurehead of the patriarchy and
introducing a retrospective view which recognizes a new identity
emerging (Harrison/Cicero).

Here's his dad again, now a lonely old man with no come-back
but to gripe:

> *Ah can't stand it no more, this empty house!*
> *Carrots choke us wi'out your mam's white sauce!*
> *Them sweets you brought me, you can have 'em back.*
> *Ah'm diabetic now. Got all the facts.*[29]

That sounds exactly right, there's an infallible ear hearing and
recalling, catching the phrasing and the pauses (indicated by the
line-spacing). For instance, the way he first establishes the matter
in hand: 'Them sweets you brought me', and then follows with
an abrupt statement: 'you can have 'em back', is a gesture of
speech characteristic of his generation, and possibly of later ones.
It has such a direct, basic thrust, is so utterly ungracious and so
true to type (he means no offence), you have to smile.

Discussing the poetics of this technique with Jeffrey
Wainwright, Harrison insisted on the coincidence of life and art,
everyday speech and verse:

> *But your father was a simple working man,*
> they'll say, *and didn't speak in those full rhymes.*
> *His words* when *they came would scarcely scan.*

> Mi dad's did scan, like yours do, many times![30]

It is difficult to disagree. The lines just discussed not only ring true, they are also iambic pentameters. This father's line on sweets, for instance, scans as follows:

> Them sweéts you broúght me, yóu can háve 'em báck.

Nevertheless, this can only work selectively, as 'many times' acknowledges, and it is not true of rhyme which only arises spontaneously on the odd occasion when 'he's a poet and doesn't know it'. Poetically, these snatches of vernacular have the value of things said and recalled, which marks them off both from dramatic diction and from deploying a familiar style. Rhyme marks a difference, and so, too, does the topography. Generally, Loiner is set off in italics from schooled English, making a visual and, by implication, aural distinction, like Bobrowski's technique of setting off Old Prussian words from the German text. The parallel is perhaps not entirely fortuitous. In both cases the language of dominance provides a context for words spoken by those who have gone under or are at the bottom of the pile. Though Loiner is still spoken in Leeds, these days by a multiracial population, one of the effects of quoting, and placing the quoted words in italics, is to bring out the contrast between the implicit present of the poet's thoughts and the words spoken. Though still within the earshot of memory, they belong to the past, and there is grief and an impulse of atonement in recalling them.

Agenda

In saying this I am generalizing about a particular group of poems, not about the use of italics – which indicate Loiner in '*v.*' without creating this effect. In this context, it is all aggressive presence, a raucous voice of protest. Similarly, the use of the 'forged music' of a sledgehammer in 'On Not Being Milton'[31] as a metaphor for Leeds stress points to a radical reprogramming of English poetry. 'Them & [uz]'[32] rehearses a spontaneous and arrogant elocution lesson, delivered in the middle of an Eng. Lit. class. I do not recall anything as crass as the episode re-enacted in this poem, and at one time had a maths master who would begin a class by saying, for example: 'Today, lads, ah think we'll do a little bit of algebra' in his slow, careful Yorkshire voice which dwelt, almost lovingly, on each syllable of the last word. Clearly, that was unusual and made an impression on me that has remained ever since. I also remember watching the way I spoke, putting myself through a process of learning and unlearning, though my vowels were still deemed outlandish by the English teachers in the German school where I went as an English assistant. So there we were, being induced to hide, as if ashamed, what spontaneously filled us with pride and loyalty, and in the act learning the shame, and being shamed by that shame. 'I doffed my flat "a"s (as in flat cap)' is patently not a random example; in doffing one, you doff the other, shed your working-class identity. The backlash comes in Section II when literature is reclaimed in the name of the dispossessed, but not in those terms, which belong to the habit of possession:

> So right, yer buggers, then! We'll occupy
> your lousy leasehold Poetry.[33]

These are brave and confident words, with the vigour of reasserted pride and independence, robustly assessing poetry in its present alienated state as a 'lousy leasehold'. However, apart from the 'we' implicit in '[uz] can be loving as well as funny', this 'we' gives way to 'I' in the following lines: 'We'll occupy', but 'I chewed up litterchewer . . . used my name . . .', etc. To move in this way from 'we' to 'I', it seems to me, is true to the record. In this context, sadly, more than sadly, speaking on behalf of '[uz]' is very much a matter of going it alone, the odd man out acting on behalf of the rest. This is one of the reasons why a wry, ironic note is sounded at the end, signalling the power of conformist pressures and a class division constantly being reaffirmed on both sides:

> My first mention in the *Times*
> automatically made Tony Anthony!

Keats's Cockney and Wordsworth's northern vowels testify that poetry written in English has its roots in local speech, which re-

inforces the implication that this act of rebellion is simultane-
ously an act of restoration, or would be if it could be. The
movement of the poem bears witness to the difficulties, and they
are faced in 'A Good Read', where Harrison's father again speaks
with a communal voice and from within the working class
endorses a division his son first encountered in the educated
accents of the classroom:

> That summer it was Ibsen, Marx and Gide.
>
> I got one of his you-stuck-up-bugger looks:
>
> *ah sometimes think you read too many books.*
> *an nivver 'ad much time for a good read.*[34]

That touches on the pathos of dispossession, but only just
audibly, in the far distances. It is a little bit of martyrdom he is
enjoying, and in the poem he is not allowed to get away with it:
'*Good read! I bet! Your programme at United!*' This is spoken in
a Leeds voice, hence the italics, as the son comes back at his old
man, though, as a kind of stage direction indicates, 'All this in
my mind'. The orchestration is pretty elaborate. A few lines
further on the italics are dropped and with them the Leeds voice.
It is then, in his 'normal' voice, that the son admits he has come
round to his father's position on literature, only he says so in
poems, and goes on to suggest that these poems should make
good reading on the bus into town for his father and 'people with
no time like you in Leeds', and 'should' is decidedly ambiguous.
No matter how much he keeps faith with his origins, to his father
his poetry is alien territory, and his father is the rule that proves
the exception. At moments that ambivalence tilts over into a
sense of betrayal:

> . . . and *me*, I'm opening my trap
> to busk the class that broke you for the pence
> that splash like brackish tears into our cap.[35]

The self-accusation in the emphasized 'me' and the dismissive
'opening my trap' modify into a sense of helplessness, for he is
earning his pennies busking, instead of baking like his dad. The
phrase which registers solidarity, 'our cap', is so complete an
identification it curbs any sense of betrayal, unites father and son
beneath an emblem of working-class identity and places them in
a shared dilemma, always allowing that the busker has an easier

life than the baker and can shed brackish tears while the other could only stiffen his back. If it's no good pretending you are working class,[36] it is worse to exaggerate the differences. That can be left to the lower middle class, with their warped view of their role and status. 'Busk' is more perceptive, a more realistic assessment, though it not only closes family ranks, it identifies his audience as, say, readers of *The Times*.

In the teeth of these difficulties a poetic is being worked out in which raids on the inarticulate are being construed as raids on the articulate for the inarticulate. Sounds and voices are heard in the night of the past, with a sense of presence and distance as the stage mutterings ('rhubarb, rhubarb') are converted to a rebellious Leeds 'tusky, tusky'. Memories of exploitation and injustice are everywhere, chiming in with rebellion and chafing at the underdog's slowness to bite back. This is still traced through the medium of language. A Cornish proverb is quoted and translated into English as: 'The tongueless man gets his land took'[37] and in an elegant gesture of defiance in defeat we are told to 'mourn in Latin' the imminent death of threatened species, 'then translate these poems into *cynghanedd*'.[38] The 'gob' (= 'mouth', and, as explained in a note, 'hole hewn in a coal face') is 'worked out',[39] which equates natural with human resources and using them with their destruction, thus maintaining the link between language and exploitation.

The Dada montage of 'The Ballad of Babelabour' invokes the notion of a primal language via German '*Ursprache*', positing class division at the origin of language by turning 'ur-' into an English 'er', like 'cur', and using Yorkshire 't' (for 'the') as a symbol of working-class speech. The diction is shattered, fragmented, a multilingual growl-cum-cry. The mingling of tongues contributes to the harsh disjointed sound and indicates the international scale of the processes invoked and the vision taking them in:

> What ur-𝔖pradje did the labour speak?
> ur ur ur to t'master's 𝔖pradje
> the hang-cur ur-grunt of the weak
> the unrecorded urs of gobless workers[40]

The heavy, jagged stress is carried by anger and protest, drawn from the long history of toil which has been accompanied latterly by the repetitive thud and clang of machines. This unrelenting rhythm carries through to images of desolation and disaster, end-product of exploitation swept along by its own momentum, 'creation of wealth' until the earth is worked out:

> by the time the bards have urd
> and urd and urd and Sprachered
> the world's all been turned into *merde*
> & Nimrod's Noah's arkered
>
> sailing t'shit in t'ship they urd at
> no labour can embark her
> just try and you'll get grrred at
> the shitship's one class: Sprache
>
> Bards and labour left for dead
> the siltword's neue neue
> bard the desperate doghead
> in that *negra negra* Goya.[41]

Bards are equated with labour in so far as they 'urd' (erred) and contrasted in so far as they 'Sprachered' (did the done thing). They are united again in the last stanza, though in defeat. They are both excluded from the same boat which is sailing the globe and sinking under all the man-made detritus.

The themes of this ballad are close to those of '*v.*',[42] an encounter with another member of the Leeds working class who is allowed to speak his own language. Before the poem was sent out on Channel 4, protests were made at the liberal use of four-letter words, and a new edition has come out documenting opinion for and against. One of the strange things about 'obscene' language is that it is used liberally not only by skins, fans and hooligans but in work-sites and on shop floors the length and breadth of the country. If we believe language is a means of communication, rather than raising hands in horror and attempting to shut out sexual imprecations, it would be better to ask why a good percentage of the nation is foul-mouthed, including our brave boys fighting in the trenches. One very good reason why this language plays a dominant role in working men's speech is that it articulates an outflow of aggressive energy, and without that you do not get the job done. David Dabydeen makes the same point, only more forcefully, about Creole:

The canecutter chopping away at the crop bursts out
in a spate of obscene words, a natural gush from the
gut. It's hard to put two words together in Creole
without swearing.[43]

It also displays virility and a contemptuous disregard for upper-
crust niceties. The flow of obscenities is so mechanical and
repetitive, like the flow of energy, 'on on on',[44] it is readily
dismissed as 'mindless', without purpose or meaning – which
explains precisely nothing. Though this epithet is used in the
poem, it does not fit the skin. At the point where the argument
comes to a head he gets the better of the poet (which is not
surprising, since he is the one offended against, though not by the
poet). He knows where to hurt and disposes of the poet's vague
pieties with trenchant vigour:

> What is that these crude words are revealing?
> What is it that this aggro act implies?
> Giving the dead their xenophobic feeling
> or just a *cri de cœur* because man dies?
>
> *So what's a* cri de cœur, *cunt? Can't you speak*
> *the language that yer mam spoke. Think of 'er!*
> *Can yer only get yer tongue round fucking Greek?*
> *Go and fuck yourself with* cri de cœur
>
> 'She didn't talk like you do for a start!'
> I shouted, turning where I thought the voice had been.
> *She didn't understand yer fucking 'art'!*
> *She thought yer fucking poetry obscene!*
>
> I wish on the skin's word deep aspirations,
> first the prayer for my parents I can't make,
> Then a call to Britain and to all the nations
> made in the name of love for peace's sake.
>
> *Aspirations, cunt! Folk on t'fucking dole*
> *'ave got about as much scope to aspire*
> *above the shit they're dumped in, cunt, as coal*
> *aspires to be chucked on t'fucking fire.*[45]

This is a voice from the present, the terraces of Elland Road,
forcing itself on the poet's inner ear, a voice in the mind, and it
consistently rings true. The skin's 'crude words' feed into his no-
nonsense aggression, stem from an angry knowledge of who and

where he is – dumped in the shit –, and he refuses to be further spat upon by some poet with his fancy words. He, seizes on 'aspirations' and repeats it mockingly, abrasively dismissive, holding it up with contemptuous irony at the line end: 'aspire', finishing with a scathing use of 'chucked' and as domestic and familiar, as telling a simile as you could ask for. He goes on to make a specific case, again eloquently, if we use the word to describe articulate feeling: 'me, I'll croak doing t'same nowt ah do now as a kid'.[46] When he attacks with this weapon on his tongue, the poet is lost for an answer and retaliates with aggression: '"Listen, cunt" I said', he turns condescending – he's trying to 'give ungrateful cunts like you a hearing' – and arrogantly dismissive: 'yobs like you . . . you wouldn't know / and it doesn't fucking matter if you do.' That mimes a common antagonism, spells out the aggression and evasion encapsulated in the word 'yob'.

In the closing section Harrison's poet persona is left to sort himself out again after the roughing-over he has had. He returns to the Wordsworth and the Byron buried near the Harrison grave, celebrating 'the shit' and the poet grown out of it. Though this echoes the skin's description of his own situation, there's little chance of him or others like him turning this to fertile use, ''oss muck in his shoes'. Accordingly, the poet is jolted by the skin's voice once more breaking into the bliss of his solitude; he is acutely aware of the distance between his personal fulfilment and the world the other inhabits, the shit he is dumped in.

'[uz]' words

In a review of Harrison's *Selected Poems* Jeffrey Wainwright feels that the use of 'mam' in the last line of 'Wordlists II' 'courts sentimentality and mawkishness' and conjectures that 'the word *mam* might seem unacceptable in a serious poem, although it is a real and deeply used word carrying the profoundest emotions and associations'.[47] That might be paraphrased by saying '[uz]' may be loving as well as funny, but you cannot bring that out in serious poetry. This is a central issue which includes the assumptions underlying 'sentimental' and 'mawkish', both of which are culturally laden. There is, of course, something of a tautology here: Harrison challenges those assumptions and is in turn ques-

tioned by them. It is not just the phrase 'mi mama's' (not itali-
cized) and the conclusion that are involved, it is the whole poem
which by the end seems like a single rhetorical gesture building
up progressively to the last line. At the same time the rhetorical
movement is revealed as a temporal structure, the cumulative
movement of acquiring languages is identical with a movement of
transience and loss, which justifies the sudden shift from
languages deliberately acquired to a language learned sponta-
neously as a child, a mother tongue, of which 'mi mam's' is a
small, emblematic fragment, a relic. The placing of this phrase is
as aware as it is emotive, it is exact, it invokes and enacts. To say
this may only repeat the tautology,[48] and that is very much the
point of a poem which exactly inverts the values attributed to
serious poetry here and places its seriousness differently and else-
where.

Force fields

More than once I have related these poems to a force field,
though on each occasion with reservations. They have a wide
reach, extending from the desperate rawness of 'I'll croak / doing
t'same nowt ah do now as a kid' to glimpses of dulciloquy and
the espousal of 'language near extinction'. My resistance to 'force
field' derives from a sense that this would need to be complete,
self-contained, a balance of forces, possibly evolving progres-
sively, like Goethe's polarity, structured, whereas the forces I feel
sweeping through these poems are strife-ridden and disruptive,
and I do not find that the moments of integration are able to
contain the turbulence admitted.

Beeston Cemetery with its blackened, gap-toothed tombstones
would have seemed the place where these energies meet, merge
and collide. Harrison has recently offered an alternative, which
he called his 'orchestra' when he discovered the Greek sense of
'circular dancing place': the street fire on VJ night, and the black
circle left on the street cobblestones, one intense, joyous, the
other a deep emptiness, both later linked with Hiroshima and
Nagasaki, and later still with the Greek amphitheatre open to the
sky, filled with light, a 'shared space and shared light'[49] in which
'the division between tragedy and satyr play, "high" art and
"low" art'[50] would have made no sense. This is an eloquent and

revealing statement, which evidently describes a force field, and recalls a communal art indifferent to the division between them and '[uz]'.

A shift of emphasis from integration to schism yields an image of the present-day world and the divisions it inflicts on the inner self:

> Half versus half, the enemies within
> the heart that can't be whole till they unite.[51]

Towards the end of '*v.*' Harrison takes leave of his home town until the day he is buried there. It goes without saying that he takes it with him, together with a hope that 'v' for 'versus' will give way to 'v' for 'victory', for 'vast, slow, coal-creating forces',[52] a formulation that implicitly expands on its own improbability.

Postscript

When I sent a copy of this paper to Tony Harrison, he opened it by chance at the passage about 'paper chips' (p.233) and wrote to say that, alas, it *is* adjective + noun; his mother showed him a way of screwing up newspaper to make a 'paper chip' in order to save wood. I know the kind of thing he means well enough but I am not familiar – evidently – with the name. (His comment was confined to this passage, and it would be wrong to assume that any other reading put forward here has received his tacit approval.) My misreading reveals how familiar language may switch suddenly, even imperceptibly, into the unknown, and Tony Harrison's gloss helps to bring out the memories, the family lore, that may attach to a seemingly humdrum phrase. Though they are not always accessible to a reader, we can still be aware of their possible presence, there is a space for this dimension of ordinary speech in our imagination.

Notes

1 Three publications are referred to repeatedly. Bibliographical details, are as follows: Tony Harrison, *The Loiners* (London, 1970); *from The School of Eloquence and other poems* (London, 1978); *Selected Poems* (Harmondsworth, 1984).
2 Tony Harrison, *The Loiners*, 40–46; *Selected Poems*, 35–7.

TONY HARRISON AND THE POETRY OF LEEDS 249

3 Tony Harrison, *The Loiners*, 30; *Selected Poems*, 28.
4 In 'The Death of the PWD Man', *The Loiners*, 56, 59; *Selected Poems*, 46, 49.
5 In 'Marked with D.', *Selected Poems*, 153.
6 Harrison, *from the School of Eloquence and other poems*, 18; *Selected Poems*, 120. The phrase is Burke's, quoted in 'Classic Society'.
7 Harrison, *Selected Poems*, 59.
8 Cf. 'Poësie ist *Darstellung* des *Gemüths* – der *inneren Welt in ihrer Gesamtheit*. Schon ihr Medium, die Worte, deuten es an, denn sie sind ja die äußere Offenbarung jenes inneren Kraftreichs' (Novalis, *Schriften III* [Darmstadt, 1983] 650), and: 'der ächte Dichter ist *allwissend* – er ist eine wirkliche Welt im Kleinen' (Novalis, *Schriften II* [Darmstadt, 1981] 592).
9 Harrison, *The Loiners*, 86; *Selected Poems*, 67.
10 Ibid.
11 Harrison, *The Loiners*, 86; *Selected Poems*, 66.
12 Harrison, *The Loiners*, 51; *Selected Poems*, 41.
13 Harrison, *The Loiners*, 52; *Selected Poems*, 43.
14 Harrison, *The Loiners*, 53; *Selected Poems*, 44.
15 Harrison, *from The School of Eloquence and other poems*, 7; *Selected Poems*, 111.
16 Thomas Mann, *Gesammelte Werke in zwölf Bänden*, Band VIII: *Erzählungen* (Oldenburg, 1960), 289.
17 Cf. 'Entbürgerlichung – aber nicht zum Bourgeois oder zum Marxisten, sondern zum Künstler, zur Ironie und Freiheit ausflug- und aufflugbereiter Kunst'. Thomas Mann, 'Lübeck als geistige Lebensform' [1926] in *Altes und Neues* (Frankfurt am Main, 1953), 314.
18 In 'Wordlists I', *from The School of Eloquence and other poems*, 16; *Selected Poems*, 117.
19 This is not to suggest that the usage is exclusive to Leeds. The OED describes it as '*arch.* and *dial.*' I've noticed it quite often in TV weather forecasts, and if it's on TV there's every chance of it becoming as common as 'she invited Jean and I', etc.
20 In 'On Not Being Milton', *from The School of Eloquence and other poems*, 11; *Selected Poems*, 112.
21 Harrison, *Selected Poems*, 159.
22 Harrison, *Selected Poems*, 141.
23 Harrison, *from The School of Eloquence and other poems*, 29; *Selected Poems*, 107.
24 'loiner. *slang.* [Origin uncertain.] An inhabitant of Leeds, W. Yorkshire' (OED). I write 'Loiner' and associate it with a way of speaking. I would not use it of people with traces of, say, Belfast or Glasgow in their speech, even though they have lived in Leeds for years.

25 In Tony Harrison, *Theatre Works: 1973–85* (London, 1986), 321–61.
26 Harrison, *Selected Poems*, 151.
27 Harrison, *from The School of Eloquence and other poems*, 15; *Selected Poems*, 116.
28 Edgar Allan Poe, 'The Philosophy of Composition', in G. R. Thompson (ed.), *Essays and Reviews* (New York, 1984), 18.
29 In 'Long Distance I', *Selected Poems*, 133.
30 In 'Confessional Poetry', *Selected Poems*, 128.
31 Harrison, *from The School of Eloquence and other poems*, 11; *Selected Poems*, 112.
32 Harrison, *from The School of Eloquence and other poems*, 20–21; *Selected Poems*, 122–3. The poem is dedicated to Professors Richard Hoggart and Leon Cortez. '"Them" and "Us"' is the title of a chapter in Hoggart's *The Uses of Literacy* (London, 1957; rpt. 1958, 1984 and 1990). Values and attitudes are illustrated throughout by characteristic sayings drawn from working-class areas of Leeds, Manchester, Sheffield and Hull. The parallel with Harrison's poems is evident, as is the difference between modes of quotation. Hoggart is detached, illustrative, quite unlike the technique I've tried to describe in 'Voices, 3'.
33 Harrison, *from The School of Eloquence and other poems*, 21; *Selected Poems*, 123. It is perhaps worth adding that I take 'you' in the third stanza to be unspecific. So the poem moves from 'we' in the first stanza to 'I' in the second and 'you' in the third, ending in the fourth with an implicit 'I': 'My first mention. . .'
34 Harrison, *Selected Poems*, 141.
35 In 'Turns', *Selected Poems*, 149.
36 Cf. the opening lines of 'Turns': 'I thought it made me look more "working class" / (as if a bit of chequered cloth could bridge that gap!).' Ibid.
37 In 'National Trust', *from The School of Eloquence and other poems*, 19; *Selected Poems*, 121.
38 In 't'Ark', *from The School of Eloquence and other poems*, 28; *Selected Poems*, 178.
39 In 'Working', *from The School of Eloquence and other poems*, 22; *Selected Poems*, 124.
40 Harrison, *from The School of Eloquence and other poems*, 48–9; *Selected Poems*, 102–103.
41 Ibid.
42 Tony Harrison, *'v.'* (Newcastle upon Tyne, 1985; 2nd edn., 1989, with press articles).
43 David Dabydeen, 'On Not Being Milton: Nigger Talk in England Today', *Landfall* 43.2 (Christchurch, New Zealand, June 1989), 180.

44   In 'Me Tarzan', *from The School of Eloquence and other poems*, 15; *Selected Poems*, 116.

45   Harrison, '*v.*' The pages are not numbered in the 1985 edition; 1989 edition, 17.

46   Ibid., 18.

47   Jeffrey Wainwright, 'Linkwords', *Poetry Review* 74.3 (1984–5), 75.

48   Cf. Wainwright: 'The pressure upon that word *mam* put in this context, show[s] what a culture forces through words, how any words are veined through their social being'. – 'Veined' brings in the body and what is in the blood, at least in the sense that it's thicker than water.

49   Tony Harrison, *The Truckers of Oxyrhynchus* (London, 1990), xiv.

50   Ibid., xxi.

51   Harrison, '*v.*', op. cit., 23.

52   Ibid., 32.

13

Waldo Williams – In Two Fields

NED THOMAS

1

This chapter approaches one of the most discussed and difficult poems in modern Welsh, Waldo Williams's 'Mewn Dau Gae' ('In Two Fields'), from the point of view of comparative cultural criticism. It does not attempt a full appreciation or explication – which is just as well, since Anthony Conran's excellent English translation,[1] on which many readers of this book will have to rely, is inevitably itself 'a reading', an interpretation of the original text. But I believe it will serve adequately my more limited purposes: to show how the perception of one very specific place implies a whole set of cultural values; and to show Welsh writing as existing not on a unique cultural island but at a unique cultural crossroads, relating to English literature and to wider European literary currents as well as to Welsh traditions, and relating also to the wars and public events of our century. When something new is made in the Welsh language out of all these elements, consciousness is extended, the culture develops.

That might seem to be an obvious thing to say about successful poetry in any language. To say it of a work of literature in a minority language, however, is to redress an imbalance and to resist stereotyping. Although stereotyping of course occurs wherever cultures look at each other, majorities have so much more power than minorities that they can often project their view of the minorities into the minorities themselves through the education system, the press and the media, and even influence the minorities' self-perception.

Until the end of the eighteenth century, the Celtic cultures of the British Isles were – in varying degrees – the objects of blatant prejudice and discrimination following earlier military conquest. But as these cultures weakened it became possible to sentimentalize and poeticize them.

The Romantic movement in England had in its early days briefly prophesied revolution and social transformation, but it soon adopted a more individualistic stance. The cultivation of the feelings – associated with Nature and everything that was sublime, picturesque, ancient and mysterious, was to be the realm of poetry while science and politics moved society inexorably forward on the iron rails of progress.

Within this frame, as the nineteenth century progressed, the Celtic peoples were allocated a special place. Translation and scholarship had revealed their ancient literatures, and their scenery was (by judicious selection) found to be picturesque. In short they had the qualities felt to be lacking in the 'modern world' of the centre. What David Jones was later to call 'the bland megalopolitan light' badly needed the 'Celtic Twilight' as an area of retreat and spiritual restoration – rather as it needed poetry. But the obverse of this seeming compliment to the special qualities of 'the Celt' was contempt. These peoples were not fit for modern life, and the best that could be expected of their ancient cultures was to become objects of study and to be a contributory stream to a modern culture in the English language. Matthew Arnold in his *Lectures on Celtic Literature* (1867) made the case for studying early Celtic literature while at the same time urging schools and traders to hasten the demise of Welsh as a living language.[2]

Welsh literature had no early Romanticism of its own. In Wales the late eighteenth century saw the Methodist Revival which indeed offered an interpretation of inner feeling but within a theological and collective context, not in secularizing and individualistic terms. Though at the turn of this century there was some imitative late Romanticism borrowed into Welsh poetry, it is my argument that only in the mid-twentieth century, and particularly in the work of Waldo Williams (writing in Welsh) and in some of the work of R. S. Thomas (writing in English) does Wales acquire a kind of early Romantic poetry of its own, something transplanted not borrowed, creating a centre of consciousness here, not a twilight horizon over there. Indeed, in its vividness it contrasts sharply with the tired sensibility of the late Romantic outsiders who sought relief in the Celtic twilight. In late colonial writers in English – whether Yeats, R. S. Thomas or Derek Walcott – one can often see a *conflict* of Romanticisms – a progressive rejection of the Romantic perceptions those others have of *us*, but a return to the early philosophic roots of Romanticism and a transplanting of those roots to our own soil. Waldo Williams's case is a simpler one. Writing in a language which has stronger religious resonances to draw on and less literary Romanticism to react against, he provides more direct evidence of how similar conditions may produce similar movements of feeling.

2

Waldo Williams was born in 1904 and died in 1970. His only collection of poems, *Dail Pren* ('Leaves of a Tree'), appeared in 1956,[3] and 'Mewn Dau Gae' was one of the poems he wrote in that year for inclusion in the volume alongside the work of a quarter century.

Waldo Williams was brought up in an English-speaking home, and had his father not moved a few miles out of the town of Haverfordwest in Pembrokeshire when Waldo was seven to be headmaster of a rural school in the Preseli hills, it is unlikely that Waldo Williams would have spoken Welsh. Nor is his an isolated case within the modern Welsh situation. English critics are well used to writers of English 'emerging' from a Welsh or Yoruba or Bengali background, but they will tend to regard those who continue to write in those languages as part of a solid ethnic bloc. But wherever languages coexist there will be some movement of individuals, even against the general drift of assimilation. Waldo Williams's background may well have given him a heightened sense of pluralism and solidarity across boundaries, but because he writes in Welsh this becomes, in the first place, a gift to Welsh culture.

Waldo's parents were pacifists during the First World War, and the poet was himself a lifelong committed pacifist and in his later years a Quaker. In the Second World War Waldo was a conscientious objector and at the time of the Korean War he refused to pay his income tax and was briefly imprisoned. Of the poem 'Mewn Dau Gae' he once said that its meaning was that young

Welsh soldiers were currently at war in Cyprus in our name. Conscription of young Welshmen to the British army he held to be a double evil. Conscience was forced and by a state which was not our own.

> Although I was sorry to see young English conscripts, some of them friends of mine, pressed into the armed forces, I did not feel certain that I had the right to interfere in the matter in England. The connection between the two nations is an accident of history. The right of every nation to its own life is a matter of principle. I decided to take my stand on this principle. It is difficult to separate these three things – nationalism, pacifism and democracy, when thinking of young Welshmen being ordered to maintain the imperial yoke on other countries – but there is no need to elaborate on this when Cyprus is daily before our eyes.[4]

But it would be wrong to present Waldo's pacifism as a wholly individual or family matter. The religious traditions of Nonconformity in Pembrokeshire among the Baptists and Independents went back to the seventeenth century and contained strong anti-state, egalitarian and pacifist strands. In the article quoted above (which is roughly contemporary with 'Mewn Dau Gae'), Waldo implied that the rural community of smallholders based on mutual aid which he had known on the Preseli hills was essentially good, and that evil came from outside, from the state and its structures of authority.

> There are those who see war as the sum total of our individual weaknesses, or an extension of our worst tendencies, the result of corrupt human nature if you like. But it was difficult for me to accept this explanation when I contrasted the things done in Korea with the customary behaviour of the ordinary people in whose name these acts were perpetrated.[5]

If this formulation makes Waldo's position sound like rural anarchism, we must remember that the community in which Waldo was brought up would have made the same points using a religious and apocalyptic vocabulary – echoes of the Book of Revelation, references to the humbling of the proud, the overturn of princes and potentates and of the powers of this world, and to the coming of judgement and of a time of universal brotherhood. Indeed, a reading of the Welsh denominational press for the period of the First World War supplies evidence that, particularly in poor areas of Wales (as the Preseli was), as the war brought news of increasingly heavy losses to every village, the apocalyptic strain in Nonconformity gathered strength, leading some to expect the imminent end of the world. Waldo, who was twelve in 1916, can hardly have escaped the sense of crisis and loss in the community nor the heightened atmosphere. The death of his elder sister at home in that same year was a more personal wound. But Waldo's parents would scarcely have taken apocalypse literally. They were educated progressives of their day, who kept in touch with religion but preferred 'modern technology' and the 'social gospel'; who favoured a metaphoric rather than a literal interpretation of the Bible, and who read widely – William Morris and Edward Carpenter, Ruskin, Keir Hardie, Shelley and Tolstoy.

When Waldo went to the University College of Wales at Aberystwyth it was to study *English* literature. His social life was lived in Welsh and he wrote poems in Welsh, yet it was not until much later in life that he read Old and Middle Welsh Poetry. But *Piers Plowman* was on the syllabus in the English department as were, of course, the English Romantic poets. These, and particularly Shelley, were his enthusiasms. What Walcott calls 'a sound colonial education' will always perhaps be a little conservative by the standards of the metropolis. There by the mid-1920s the vanguard was turning against nature poetry and Romantic ideas. Yet on the periphery a young Welshman was finding different elements in that tradition that were relevant to his personal and social experience. Roy Pascal wrote of the authors of the German *Sturm und Drang*:

> All are convinced of the primacy of feeling, of intuition, among human values. Nurtured in pietism, and constantly stimulated by religious experience, this conviction widens and deepens under the influence of the boldest thought of their times . . .[6]

This would not be a bad description of Waldo's own background and development, the ground from which Romanticism springs.

3

The first three stanzas recall and question experiences of a mystical kind associated with two named fields. We know these to

Waldo Williams
Mewn Dau Gae

O ba le'r ymroliai'r môr goleuni
Oedd a'i waelod ar Weun Parc y Blawd a Parc y Blawd?
Ar ôl imi holi'n hir yn y tir tywyll,
O b'le deuai, yr un a fu erioed?
Neu pwy, pwy oedd y saethwr, yr eglurwr sydyn?
Bywiol heliwr y maes oedd rholiwr y môr.
Oddifry uwch y chwibanwyr gloywbib, uwch callwib y cornicyllod,
Dygai i mi y llonyddwch mawr.

Rhoddai i mi'r cyffro lle nad oedd
Ond cyffro meddwl yr haul yn mydru'r tes,
Yr eithin aeddfed ar y cloddiau'n clecian,
Y brwyn lu yn breuddwydio'r wybren las.
Pwy sydd yn galw pan fo'r dychymyg yn dihuno?
Cyfod, cerdd, dawnsia, wele'r bydysawd.
Pwy sydd yn ymguddio ynghanol y geiriau?
Yr oedd hyn ar Weun Parc y Blawd a Parc y Blawd.

A phan fyddai'r cymylau mawr ffoadur a phererin
Yn goch gan heulwen hwyrol tymestl Tachwedd
Lawr yn yr ynn a'r masarn a rannai'r meysydd
Yr oedd cân y gwynt a dyfnder fel dyfnder distawrwydd.
Pwy sydd yn sefyll ac yn cynnwys?
Tyst pob tyst, cof pob cof, hoedl pob hoedl,
Tawel ostegwr helbul hunan.

Waldo Williams
In Two Fields[*]

Translated by Anthony Conran

Where did the sea of light roll from
Onto Flower Meadow Field and Flower Field?
After I'd searched for long in the dark land,
The one that was always, whence did he come?
Who, oh who was the marksman, the sudden enlightener?
The roller of the sea was the field's living hunter.
From above bright-billed whistlers, prudent scurry of
    lapwings,
The great quiet he brought me.

Excitement he gave me, where only
The sun's thought stirred to lyrics of warmth,
Crackle of gorse that was ripe on escarpments,
Hosting of rushes in their dream of blue sky.
When the imagination wakens, who calls
Rise up and walk, dance, look at the world?
Who is it hiding in the midst of the words
That were there on Flower Meadow Field and Flower Field?

And when the big clouds, the fugitive pilgrims,
Were red with the sunset of stormy November,
Down where the ashtrees and maples divided the fields,
The song of the wind was deep like deep silence.
Who, in the midst of the pomp, the super-abundance,
Stands there inviting, containing it all?
Each witness' witness, each memory's memory, life of eachlife,
Quiet calmer of the troubled self.

Nes dyfod o'r hollfyd weithiau i'r tawelwch
Ac ar y ddau barc fe gerddai ei bobl,
A thrwyddynt, rhyngddynt, amdanynt ymdaenai
Awen yn codi o'r cudd, yn cydio'r cwbl,
Fel gyda ni'r ychydig pan fyddai'r cyrch picwerchi
Neu'r tynnu to deir draw ar y weun drom.
Mor agos at ein gilydd y deuem –
Yr oedd yr heliwr distaw yn bwrw ei rwyd amdanom.

O, trwy oesoedd y gwaed ar y gwellt a thrwy'r goleuni y galar
Pa chwiban nas clywai ond mynwes? O, pwy oedd?
Twyllwr pob traha, rhedwr pob trywydd,
Hai! y dihangwr o'r byddinoedd
Yn chwiban adnabod, adnabod nes bod adnabod.
Mawr oedd cydnaid calonnau wedi eu rhew rhyn.
Yr oedd rhyw ffynhonnau'n torri tua'r nefoedd
Ac yn syrthio'n ôl a'u dagrau fel dail pren.

Am hyn y myfyria'r dydd dan yr haul a'r cwmwl
A'r nos trwy'r celloedd i'w mawrfrig ymennydd.
Mor llonydd ydynt a hithau a'i hanadl
Dros Weun Parc y Blawd a Parc y Blawd heb ludd,
A'u gafael ar y gwrthrych, y perci llawn pobl.
Diau y daw'r dirháu, a pha awr yw hi
Y daw'r herwr, daw'r heliwr, daw'r hawliwr i'r bwlch,
Daw'r Brenin Alltud a'r brwyn yn hollti.

(*Dail Pren*, 1956)

have been real fields on the land of a neighbour and we know the
time to have been in the poet's early adolescence. It was in the
gap between these two fields, Waldo recalled, that he first sensed

Till at last the whole world came into the stillness
And on the two fields his people walked,
And through, and between, and about them, goodwill widened
And rose out of hiding, to make them all one,
As when the few of us forrayed with pitchforks
Or from heavy meadows lugged thatching of rush,
How close we came then, one to another –
The quiet huntsman so cast his net round us?

Ages of the blood on the grass and the light of grief,
Who whistled through them? Who heard but the heart?
The cheater of pride, and every trail's tracker,
Escaper from the armies, hey, there's his whistling –
Knowledge of us, knowledge, till at last we do know him!
Great was the leaping of hearts, after their ice age.
The fountains burst up towards heaven, till,
Falling back, their tears were like leaves of a tree.

Day broods on all this beneath sun and cloud,
And Night through the cells of her wide-branching brain –
How quiet they are, and she breathing freely
Over Flower Meadow Field and Flower Field –
Keeps a grip on their object, the fields full of folk.
Surely these things must come. What hour will it be
That the outlaw comes, the hunter, the claimant to the breach,
That the Exiled King cometh, and the rushes part in his way?

* *Weun Parc y Blawd* and *Parc y Blawd* – two fields in Pembrokeshire

the brotherhood of all human beings. It is interesting that the
event occurred in the gap, and that in the third stanza of the
poem the fields are seen as being divided from each other.

The imagery of light and of quiet strongly suggests the Quaker tradition, and the poem in general is consonant with a Christian interpretation. But that interpretation is not forced upon us. The poem is not dogmatic. Its syntax is affirmative in respect of the experience, but questioning in respect of the source of that experience. As in so many Romantic poems we are dealing with a transaction between the world of inner feeling and the outer world of nature. Is the light an inner light or an outward sea of light? There is no third force present in the form of the Church or the Bible to give authoritative interpretation. Discussing 'the inner light' in his essay 'Paham yr wyf yn Grynwr' ('Why I am a Quaker') Waldo wrote:

> and we believe that it comes from God. How do we know that we are not deluding ourselves? In the end we have nothing but our experience to depend on. In the end those who accept the most traditional kind of religion have nothing else to go on.[7]

The poem seems to recall a series of mystical experiences, but two in particular. One, described in the second stanza is set in late summer and appears to record the birth of his poetic faculty, the awakening of the aesthetic imagination. The second, set in November has a more sombre and troubled tone. Is it too much to see the blood of the first Battle of the Somme as well as the end of the world reflected in the red clouds of the third stanza? The questions asked in the last four lines parallel those asked in the last four lines of the second stanza, but the quest now seems to belong to the realm of the moral rather than the aesthetic imagination.

The transition from the third to the fourth stanza moves from memory to vision. The words 'barc' and 'bobl' are the mutated singular forms of the plurals that appear in the final stanza and which Anthony Conran translates there as 'the fields full of folk' a phrase familiar to us from *The Vision of Piers Plowman*. We know that Waldo Williams had been reminded of this poem when he looked out of his bedroom window in Llandysilio and saw the Norman Tower of Roch Castle and a sloping field below it with an outcrop of rock. In a long poem 'Y Tŵr a'r Graig' ('The Tower and the Rock') he made these objects into symbols of military power and of the long-suffering people respectively. In 'Mewn Dau Gae' the people are the people of the whole world, but the feeling of brotherhood in the simile introduced by the fifth line is that which he had known in the neighbourly co-operation of the farmers of the Preseli.

The word 'awen' in line 4 of this stanza is worth closer attention. This would normally translate into English as 'The Muse' or 'poetic inspiration', and another translator has indeed used the word 'Muse' at this point. (Etymologically *awen* is related to *awel*, breeze.) But here Waldo has extended the meaning of the word in two ways. In 'Mewn Dau Gae' the context makes it (a unique usage in Welsh, so far as I know) a collective phenomenon, something which binds people together rather than something which inspires a single and special individual. At the same time the word has moved from the realm of aesthetic feeling to that of moral feeling – though not towards any moral rules or precepts. A comparison can perhaps be drawn here with Schiller's *An die Freude* where the spells woven by joy bind together what habit has left divided – and again within an atmosphere of universal brotherhood:

> Deine Zauber binden wieder
> Was die Mode streng geteilt,
> Alle Menschen werden Brüder
> Wo dein sanfter Flügel weilt.

The fourth stanza opens with an echo of one of the earliest Welsh poems from *Canu Heledd* (collected in *Canu Llywarch Hen*).[8] This is the phrase 'y gwaed ar y gwellt' ('the blood on the grass'). The use of a phrase from a poem of the Welsh Dark Ages emphasizes the point that is being made about the long centuries of bloodshed. Yet faced with that history of violence Waldo can still assert our common humanity which can respond to others across all barriers and divisions.

Even in this superficial age, an age of planning and systems, there remains in our nature some unquenchable freedom. The spark or realization is struck quite unintentionally. That is the history of experience and the experience of history. Our person responds directly and immediately to our environment, and if we don't trust this reaction then all other help is vain. These days such a reaction is called romantic, ecstatic, over-individualistic, irresponsible, – but that is only the falsetto voice of an artificial age denying nature its place, and if it persists in this denial it will learn to repent in ashes or else withdraw its contempt: it is a case of our expectant 'being' becoming ready to receive the unknown essence. But it has to seek and experience it, and interpret if for itself.[9]

The whole article quoted from above is in fact an extended gloss on 'Mewn Dau Gae', and its concluding paragraph relates directly to the final stanzas:

The only thing that will free us is a response between people. Sensitivity to the sufferings of others can lead us through places where reason founders unless awoken by imagination. There is no alternative but to face our guilt and from that guilt to forge conscience and from conscience responsibility. Then our responsibility changes into vision. But that is what we find hard.

> Sometimes when alone
> At the dark close of day
> Men meet an outlawed majesty
> And hasten away

wrote the Irish poet A. E. It is only this being alone that can bring us, through the Exiled King, into a right relationship one with another.[10]

In the penultimate stanza, of 'Mewn Dau Gae', Anthony Conran translates 'adnabod' well in the context as 'recognition'. It is the infinitive form of the verb meaning 'to know (people)'. (Another word, 'gwybod' is reserved for 'knowing facts'.) Characteristically, it is not sentries but the deserters from armies who recognize each other. Characteristically, too, in the last three lines of this penultimate stanza, this recognition of common humanity becomes general. Again Waldo is the only person, so far as I know, to use the word *cydnaid* ('leaping together') though compounds with *cyd* are in common use (e.g. *cydymdeimlad*, 'sympathy') and are very common in Waldo's work.

The leaping together of hearts is depicted as a fountain bursting towards heaven as the ice thaws; but, in falling back, its tears are 'like the leaves of a tree'. It is not difficult to find a biblical origin for the image of water breaking from a rock, but it became a favourite Romantic image as well, as did sparks from one hearth, or the tree from one root. Indeed, in an English essay, 'The Function of Literature', Waldo uses the image of the fountain in the context of a discussion of Romanticism:

What is this energy springing from within and like a fountain acquir-
ing relevant form without losing its dynamic? Coleridge derived from
Kant his own idea of the kinship of the energy of literature with that
of life.[11]

and Coleridge himself had written in 'Dejection: An Ode'

> I may not hope from outward forms to win
> The passion and the truth whose fountains are within.

Waldo's volume carries a note by its author on the phrase 'fel dail
pren' (like the leaves of a tree). Translated, it reads simply:
'*Revelation 22.2*: 'And the leaves of the tree were for the healing
of the nations', a verse well-known to Quakers. But Waldo was
equally aware of the famous phrase in Keats's letters: '. . . if
poetry comes not as easily as leaves to a tree it had better not
come at all.'[12] After all he called his only volume of poems *Dail
Pren* ('Leaves of a Tree') which may in the context of our poem
suggest a wider attempt to unite the moral and the aesthetic
imagination for a transformational purpose.

The final stanza opens with some rather obscure images which
are illuminated by Waldo in a letter to the late Bedwyr Lewis
Jones.[13] In relation to the first line he quotes from Wordsworth's
'The Excursion', saying that he had a similar idea in mind

> Descend prophetic spirit that inspirest
> The human soul of universal earth
> Dreaming of things to come.

The second line he explains as an image of the stars like cells of
a brain on the branches of one tree. These very expansive images
are then linked back to the two fields and the vision of the field
full of folk. The poem ends apocalyptically. The 'One' who was
questioned at the beginning of the poem becomes the exiled king
returning to claim his kingdom.

There is always an individualist and a collective interpretation
to this kind of imagery. Does some change of feeling enter the
individual heart or is there a social transformation? The medieval
'field full of folk' and the many collective elements and words in
the poem suggest a coming of the social kingdom, yet there are
elements of personal memory and feeling as the poet meditates
on the experiences of his youth, and these take the individualist

direction in which English Romantic poetry later developed. But in its beginnings the Romantic movement held together the hope of social transformation and poetry springing from the individual heart as Waldo does. This moral and collective emphasis in the Welsh poem derives from the nature of the society which produced it – a society that had been kept under hatches, that had found strength in its own brand of rebellious Christianity and that was moving towards secularism and nationalism. This is what gives the poem such energy and sets it apart from the languors and melancholy of those who romanticized the Celtic countries from outside.[14]

Notes

1 In *Welsh Verse*, translations by Tony Conran (Bridgend, Seren Books, 1992). This volume includes translations of two other poems by Waldo Williams.

2 See Ned Thomas, 'Renan, Arnold, Unamuno: Philology and the Minority Languages', in *Bradford Occasional Papers No. 6* (1984).

3 *Dail Pren* (1st edn. Llandysul, 1956).

4 'Paham y gwrthodais dalu treth yr incwm' in *Y Faner*, 20 June 1956, translated by Ned Thomas as 'War and the State' in *Planet*, no. 37/38, 11 May 1977.

5 Ibid., 11.

6 Roy Pascal, *The German Sturm und Drang* (Manchester, 1953), 40.

7 These lines are translated from the broadcast talk *Paham yr wyf yn Grynwr* ('Why I am a Quaker') collected in the volume *Waldo*, ed. James Nicholas, Llandysul, 1977. There is no English translation available of the full text.

8 *Canu Llywarch Hen*, ed. Ifor Williams (Cardiff, University of Wales Press, 1990).

9 'War and the State', op. cit., 10.

10 Ibid., 13.

11 'The Function of Literature', in *Waldo*, ed. James Nicholas (Llandysul, 1977), 256.

12 John Keats, letter to John Taylor, 27 February 1818, in *The Letters of John Keats 1814–1821*, vol.1, ed. H. E. Rollins (Cambridge 1958), 238.

13 From a copy of the letter supplied to me by the recipient.

14 The cultural framework within which I set Waldo Williams's work is elaborated on in my Welsh volume *Waldo*, (Cyfres Llên y Llenor, Caernarfon, Gwasg Pantycelyn, 1985).

14

The poetry of Gillian Clarke

K. E. SMITH

1

In an age of rapid change the needs of readers may seem contradictory. There is a constant search for the new, the strange, the freshly observed, the exotic even. And, in reaction, there is a quest for the traditional, the firmly rooted, a cult of nostalgia. In aesthetic terms we see a corresponding dichotomy between a distrust of closure and search for open forms on the one hand and a yearning for shapeliness and coherence on the other. Pursued exclusively, the first elements in these twin disjunctions lead to restlessness, instability, the hunger for novelty above all else, while the second lead towards separateness, exclusion, an Olympian view of art.

Poetry as an art form may seem intrinsically well-suited to linking these sets of impulses. New in its fresh observations, novel diction and surprising metaphors it yet joins us to the deepest traditions and rituals through its heartbeat rhythms, its use of recognizable formal structures and patterns, its reference to symbols that have endured through many cultures. More specifically, we may at this juncture value specifically those poets who affirm the value of their own and other individual lives in specific places (the matter of the so-called periphery) while exploring the larger, most pressing problems of the age (the matter of the so-called centre). In this context the contribution of a poet in one of the oldest poetic traditions, that of Wales, who writes out of newly explored female identity, may seem particularly well-placed to speak to us of the old, of the new and of the connections between them. But this is all by way of saying that Gillian Clarke, a contemporary woman poet, proudly Welsh-speaking yet confidently writing in English, is well worth our initial attention. In what follows we may see just how much her already considerable output repays more prolonged scrutiny.

2

Born in 1937 in Cardiff, speaking English as her first language but aware of a Welsh-language inheritance she would later recover, Clarke describes herself as a late-developing writer. Indeed, she draws attention to general forces which in her generation hindered her and other women from developing artistic confidence at an early stage: 'But being a woman and Welsh and therefore in two senses not wholly ready to count as myself one of the grown-ups, not easily able to feel I was permitted to be myself, to be a writer, an artist, I was a very late developer.'[1] Yet there were mentors and inspirations from two different sources: 'So in one sense, the woman writer begins to write coming across Sylvia Plath, Anne Sexton, Anne Stevenson; in another sense, the writer begins to write coming across poetry written by other Welsh people in the English language.'[2] Ultimately, though, what is most striking about Clarke's early poetic output is its individuality, its announcement of a new voice. While we must take seriously the difficulties which the author describes as attending her long gestation as a writer we may also observe how much experience she brings to her poetry from the outset, how much sense she gives of a distinctive voice and stance.

It is tempting to characterize Clarke's first full collection, *The Sundial* (1978), in terms of particular subject-matters – sorts of emphasis which will recur throughout her *oeuvre*. Thus, we might say, there are the poems of intimate human relationship, the memory of place poems and the direct nature – bird, beast and flower – poems. While this description may serve to organize a more detailed study it is also reductive in ignoring the common factor in all these poems – a search for connection between the human and non-human worlds which involves a search for an authentic personal language. In passing, it may be of interest to note that this quest in very different forms has been a common factor in English-language poetry in Wales. Shared by poets as different as the three unrelated Thomases, Edward, Dylan and R. S., it may be seen in them as in Gillian Clarke as embodying the distinctively post-Protestant (even in R. S. Thomas) yet still questingly spiritual sensibility so characteristic of modern Wales.

What this sensibility reveals is a universe which lacks special providence or even justice and yet is intensely meaningful and interconnected. If one of Clarke's mentors is Edward Thomas she moves from his watchful male stance, edged with light and darkness, negotiating ecstasy and stoicism in the face of nature, towards a woman's sense of fluidity, relationship, changing boundaries. A poet who embodies rather than preaches the Gaia hypothesis she is also intensely aware of the vulnerability of single lives beyond her own and thus is not tempted by a facile affirmation of cosmic unity.

What distinguishes Clarke's larger sense of process in the world, though, is her way of coming at it through slices of the life she observes and experiences. Her poems both contain vivid details and narrate stories that compel our interest. In 'The Sundial' itself we can see all these things along with an intimacy of tone, moving between gravity and quiet wit, that distinguishes much of her best work. There is the unfussed plain-spun opening, sounding like a shared confidence in the street or on the telephone:

> Owain was ill today. In the night
> He was delirious, shouting of lions
> In the sleepless heat.

As the boy makes his sundial on the lawn the description moves into a more inward mode, stressing personal growth:

> He looked up, his eyes dark,
> Intelligently adult as though
> The wave of fever taught silence
> And immobility for the first time.

The poem progresses further towards a conclusion which is an early example of that naturalistic symbolism which allows the poet to stick closely to what she observes while leaving with us broader implications about growth, life, time and death if we want to take them on board. That the poem seems content to leave us to make these inferences is, though, part of its power:

> All day we felt and watched the sun
> Caged in its white diurnal heat,
> Pointing at us with its black stick.

Clarke's handling of children and children's experience in these early poems is noteworthy in two respects. First, she gives the sense of honouring the child's world in its separateness and distinctness – here are dreams, anger, concentration, creativity. Thus she takes us beyond the assumptions of the adult world. But, having done justice to the child's otherness, she can legitimately use the child's experience to access connections in her own mind which are otherwise hidden. The child diverts the mind away from what may seem authentic responses, but are in fact taken-for-granted ones, and towards new perspectives. Thus 'In Pisgah Churchyard' sees the poet's, and by implication the reader's, conventionally solemn response to the graveyard waylaid by the child's emphasis on growth:

> Dylan tells me this is a church garden.
> Indeed these bones, ground seed small, seem neither
> Static nor dead.

It should be emphasized that although there is an indebtedness to the Romantics' stress on the naturalness and freshness of childhood the core of these poems of childhood is often a relationship. That the focus is on interaction rather than on a separate 'subject' – in a psychological and a poetic sense – leads us towards that more developed green feminism, that implicit stress on interconnection, which underlies the later *Letter from a Far Country*.

But before moving on to that volume and poem it is worth noting that an apparently quite different sort of poem can be seen as leading in the same direction. For Gillian Clarke's creature poems, although having a real relationship to the traditions established by D. H. Lawrence and Ted Hughes, have a subtly different flavour. The energy and violence of nature are here but so also are its protectiveness, nurturing and hunger for continuity, as in 'Curlew':

> Dusk blurs
> circle within circle till there's nothing left
> but the egg pulsing in the dark against her ribs.
> For each of us the possessed space contracts
> to the nest's heat, the blood's small circuit.

Here, as throughout *The Sundial*, Clarke focuses on a specific interaction, a mode of relating. It is as if, having established these tactile solidities, she is now ready 'for longer flight'.[3]

3

The volume *Letter from a Far Country* (1982) is very recogniz-ably from the same pen as *The Sundial*. Beyond the title poem itself, it contains a range of vivid poems imaging forth Clarke's hill-country world. 'Bluetit and Wren', 'Ram' and 'Buzzard' show the same fascination with pinpointing the borders of life and death through precise images. From the last mentioned we have this unflinching yet finely-honed opening:

> No sutures in the steep brow
> of this cranium, as in mine
> or yours. Delicate ellipse
> as smooth as her own egg
>
> or the cleft flesh of a fruit.
> From the plundered bones on the hill,
> like a fire in its morning ashes,
> you guess it's a buzzard's skull.

Yet there is also a broader, more explicit humanism in the volume. This is partly seen in the poet's attempt to bear witness to pain in the community at large ('East Moors') or individual strangers ('Suicide on Pentwyn Bridge'). In completely contrast-ing mood and subject-matter, but still registering an extended grasp and ability to dramatize, is the relaxed but alert registering of French scenes in 'A Journal from France'. Here, perhaps released by this fresh scene of action, the poet's painterly quali-ties are harnessed to a new expressive richness:

> Embroidery cloths abandoned
> at the roadside table; a weir
> of lace falls from her chair; silks
> spill blossoming from a basket.
> Under its turning ribbon of gauze
> her tea cools in a white cup.
>
> She sings in the dark interior.

This particular section, 'Seamstress at St Leon', gives us the opportunity to note significant aspects of Clarke's poetic technique. Given the recurrence in her work of lyrics in unrhymed lines of varying lengths it is tempting to think of hers as a spontaneous voice and leave it at that. Yet in this poem and elsewhere one sees the use of stanzas to shape and structure an apparently informal utterance. Additionally, she herself has remarked on the half-conscious influence of Welsh poetry on her style: the use of the seven-syllable line and of *cynghanedd's* alliteration and vowel-music as a repertoire which may put 'an extra tremor or richness in a line'.[4] That this is not just theory but practice we may see from the closing of 'Seamstress at St Leon' where each line contains a chain of contrasting vowel-sounds and where the whole is bound together by recurrent consonants – 'l' and 'f' at the beginning of the stanza, 'b', 'd' and 's' towards its end:

> Lace glimmerings at dusk. A foam
> of linen, flowers, silences.
> Sunlight has flowed from her sills
> of yellow stone. Bats are shuttling
> their delicate black silks to mesh
> that dark doorway on her absence.

Still, it is the title poem itself which dominates the volume and not only in its greater length and scope. Whether 'Letter from a Far Country' is adequately described in its author's characterization of it as 'an epic poem about housework'[5] must emerge from our larger discussion in due course. But for the moment we can begin by noting a number of more specific things about it. Firstly, it is a poem for voice, both in having been written for radio and in a more intrinsic, tonal sense. Secondly, it is a poem with a much richer structural pattern than anything the author has so far attempted. And thirdly, it is a poem which brings together the two crucial sides of Clarke's cultural lineage: her Welshness and her sense of female solidarity.

It is, then, very much a heard or overheard poem, aural as well as oral. Doubtless the poet's own reading would bring this out very directly. But the deeper point, equally valid for those who like myself have never heard her read it, is that the poem has its own inbuilt cues, its implicit markings which tell us how it should sound in our heads:

> They have gone. The silence resettles
> slowly as dust on the sunlit

surfaces of the furniture.
At first the skull itself makes
sounds in any fresh silence,
a big sea running in a shell.
I can hear my blood rise and fall.

Such passages at this opening show that it is not just imagery but also tone which make the poem's impact, with a strong sense of the narrator feeling blessed by the quiet she finds for contemplation yet also knowing she must face the troubled aspects of existence. Upon the relaxed beat of a line that hovers around four beats and seven or eight syllables (drawing on both English and Welsh measures in a fresh blend) the poet builds verse paragraphs just long enough to follow a particular train of thought before a lateral connection is made in the next section. Enjambment flowing across the lines makes for a sense of spaciousness appropriate to time felt as a kind of bonus (a bonus whose preciousness stems precisely from its contrast with a woman's busy life). Indeed it is precisely the narrator's own work and that of generations of other women which makes the most obvious focus of her poem and appears to justify the 'epic poem about housework' summary:

Familiar days are stored whole
in bottles. There's a wet morning
orchard in the dandelion wine;
a white spring distilled
in elderflower's clarity;
and a loving, late, sunburning
day of October in syrups
of rose hip and the beautiful
black sloes that stained the gin to rose.
It is easy to make of love
these ceremonials. As priests
we fold cloth, break bread, share wine,
hope there's enough to go round.

These passages are set into a larger structure which orchestrates them into a cumulative pattern rather than a logical sequence. We are reminded of the author's belief, quoted in the symposium 'Is There a Women's Poetry?' that women writers often give a 'sense of moving from one image to another as if searching, as if not fully committed to a role, the metaphor not seen but felt'.[6]

Here also we feel a moving and a searching through a number of key foci which might be summarized as: the writer herself in her various roles, most notably as poet and houseworker; the Welsh landscape and natural life, so often a touchstone of reality in her work; all the Welsh women of the past; the 'traditional' Welsh heritage. Separating the last two does not imply some female equivalent of a Caradoc Evans debunking of shibboleths. Rather the relationship between Welshness and womanhood is a matter for serious interrogation. Neither herstory nor Welshness is dispensable, indeed both in different ways are worthy of praise, but how and to what degree can they be made compatible?

The issue has a peculiar resonance in face of a culture which arguably has a dual face. On the one hand, Welshness is associated with rootedness, kindred, co-operativeness, with imagination, spirituality and the arts – in short with an agenda more apparently compatible with feminism than the cultures of more imperialist, competitive, instrumental societies. On the other hand the roll-call of eminent Welsh people is markedly masculine and the very myths of Welsh distinctiveness have attached themselves to male archetypes, such as the medieval bard, the Nonconformist minister or the coalminer. It is interesting that similar concerns appear to have arisen in the attitude of some Irish women writers to the recent Field Day anthology of Irish writing. How to do justice to the special, cherished national history while firmly registering the centrality of women within it?

Two radical rewritings of Welsh history are present in 'Letter from a Far Country'. First there is a drawing of attention to women's pain, as indisputable in small-town Wales as in the world of Sexton or Plath. Two women's suicides are recounted mid-way through the poem. The first is that of a poor woman overwhelmed by isolation and illness, the second that of a woman who, in terms of respectable opinion, had a good life ironically imaged by the poet as 'A village house with railings'. Woman as oppressed labourer, woman as the doll in a doll's house, these have been found in Wales as anywhere else. The poet's unshakeable commitment to her native country and culture goes along with a commitment to dramatizing such painful unreported histories.

The very presence of such elements undermines the criticism, made by Stephen Tunnicliffe, of this poetry working 'perhaps with a touch of middle-class sentimentality for good measure'.[7] But his characterization of the poem's keynote as reassurance is doubly wrong, because the second, positive rewriting of Welsh history is also far from merely cosy or comforting. It is, as an earlier quotation with its invocation of a priestly role may have suggested, much better described as celebratory, ritualistic. Here the Welsh tradition of praising is put at the service of a previously undervalued aspect of Welsh life. It is not just a case of acknowledging that women's work is important but of affirming that it is central to community, to Welshness. Indeed the poem goes further in suggesting that it is women's actions, at least as much as men's preachings, that have put the culture in touch with the ultimate sources of life:

> Into the drawers I place your clean
> clothes, pyjamas with buttons
> sewn back on, shirts stacked neatly
> under their labels on the shelves.
> The chests and cupboards are full,
> the house sweet as a honeycomb.
> I move in and out of the hive
> all day, harvesting, ordering.
> You will find all in its proper place,
> When I have gone.

That 'when I have gone' reminds us that valuing past and present does not itself suffice to answer the questions of the future. What happens when the woman moves, literally and metaphorically, and shares the public stage, when she is a partner in, rather than the all-in-one support of, family life? The poem at once suggests a high valuation of what women have done in the home and of what many women continue to do along with a clear sense that they are going beyond this. (Much of the poet's own energy has been devoted to domesticities: now more is being devoted to her own poetic art. She values both contributions.) It is interesting to note that when the 'Letter' reappears three years later in *Selected Poems* it has acquired an envoi. Rather than concluding with the downbeat social realism of its being 4 p.m. and time for children to come home from school the poem continues to a string of emphatic, rhymed questions:

> Will the men grow tender and the children strong?
> Who will teach the Mam iaith and sing them songs?

> If we adventure more than a day
> Who will do the loving while we're away?

The general burden is inescapable and in one sense universal – challenging the male reader to share equally in the work of home and family as women share in the worlds of politics, art, science and so on. But in a Welsh context there is a more specific resonance, again double-edged. What of the mother tongue, the *Mamiaith* itself? Has it not been women who have ensured the continuance of the language and culture at its most basic level? And if women now become, say, preachers and bards must not some of those males who have seen themselves as the guardians of the Welsh language accept that they must help preserve the language at a more basic level – by teaching it to their children? To use an image from elsewhere in Clarke's poetry the world of Dyddgu must be acknowledged as being equal in significance to that of Dafydd. Those two crucial things which go together, nurturing the child and teaching language, are seen as tasks for men as well as for women.

4

It is tempting to see 'Letter from a Far Country' as aiding the poet's ability to recover and render her own Welsh family history in 'Cofiant', the long sequence which concludes *Letting in the Rumour* (1989). Traditionally, the *cofiant* is a particularly Welsh form of memorial volume, a composite tribute invoking and praising a prominent member of the community such as a Nonconformist minister. While honouring the broad concept Clarke moulds it very much to her own purposes, at once democratic (including a sailor, a railwayman, the thrice married Jennet), ungendered (giving equal prominence to women) and collective (recalling a family rather than a specific individual).

The texture of the poetry here is very different from the free, lyrical musing of the 'letter'. Rather, we encounter compressed, vividly imaged epitomes of particular lives as with the poet's evocation of her father in 'John Penri Williams (1899–1957)'. The poet still quests, but at once narrows and deepens her vision to produce a hypnotically vivid dramatization of her father's world in so far as she can empathetically reconstruct it. One may

note again how the confident handling of a long stanza form
serves to enclose and shape the significant details:

> Chapel boy from Carmarthenshire
> locked in his cabin, writing home,
> 'Annwyl Mam', shocked by crew-talk,
> or tapping morse as the world burned.
> He drummed bad news on the sea's skin,
> his air-waves singing over the roof
> of the whale's auditorium. Only his heart,
> the coded pulse over dark water
> to a listening ship and the girl at home.

Beyond this precision an allusive intensity also enters the
sequence as when Annie, 'A widow nearly forty years', becomes
identified during her stay in hospital with the old doll which she
once gave the narrator: 'Then she was lost or somebody gave her
away.' The simplicity and absoluteness of the line takes us
beyond the poetic conceit to a simultaneous sense of the sheer
pain of childhood loss and of the absoluteness of death. It is
above all the poet's control of tone, combining gravity and imag-
inative response, that one registers here. This strength may be
connected with the writer's sense that, relatively newly in Welsh
history, it is the woman's task to fulfil the bardic role of remem-
bering and praising the dead. Here the poem's ending with a
genealogical table is significant. Nothing could be more tradi-
tionally Welsh. Yet as we go down the list of male progenitors the
full significance of the poem's opening line becomes clear to us:

> Daughter of Penri Williams, wireless engineer of
> Carmarthenshire and Ceinwen Evans of Denbighshire

What is clear here is a new kind of engagement with Welsh
history and culture, as the poet acknowledges in her conversation
with Susan Butler: 'The . . . thing I am certain of since writing
"Letter from a Far Country" is that the right way forward is to
be more and not less oneself. If I'm Welsh, and if I'm a woman,
then what I must not try to be is a perfect English man poet and
to model myself on what's going on among the men.'[8] As with
any active creative artist it is not possible to say where this confi-
dence will lead, particularly as there are other green shoots in
Letting in the Rumour. Specifically, we see in the title poem and
elsewhere the writer searching to connect the basic simplicities of

Welsh hill life to a world in which the voices of human pain
know no boundaries, in which the threat of a Chernobyl does not
respect national territories. Other poems register a self-conscious
preoccupation with the art of painting, a natural development
from a poet who always, in Cynthia Fuller's words 'uses images
which bring detail into sharp focus, making the reader see things
freshly'.[9]

However, *Letting in the Rumour* shows continuity as well as
change in Clarke's poetry. There is still the need to register the
processes of life and death in the Welsh hills and thus short
lyrics registering birds, beasts and flowers remain important.
That lambs are born, hares killed, slates laid in place, these
things recur and need to be witnessed. The poet changes never-
theless, develops her sensibility and expression, often given
rise to an etched, calligraphic style. In 'Gannet' the bird's swoop
is registered with brief intensity but also with symbolic reso-
nance:

> The black wave,
> a white-hot knife of light,
>
> sea's retina dazzled
> by the sign of the cross.

In a sense the very confidence which underlies such a poem is a
product of the earlier, more literal and expansive poems, the
implied meaning built on the more explicit consummations of
significance which close earlier natural sightings in Clarke's
work.

5

An active poet cannot be summed up, still less predicted. In
Gillian Clarke's case all we can do is to note significant achieve-
ments and their counterpointing of each other. Throughout there
are the sightings, the poet's creation of refreshing natural images
through her blending of vowel-consonant music and receptive
eye: these sightings, we have seen, themselves become less
framed, more implicit in their significance. Then, intermittently,
the poet's focusing seems to have generated the need for some
longer, interleaved narrative: the need to tell some larger, unpara-
phrasable human story gives rise to 'Letter from a Far Country'

and to 'Cofiant'. How these aspects of her creativity relate to each other one can only guess. It is as if Clarke sees her conscious work as a poet – her daily task as she puts her craft at the service of her vision – as concerning the creation of the shorter, lyric poems. Then it appears that, from time to time, the poetic process gathers some larger momentum and scope. What she guarantees us – and it is in itself enough for us to be grateful – is her daily witnessing of life. But, in addition, she has given and may give us from time to time the something other, the more inclusive vision which cannot be willed but which we know she will craft and shape with all her hard-won abilities if and when it arrives.

In broad terms the poet herself is very clear about the relation between her selfhood, her lifestyle in the Welsh hills and her creativity as an artist. Her self-descriptions thus convey a mixture of vocational commitment and quiet confidence. Although this is hard-won and the poet has known the struggles that can still surround a woman's assertion of herself as an artist, Gillian Clarke's artistic world is very much her own:

> I do not need to be hurt into poetry, as Yeats put it. Neither do I need ideas, as such. I store things in memory. The red and white hens and other images from 'Letter' for example, have been in my memory since early childhood. I have kept journals and diaries since I was fifteen, and I re-read them and things spring to life and poetry from those pages. I take photographs and make what I call my picture books. Looking at them reminds me there are things I want to write about when the image/energy/idea meet at the right force.
>
> Then there's the sheet of paper. There are *words*, the paraphernalia of words, books, sermons, conversations, eavesdroppings, note-books, pens. After pen and paper, the beauty of the empty cleanness, there is energy. It sets me thinking. I try the paper to see what the words will do. It must be like drawing . . . try the line, see what happens.[10]

But this commitment to the artistic vocation is always at the service of a purpose stretching beyond the poet herself, that of using poetry as a mediation between her own vision, the world around her and the mind of the reader. The absorption in her own vision does not end in itself but issues forth in a gift of awareness and insight, a process which the poem 'My Box' from *Letting in the Rumour* seems to encapsulate in symbolic

language. The concluding stanza may serve as a brief epitome of
Gillian Clarke's artistic achievement thus far:

> On an open shelf I keep my box.
> Its key is in the lock.
> I leave it there for you to read,
> or them, when we are dead,
> how everything is slowly made,
> how slowly things made me,
> a tree, a lover, words, a box,
> books and a golden tree.

Notes

1 'An Interview with Gillian Clarke', in Susan Butler (ed.), *Common
   Ground: Poets in a Welsh Landscape* (Bridgend, 1985), 196.
2 Loc. cit.
3 Andrew Marvell, 'The Garden', l.55.
4 *Common Ground*, op. cit., 196.
5 Ibid., 195.
6 *Poetry Wales*, XXIII, 1, 1988, 44.
7 *Poetry Wales*, XVIII, 4, 1983, 98.
8 *Common Ground*, op. cit., 197.
9 *New Welsh Review*, II, 3, 1989–90, 82.
10 *Common Ground*, op. cit., 198.

Further reading

1. Individual Volumes:
Gillian Clarke, *Snow on the Mountain* (Swansea, Christopher Davies,
   1971).
— *The Sundial* (Llandysul, Gomer Press, 1978).
— *Letter from a Far Country* (Manchester, Carcanet, 1982).
— *Selected Poems* (Manchester, Carcanet, 1985).
— *Letting in the Rumour* (Manchester, Carcanet, 1989).

2. Anthologies:
Poetry Introduction 3 (London, Faber and Faber, 1975).
Raymond Garlick and Roland Mathias (eds.), *Anglo-Welsh Poetry
   1480–1980* (Bridgend, Poetry Wales Press, 1984).
Susan Butler (ed.), *Common Ground: Poets in a Welsh Landscape*
   (Bridgend, Poetry Wales Press, 1985).
Meic Stephens (ed.), *The Bright Field: An Anthology of Poetry from*

Contemporary Wales (Manchester, Carcanet, 1991).

Beyond such surveys as Roland Mathias's *Anglo-Welsh Literature: An Illustrated History* (Bridgend, Poetry Wales Press, 1986), much of the most perceptive criticism on Gillian Clarke is still to be found in the extended reviews of her work published in *Poetry Wales*, *Anglo-Welsh Review* and *AWR*'s successor *The New Welsh Review.*

15

'The Binding Breath':
Island and community in the poetry of
George Mackay Brown

DAVID ANNWN

1

In George Mackay Brown's recent poetry, written as he approached and experienced his seventieth year, a theme which has lain latent for decades in his work begins to emerge as a rich questioning. It is one thing to be born into community and into the heterogeneous culture of the Orkney Islands: the indigenous lifestyles stemming from no 'pure' stock but from a mixture of native, Viking, Scottish, Irish, English and Romany blood. And it is part of such an origin to be simultaneously aware of one's separateness and have an intimate consciousness of one's native islands:

> The wind is rarely still. It shifts from airt to airt, and everything – flowers, clouds, birds, animals, boats – are caught up in the invisible stream . . . the evenings are marvellously tranquil, except for a broken thunder all along the West Coast of Orkney – Noup, the Brough, Marwick, Yesnaby, Black Craig, Rora . . .[1]

The recital of place-names here has no trace of the cartographer but, blending topography, weather and animals as it does, it is a linguistic evocation from the inside, from closeness and familiarity. It is one thing, as I have said, to be born into these realities, yet it is another imaginatively to step outside these circles and ask what life would be like in an existence unmediated by human culture and language at all. Such a question has, of course, occupied many writers at many times, but in Brown's work, I believe, his poems embodying this issue take us to the heart of his complex relationship with his islands and community.

There are, of course, some usual divergences in conceptions of the Orkneys' spatial context: to the earliest literate geographers and explorers they seemed remote, even at the end of the world, the last isles before *ultima Thule*. For the Norse' and saga-makers, aware of yet more remote and considerably more inhospitable lands, the Orkneys were a valuable prize, central as they were to northern trade and raiding routes. Over centuries, the islands developed a strong independent culture nurtured from a wide diversity of traditions; any sense that the burgeoning materialistic powers of Western Europe might have of Orcadian marginality, (a view perhaps shared by British publishing houses and media until recently), is offset by the islanders' sense of their own centrality: not simply invested in their own traditions, but a centrality in questions of tactical importance, the provision of oil, crops, fish, and issues of ecological balance.

As part of such awareness, it is common on these particular islands to be raised with a strong sense of the past. Brown puts it more compellingly: 'The Orkney imagination is haunted by time.'[2] The first section of Brown's personal topography: *An Orkney Tapestry*, embodies a notable consciousness of the historical islands and their people. His knowledge of events, customs, stories seems encyclopaedic and, as well as the resource of oral culture, his own first-hand awareness of island heritage is also built upon a considerable literary tradition. He cites better-known studies like Marwick's *Orkney Norn* and *Orkney Farm Names* and histories by Clouston and Firth, yet this poet has also been fascinated by island literary curiosities like *Two Old Pulpit Worthies of Orkney* or *Report of the Orkney Crofters' Commission*. He knew early on that:

> Nearly every facet of life in the islands has been described and discussed and catalogued over and over again.[3]

As part of Brown's sense of the islands, there is a tension between things seen in their elemental state and as linguistic and literary presences. His awareness then is very different from that of dis-inherited peoples or from islands where culture has been lopped off or disowned. Yet this density of literary background has never impaired Brown's ability to see the elemental condition of the land. Indeed, in his eyes, the bounded shores: the limits of island existence have isolated and concentrated his art. Isolation, even island isolation, is of course supremely relative, unless one is Robinson Crusoe or the 'Master' in Lawrence's 'The Man Who

Loved Islands'. Yet, for Brown, even that human community
which mediates such isolation, is simplified and amplified by
its being set apart. With such bounds a community becomes
a significant microcosm and individuals clearly delineated
figures.

2

If I were asked to characterize the most fundamental tendencies
of Brown's poetry, I should write on one hand of 'foldings': the
desire to gather up and preserve, and, on the other, of clear
outline and definition, the low appearance of the landscape
simultaneously enhancing and simplifying:

> But I think it is . . . the look of the islands that suggests heraldic still-
> ness and a hoarded symbolism – quarterings on the hill, pasture and
> meadow and cornfield, a slow change throughout the year; and, older
> still, the great shield of the sky swarming with azure and gule, and
> clouds like fabulous beasts rampant.[4]

The shield or targe is, of course, and old motif of Scottish poetry,
at least as far back as Dunbar. Nonetheless, this consciousness of
the symbolic nature of the land is significant in its unique time
and place. Edwin Muir, another Orcadian, sees the power of such
symbolism. In his poem 'The Emblem' a 'contracted world'
grows 'so vast' that the rest of existence seems 'a little tangled
field'. Such emblematic visions of the land then both hone down
and enhance its power; the geographical condition here defines a
poetic tendency or, at least, it is seen to do so. It is part of
Brown's self-definition as a poet.

Additionally, it is fair to say that Brown's work thrives with the
communities of the islands. It is a poetry alive with voices. If one
tendency in his poetry shares the saga-maker's preference for a
runic textual simplicity, another shows the desire to catch up the
peoples of the Orkneys in all their diversity, to celebrate and
preserve, in islands where the conditions of humankind stand out
in stark relief. This brings us to the fact of Brown's birth: in
infancy and early life he found himself deeply implicated in a
human-scape. An early poem 'Hamnavoe' finds him imagina-
tively following his father, the postman, around the town; many
sections of the working community are glimpsed here, some of

the lines ringing with echoes of Dylan Thomas's praise-poems and the poem ends with:

> And because, under equality's sun,
> All things wear now to a common soiling,
>   In the fire of images
>   Gladly I put my hand
>   To save that day for him.

Passing for a moment that dislike of Marxist homogeneity, we can see here that desire to 'fold' the community and the poet's link to that outer human circle: a father who knew each name and address, in enduring art. There is here then a sense of personal and social vocation. In a recent BBC Scotland interview, Brown says that he doubts whether he would have become a poet apart from the influence of his home island; his very first unpublished attempts at poetry were written in praise of Stromness. Moreover, if we remember the writer's father and a consciousness of the stories behind each doorway, we might also recall Brown's close attachment to his mother, a woman who could speak Gaelic and perhaps provide glimpses of human patterns from the more distant past.

It is also possible to view the word 'community' in another way; on one level it might refer to his readers in his own town and islands – neighbours aware of his art and contributions to world literature, his occasional involvement with TV, radio and the stage. For years Brown wrote short essays on local topics for a weekly newspaper, *The Orcadian* – the intention was to 'entertain a small community of 1,600 townsfolk – possibly a scattering of other islanders – also to kindle some home thoughts in the minds of the thousands of Orkney folk who live outwith the islands but keep in touch through the pages of the paper . . . reading for quiet townsfolk on a Thursday afternoon.' The articles eventually gathered in *Letters from Hamnavoe* reveal a light ear and eye in judging what would appeal to his community. These and a steady stream of visitors to his door must mean that few townspeople of Stromness remain ignorant of his name at the very least. Despite Brown's dislike of technology and any 'confessionalist' stance, which means he will never become the 'smiling public man', a brief survey reveals an admiration and liking for Brown's novels, short stories and articles yet some puzzlement as regards his poetry, as reported in *Planet* in 1977. Over the years and with the familiarity of age and the growth of his repute, one suspects continual increase in this reciprocal feeling of pride. The writer has often dwelt on his love for Orcadian speech, habits, faces and customs. Yet he has also written in a Byronic vein that he writes only to make himself 'a moment merry' and in a recent interview this attitude seems more accentuated:

Nowadays I write simply to please myself. Very selfish . . . I'm glad if readers like my work but am not the least worried if they don't.[5]

On one level, of course, such utterance is beside the point for a study such as this, which surely must concentrate on *literary* evocations of island and community. Yet such a view seems to square uncomfortably with a challenging statement from *An Orkney Tapestry*:

It is a word, blossoming as legend, poem, story, secret, that holds a community together and gives a meaning to its life.[6]

Such a view is crucial for this study and we shall return to it; yet in a written response to my own questioning of this apparent disparity, Brown has written:

I've stopped thinking too much about my community; all along the line they're happily surrendering to TV trash, pop music, supermarkets, American values. So I just sit in my anchorite cell and it may be that, now and then, here and there, some of the old ancestral strengths, if they may be called that, will be recognized. (But that is to sound too much like a seer or prophet, which I am not.)[7]

As far as this writer's external views of attitude and art in relation to community are concerned, this is a deeply telling statement. These sentiments are notable, and not simply for the fact that few living poets and novelists of the British Isles can enjoy such a close association with one particular community in the public eye: perhaps Charles Causley and R. S. Thomas might come to mind in this respect but their lives do reveal greater mobility at certain points.

These are some of the implications that Brown has discovered and explored as incumbent on his poetic identity as an Orkney Islander. He also has a growing sense of himself as a member of a literary Orcadian fellowship. In talking of this, one must immediately refute any idea of an artistic commune or group, with close association or common aims. Yet in *Portrait of Orkney*, Brown talks of his acquaintanceship and friendship with Eric Linklater, Edwin Muir, Robert Rendall, Bessie Grieve, and Ernest Marwick; Brown brings this disparate group of very different and independent writers together in his pages as an admission of affection, gratitude, admiration and, occasionally, kindred spirit. Moreover, it must not be forgotten that Brown is involved with religious fellowship on the islands. He became a Roman Catholic in 1961 after long consideration, and, of course, biblical and devotional influence does tinge his 'archetypal' visions of island life, and his perception of Everyman within the community.

From the early 1970s onwards and especially in more recent poetry, as we have said, the poet begins to explore what life would be like outside these communities, away from social and cultural ties that bind. In 'Eagle' a child is stolen by the bird of prey from the 'shadow of a barley stook'. The poetry sings and soars in the resultant conflict between human and animal nurturing. The mother

> Lifted the boy like an egg
> From the broken
> Circles of beak and claw and scream
> She brought him down
> To her nest of crib and milk.

After the baby's rescue we are shown his 'grand-da' wondering whether it would not have been better for the boy: 'That freedom of rock and cloud' rather than human existence:

> Ten thousand brutish days
> Yoked with clay and slime.

Such speculation might pass for a mere aside if it were not repeated in several ways throughout the book. The title poem shows the formula from a different viewpoint: a child caught in a wreck, seemingly lost and the property of the waves and 'circling wolves of wind' is won back to society. That which was nearly lost to the elements, a 'thin cold flame', is brought to a human hearth:

> He endured there
> The seventy ploughtimes, creeltimes,
> Harvests of fish and corn,

His feet in thrall always
To the bounteous terrible harp.

The plangent final lines compound the meaning. For Brown, the human island is a central presence, yet, because of the elemental oneness, as he regards it, of all life, for community to remain meaningful, it must also remain close to those non-human elements. These beliefs have crucial implications for his art and use of language. Brown's work abounds with folk narratives, riddles, fairy tales, yet it is interesting that one dominant motif remains the Celtic wonder-tale of the child stolen by non-human forces, a motif recurring in Scottish, Irish, Breton stories and in *The Mabinogion*. Any consideration then of Brown's sense of community and nationhood, and of his position within those realities, has to be tempered by his testing and questioning that which lies outside those allegiances, free of what Stephen Dedalus called the 'nets' of society. Brown's path has not been one of Dedalian flight; quite the opposite. Yet, nonetheless, any enquiry into Brown's role as a writer in relation to his folk, must take into account his sense of existence outside the societal forces that 'bind the breath' to a local habitation.

3

Yet before we proceed to consider how these tensions have emerged to energize these concepts in his work, there are other basic issues to broach. It is one thing to ponder evidence from interviews and critical writings, yet how does the figure, or, more correctly, do the figures of the poet in relation to island and community emerge in the poems themselves? For it is here we shall find the most subtle probings of identity and vocation. And what of Island? What are Brown's views of the specific qualities and cultural heritage in which he as an insular poet is involved? To what views and images of the literary islands does he accede? Does he as a writer involved in the 'Matter of Orkney', view himself, or his work, as epistemologically distinct from writers from other islands, and from those land masses we call continents? Indeed, are such distinctions significant at all in an ideological or lexical sense?

In 1952, when a student at Newbattle Abbey, Brown wrote the

'Prologue' for his first small collection of poems, *The Storm (& Other Poems)* which was not to be published until two years later. The characteristically straightforward voice attended by internal subtleties is there from the start:

> For the islands I sing
> and for a few friends;
> not to foster means
> or be midwife to ends.

The poet has no taste for Marxist 'anthill dialectics' nor for Lawrentian extravagance: in such disavowals he was also distancing himself from much that was current in Scottish literary life at the time, in a style which echoes the Neo-Celtic praise-poems of Yeats and Dylan Thomas. In stanza four he returns to positive assertion:

> For Scotland I sing,
> the Knox-ruined nation
> that poet and saint
> must rebuild with their passion.

Even this far into the poem the web of allegiance is complex: this writer has often written of his Orcadian patriotism, proud of its intellectual and spiritual traditions, yet the poet's mission here includes a commitment to the restoration of mainland Scotland, viewed as a victim of religious despoilment. An examination of the mixed feelings with which Orcadians regard Scotland would occupy a book in itself: mistrust, regret, affection, pride of kinship, yearnings for a lost cousin, admiration and pain, yet Brown here does state a pledge after a fashion, a gesture of affiliation. The 'Prologue' goes on to invoke 'workers' in field/ and mill and mine'. It finishes:

> Praise tinker and saint
> and the rose that takes
> its fill of sunlight
> though a world breaks.

The image of the rose perhaps again stemming from Yeats and Eliot; two years later Edwin Muir was to present his vision on Sicily, an island of the south, which served to externalize his feelings of the continuities of insular life, and in words which anticipate Brown's style of the 1970s:

> Men are made of what is made
> The meat, the drink, the life, the corn,
> Laid up by them and in them reborn.

Muir finishes his vision of the ageless island with:

> indigenous art
> And simple spells make unafraid
> The haunted labyrinths of the heart,
> And with our wild succession braid
> The resurrection of the rose.

Though 'the rose' as a central presence was a stock emblem in writings of the forties and fifties, the spiritual affinity between 'The Prologue' and 'The Island' is obvious in the resonances clustering in the rose-image: timeless love and fidelity, human endurance and faith on the islands. For Brown, the stated allegiances are also obvious: the islands first and last, Scotland, workers, (both agrarian and industrial), 'tinker and saint', (both in their own ways walkers at the margins of society), and the deathless rose at the heart of existence. So, a highly literary style of pledge and to a peopled island: 'a landscape that has shaped them and been shaped by them.'[8]

If we compare Brown's conception of the Orkneys with V. S. Naipaul's words about his own birthplace we can see what might apparently seem to be diametrically-opposed views and cultural conditions: 'History is built around achievement and creation and nothing is created in the West Indies.'[9] In *Derek Walcott, Poet of the Islands*, Ned Thomas goes on to write of Naipaul's 'feelings of contingency and rootlessness [which are] endemic in the Caribbean'; the result of this is to 'make the west Indian a prototype of the culturally-displaced person.'[10] Of course, the whole relationship between Naipaul's and Brown's archipelagoes with early iron-bearing kingdoms, mercantile nation-states from the fifteenth century onwards and the emergent imperialistic powers and colonizers of the eighteenth and nineteenth centuries, has been entirely different. Both groups of islands have seen violence, piracy and intermarriage and the respective regimes of planters and dynasties of lairds. Yet Brown writes of raids and incursions, rather than massacres and slavery and is able to aver that Orcadians 'probably have as much Pictish blood in us as Norse'; whereas the native Arawaks were exterminated and

Caribs savagely hounded and constricted on Naipaul's islands. One then understands Nailpaul's sense of artistic isolation, his feeling that the creation of void in the past leads to continuous negation: or an absence even of that minimal tendency. His statement is, of course, also rife with irony. Yet the one converse irony is that nothingness and displacement can become a social and psychological predicament which outlasts the historical reality.

In terms of cultural identity and its influence on the writer, Brown is at pains to point out that Orkney has 'more artists, writers, musicians than most other small communities', yet he passes over the 'silent centuries' between the great medieval ballads and the 1920s. Indeed, his words about the heraldic condition of the Orkneys hint not only at a 'made' place but at lands serving as symbol for the medium of Art itself. One might of course argue that it has served as such for Brown himself and potentially so for anyone raised there – it is after all that person's living environment from which they filter their materials.

4

Yet, is this Orcadian poet right about the unique density of artistic activity and closeness of the past in his islands as compared to say Anglesey or Malta or Islas Canarias or Sado Island? A quick survey of the Western Isles might yield us Iain Crichton Smith, Aonghas MacNeacail, Derick Thomson, Ian Stephen and Sorley MacLean, just among the writers. And Brown and Muir are not, of course, the only island artists to see their land as central, revealed in an Edenic or life-giving light. One thinks of Goronwy Owen, master of the *cywydd* and *awdl* forms during one of Orkney's 'silent centuries'. He was to call his native Anglesey:

> Goludog, ac ail Eden
> Dy sut, neu Baradwys hen.
>
> [Bountiful as a second Eden
> Or an ancient Paradise.]

Note again the Paradise 'hen' translated as 'ancient' here – one of Brown's favourite words as Alan Bold has noted. The great number of Mesolithic and Neolithic sites on Orkney are often cited as singular aspects of its identity; indeed they have become recurring motifs in his work. Yet we can cite Bryn Celli Ddu and the magnificent Barclodiad y Gawres on Môn (Anglesey) and the island's classical identification with the Druids. The issue here is not a comparison of favours, or a disputing of the particular richnesses of the islands, but rather Brown's emphasis and refining of these specific elements of Orcadian life as cornerstones of his art. For, just as Naipaul isolates qualities of nothingness and displacement in characterizing the West Indies, Brown consistently posits the ancient and artistically creative aspects of the Orkneys as his aesthetic touchstone.

Such notions, held in tension with the cross-currents of Gaelic, Irish, Norse and folk traditions from which Brown draws his poems and stories, of course, go some way to defining a role, a sense of his position as an island-poet. For the writer is not simply informed by how he sees his own land and traditions, but by now he uses those realities in relation to other lands, centres and powers. In such a light it is interesting to contrast Brown's views and experiences with Jean Joseph Rabéarivelo, founder of the modern literature of Madagascar. A pure Malagasy by descent he became gradually *assimilé*, inventing a poetic idiom of his own using symbolist and native 'hainteny' ballad forms. As in Brown's case, his poems about the flora and fauna of his island stand out in wonderfully clear outline, yet Rabéarivelo regarded France as his spiritual home and committed suicide partly out of his thwarted attempts to move there. He serves again as a reminder of the seismic psychological influence of colonization, and of the inability, in his case, of the individual artist to supplant such ideals, by recasting native resources. Part of Brown's vision of his island is that of gentle resistance, of farmers and fishermen evading muster for England's war with Napoleon, of a subtle native will against corporate American homogeneity: the 'vast, bland Buddha' of consumerism.

In terms of linguistic culture, for the most part Brown's life and writing have occurred alongside a continuous fading of the different strains of Gaelic from the islands, until the very recent, heartening resurgence. In *An Orkney Tapestry*, Brown deplores the passing of the old names, names which have a power to give health to a community. Within the context of the standard English of his work he has striven to embody the linguistic formulae, speech rhythms, images of past generations, but he has fallen short of writing poems in Gaelic; his translations have been from Old Norse and English. In this, he reminds one of a less vituperative R. S. Thomas, simultaneously condemning the erosion of native speech and yet predominantly writing in forms of English which initially displaced Gaelic and Welsh. These issues are not closed in any sense: it is possible to see both poets as transitional, meeting the occasion with the persuasive powers and language which their education gave them, caught as they are perhaps between two great linguistic shifts. A good lexical study of Brown is long overdue – an examining of the recurrence of Norn, Norse, ballad, Scottish and loan-words from early and Romantic poetry might reveal another kind of subtle resistance to Americanized English.

Voice, language and varieties of speech are always vital in manifesting the writer's relationship with local and wider communities. And it is in this, as in other ways, that Brown's work is so different from that of Sorley MacLean: MacLean seems to speak from *within* a community, assuming a knowledge of specific figures, poets, woods, villages – his Gaelic is, by its very nature and strain, that of an insider – (however much he feels historical schism), speaking to others of known traditions. Brown, though, rediscovers emblems of shared values and exter- nalizes them through language, writing often as if for outsiders and strangers. It is true that the great majority of Orcadians were English-speaking even by the time of Brown's parents; Robert Rendall's dialect poems themselves could not draw a wide audi- ence and Brown's first real chances in writing came via Edwin Muir and London. Yet, viewed from another direction, he has succeeded in making native Orcadian traditions accessible to a worldwide audience.

The formula remains a complex one – an early childhood on a rural island does not, of course, necessarily produce a writer of Brown's tendencies or predispose that writer's view of his community; like Derek Walcott, he decided to stay and sing of the islands. It does not seem either that his 'island song' has a unique claim upon ancient history, Edenic grandeur, cultural cross-currents or aesthetic unity, yet he emphasizes the prepon- derance of these realities in the Orkneys and powerfully registers their presence in his work. It is the coming together of what might epistemologically be called 'island-ness' in a writer's work with the particulars of one archipelago, its haeccity or this-ness, which we find in this poetry as a whole. The thought of a small island might dispose us to notions of limits, an intimate awareness of the sea, specialization in occupations, a fine sense of topography and a knowledge of lives of families over generations. It might also lead us to posit a consciousness which stresses preponderance or lack: in a given small space points of reference might seem to cluster. For example, extant standing-stones on Anglesey might *seem* to be more numerous than elsewhere in Britain and Wales, yet Frances Llewellyn, the island's most distinguished historian, tells me this is not the case. Conversely, as in Naipaul's example, lack of cultural signs might seem to be complete.

5

Finally, in examining these questions, we must return to this poet's emphasis on the strong particularities of Orkney existence, and how these have shaped his work. If this were a different type of study we might instead look at the importance of Brown's lengthy hospitalizations or his position in his family as significant psychological ciphers to his 'island-ness'. Yet this poet would discourage such lines of enquiry and I have no need for them here, and even less for an abstraction of an 'island of words' away from substantive island and writer. Breath is 'bound' to particular affiliation; it is not for nothing that Brown chose to study G. M. Hopkins for his postgraduate research. And I am reminded of David Jones, that other insular Catholic, who wrote both of unity and 'the holy diversities'. If Jones was intent on living voices and the merging power of presences like Arthur and Christ, Brown celebrates the elemental conditions of his islands through the actions of human generation, and places St Magnus and Dietrich Bonhoeffer in Christ's order of signs. Jeremy Hooker's fine statement on David Jones is true, too, of Brown:

> . . . he restores the rich diversity . . . to the islands by using words that signify the coming together of traditions from without, and *their* coming together with traditions from within.[11]

Many of the poems in *Loaves and Fishes*, (1959) operate at an allegorical level, yet, by this stage of his art, three narratives fascinate Brown more than all others at his disposal: the voyages and death of St Magnus, other early Viking stories, and the biblical parable of the seed that must fall to earth for new life. *The Year of the Whale* (1965) finds the poet venturing into a more varied terrain of history, deepening his glimpses of island life. We also see a new self-consciousness about the poet's stance in relation to his work and the people. His frequently anthologized poem, 'The Poet', is worth quoting in full here: the poet as guitarist seems an obvious descendant of Einar, the harpist, in 'The Abbot', and he moves in a timeless pre-industrial present of 'lamps', 'masks' and 'cloaks':

> The Poet
>
> Therefore he no more troubled the pool of silence
> But put on mask and cloak,
> Strung a guitar
> And moved among the folk.
> Dancing they cried
> 'Ah, how our sober islands
> Are gay again, since this blind lyrical tramp
> Invaded the Fair!'
>
> Under the last dead lamp
> When all the dancers and masks had gone inside
> His cold stare
> Returned to its true task, interrogation of silence.

It is a revealing and notable poem, (and not just because the writer still quotes those last three words as a condition of poetry thirty years later). The poet, (here seen in musical incarnation), in his role as entertainer for a community, is wearing a mask, (and presumably a false one). The opening is an interrupted response: 'Therefore . . .' Is this because private poetic meditation has proved exhausting? Does he revisit the people for the verve and colour such contact can give? In an interview he has said:

> . . . the history of verse seems to show that once the heightened speech becomes mannered and ridiculous, it is best for the poets to go into the pubs and the smithies and farm-yards and listen to what's said there.[12]

The people of the poem praise the transforming power of the poet's music – they admire their lives and home as caught up in his tune. Yet they also see him as intrusive: both 'blind' and 'a tramp', invading the fair. His questing and values are, they know, very different from their own. The poet's true task under the mask, (for all life involves masks, cf. 'The Seven Houses' in the same collection), brings to mind Yeats again and the 'cold stare', Yeats's horseman. We are left with a picture of a poet neighbouring and partly dependent upon community, but whose characteristic task is 'interrogation' of the non-human: the stance is part-Symbolist, part-Stoic, and, if we are to believe what the Rees brothers and Stuart Piggott have written of the early practices of the bard class, part-Celtic.

'The Condemned Well' shows an even stronger self-consciousness about Brown's role emerging: the poem's structure celebrates the stories of generation surrounding a well, but the voice is overheard checking its own processes of selection:

> Shall we mention Linky the tailor
> Who stitched that silk through his rum?
> We shall not forget . . .

The poet's power of recall is summoned here – he makes a verbal memorial, a genealogy of drinkers for a threatened centre of village life, yet his efforts are checked by a cynical rejoinder:

> Fool, thou poet, thou rememberest
> Ada and Mary and Ann
> Who sank bright buckets here . . .
> Nor could thy net of words hold one.

And again:

> Fool, thou poet,
> Tomorrow is the day of the long lead pipe.

The self-mockery here, of the poet's failure in his ancestral task, to preserve, to sing generation, is new in Brown's work, as is the mockery of his vain attempts to offset the distancing power of time. The well, like the old festivals, brought the people together – made community perforce. A lead pipe will come to individual homes.

It is during the years 1971–6 that this writer comes to his most testing examination of writer and community in his poetry and prose. With *New Poems* (1971), the voices of poets associated with the islands and Scotland in the past, begin to be heard. Arnor, 'the red poet', recalls his voyages out of Orkney:

> I went the blue road to Jerusalem
> With fifteen ships in a brawling company
> Of poets, warriors, and holy men . . .

The poet of verses over the lintel of the great Maeshowe burial chamber speaks of his desire for poetry as 'a deep rune'. The poetry indeed becomes formulaic: the lines part-paraphrase, part-translation, serve as testament and memorial. 'Prince in the Heather' starts with the inset epigraph:

> The bard Alasdair MacNiall
> made this in Barra
> the day after the true
> prince left Scotland
> for France, 1746.

And this elegaic 'Keening' for the prince's departure ends with a vision of a lineage of bardic singers fading out, an invasive language demanding precedence:

> Now grandsons of hunter, fishermen, bard
> Must turn high courtesy to unction,
> A manner and a speech to please the Saxons
> A thing never known before.

These considerations of Orcadian, Viking, Scottish makars – scalds, craftsmen of kennings and runes – culminate two years later in Brown's examination of the role of a ballad-maker in his community in *An Orkney Tapestry*. The story is rooted in an attempt to 'resurrect' a great little-known ballad, 'The Lady Odivere' which Brown had read in Marwick's *Anthology of Orkney Verse*. Corson's recital of the ballad in the midst of sheriff, factor, canon makes him, ('a person of no consequence'), a man to respect:

> . . . but while the ballad lasted these great ones of Orkney were his utterly, he could make them laugh or weep as he chose, or beg for more like dogs.[13]

For the listening Canon Fulzie, Corson's ballad is dangerous and chaotic, 'a subtle searching poison' in society. Its story of the selkie and the human breaks down all barriers and 'usurps the sacred tongue of men' and is, again, that hint of kinship beyond the circles of human life. Corson, the poet, is described as an actor, ('as if he had momently changed sex, and was entered into

the secret estate of motherhood'), and musician ('How skilfully
. . . better than any flute or viol'), in one. In Brown's eyes, 'the
Reformation killed the songs and ballads of the people'.[14] Fulzie
links such ballads with the witches of the islands – image and
fable are paths to heresy. Yet Earl Patrick Stuart, also in atten-
dance, thinks:

> there is nothing like an interlude where a group of people take part,
> both as players and audience, a concert, a communion in which the
> bread of art is broken and shared.[15]

So much for 'the eye of the beholder' yet Corson is central to any
understanding of Brown's conception of poets and their place in
the islands. He symbolizes a link back through the Reformation
to the tales and songs of the fishermen and farmers – through
dialect, Norn, and Norse – to the oldest mythic tales. His words
simultaneously probe to the 'innermost sanctuaries of his listen-
ers', convicting them of their mortality yet also to reveal the
'immortal pearl' lost under the daily trivialities of existence.

Fishermen with Ploughs (1971), a poem cycle, reflects the
prehistory and history of a people from Rackwick and Hoy – his
first attempt to show a community whole, from its early begin-
nings, sailing west out of Norway in the ninth century, through
Reformation and annexation to Scotland, yet, generally, showing
the 'same people' appearing and reappearing over many genera-
tions. Given Brown's conception of himself as an island artist,
this idea of a turning wheel of generations must seem natural on
islands where, despite displacements and alterations in belief,
some stock goes back over a millennium and further into the
centuries of Pictish and Neolithic habitation. Such a notion of
Everyman echoes Muir's ideas in his autobiography: 'the life
of every man is an endlessly repeated performance of the life of
man.' The poem-cycle shows the struggle of people for material
improvement – and this is where Brown's ethos must surely set
him apart from most in the community where he lives: progress
is seen ultimately as the great evil. This feeling is shared, of
course, with other hard-core ruralists such as R. S. Thomas; the
image of tractors replacing horses in the fields is common to
these writers' work.

The hubris of 'Progress' and materialism leads to nuclear holo-
caust in the 'Return of the Women' section of the volume. It is

only through a 'terrible cleansing' or return to elemental life-patterns that the race can survive – we have heard such primitivism before – it is, amongst other things, a legacy of Romanticism. No Lawrentian golden phoenix 'flowering from blood' perhaps, yet the fire, blood, whipping, and desolations of this section are as terrifying as anything in *The Plumed Serpent*. We have already hinted that, in its exposure and closeness to the elements, Orcadian culture feels itself closer to the beginning and end of things, closer to the edges of human capacity. We certainly remember Muir's poem 'The Horses'. This gives us another hint and confronts us with the other central fact that so frustrates many of Brown's critics – his persistence in writing of the agrarian Orcadian past as it may have been two or three generations ago. Any dealing with the challenges of the present: oil, nuclear power, Uranium, tends to lead to a sharp swerve back into the nineteenth century and beyond. Even given Brown's careful distinction between a poet's and a historian's truths, there is no glimpse of a potential ecological recovery in his work, save perhaps in his story 'The Seven Poets'. His 'time-set', as it were, can be attributed to his desire to resurrect 'old strengths', to distance himself within the medium of art, to maintain his early voices as a writer, or simply as a consciously accepted convention. Orcadian art has thrived on convention rigorously adhered to; such an insistence surely affects Brown's relationship with his islanders.

6

It is in work published between 1971 and 1976 that Brown reached his most deliberate questioning of the position of poets in relation to their communities. In the final story of *The Sun's Net*, 'The Seven Poets', the narrator ranges in another post-Apocalyptic world, (more hopeful, Edenic and Muiresque in its vision of the 'ancient bond' between men and animals restored). The world is seen in terms of a network of villages, and wherever the protagonist goes, 'after the age of forty (being then too old for the delectable House of Lovers)', the subject stays in the houses of poets. The main vocation of the village poets is to write 'a masque, or chorus, or group of poems' for a midwinter performance by the villagers. In succession we are shown a poet questing after 'The Word', a wordless poet speaking of the abandonment of 'dead forms', a Neo-Futurist and the African poet who makes ten poems a day celebrating the praying mantis. In the last example, the village joins in 'the joy that the Universe felt for that stick of an insect'; this 'poet' anticipates Brown's own poems in 'Stone' where a long sequence celebrates that most basic of island substances from a wide spectrum of views. One theme which binds these sections of the story together is that of the support of the wider community for their poet, even if their ideas are radically different from his. This concept is deeply significant for this study, even given the removes of fiction and a partly Utopian setting.

The Siberian poet seems to embody that faculty which opens the human world to the influence of nature:

> There was some kind of kinship, it seemed, between the speech of a people and their natural surroundings. Birds, winds, waterfalls, the coil of a river, the shape of a hill . . . moulded speech.[16]

The 'roots of speech' we are told are 'deep in the elements'. The task of composing is an arduous one and the community's performance of the masque, difficult, but one tells the traveller:

> Always we feel that we are one with the earth . . . we re-affirm our kinship with fish and stars.[17]

In the case of the final poet – an eskimo – a whole tribe attends the performance (an integrated group of lyrics). In the seventh poet's seventh song occurs the collection's title:

> My eyes some morning
> will be caught like two fish in the sun's net.[18]

This eminently successful poet – social and sociable – attended by and approved by his people, sees it as his duty to 'attend to the pure essences'. Poetry 'ferments' inside the meaninglessness and suffering of life – it is the wine of the folk and the poet's role is to make serviceable vessels for nourishment and satisfaction.

The far northern latitude of this poet's existence is important. The simplicity of life's emphases and links with nature associate him with Brown himself, who has said that all seven poets of the story can be found in one writer's work. The heptamerous structure of the story is also crucial, for this Orcadian has said that he

likes to view a situation or character from seven different view-
points; as a result 'they seem to tremble into breath and life . . .
many of my poems seem to come in sevens'. The story ends with
a final wistful joke for Sidney Goodsir Smith and an image of the
traveller closer to home:

> Now thirty years later, I find myself for the first time among the
> nations of Scotland.[20]

We are left then with a vision of a poet who makes lyrics cele-
brating the rhythms of a community: more, an imagination that
builds about the people 'a palace of unimagined beauty'. In
Portrait of Orkney, Brown writes that 'to ignore the unity of the
tribe, the nation, the race, is to go against the grain of the human
spirit from the beginning'. Yet, he continues that we are all
united in a wider plan 'indissolubly involved in each other and in
the whole totality of human kind dead and unborn, from the
beginning to an unforseeable end. "No man is an island".' We
are reminded momently of that other islander's vision of tran-
scendant unity beyond insular rivalries, in Derek Walcott's 'The
Schooner *Flight*:'

> There are so many islands!
> As many islands as the stars at night
> on that branched tree from which meteors are shaken
> like falling fruit around the schooner *Flight*.
> But things must fall, and so it always was,
> on one hand Venus, on the other Mars;
> fall, and are one, just as this earth is one
> island in archipelagoes of stars.[21]

The seven-fold story involving poets dramatizes one poet's views
of an artist's links with his community and, taken together, they
quicken to produce a core of concerns. True art is not made to
give a moment's pleasure to a social élite – it is absolutely neces-
sary for 'the well-being and health of the community'. In
attempting this, one type of poet must seek 'The Word', expose
himself to the sounds of unhindered nature and celebrate the
tribe inside humankind whilst remaining aware of the unity of
all: these concerns are mentioned many times within Brown's
work.

Winterfold (1976) and *Voyages* (1983) do not broach these
issues as directly or self-consciously as the writings of the early

seventies. Instead, the first book examines how translations turn their original texts into discrete works of art – something different again – with Brown's version of Rognvald Kolson's lyrics and the Old English *Deor*. Representative poets who do occur resort to silence and can explain 'nothing' – for the 'best poets', the ultimate art is folded from them. All writing is a quest for the image that will reveal 'the hidden harp'. The whole tone of the *Winterfold* poems is reverential and determinedly mystical, more than anything that has appeared before. 'The Lesser Mysteries of Art' addresses 'Harp', 'Image', 'Ballad', 'Symbol' in turn, hinting at the timelessness and transforming power, the transcendence of art over and *for* generations. 'Rune' is typically compact:

> Obliterator
> of a thousand questing mouths,
> and sevenfold silence still.

One is tempted to ask that, if art is to be efficacious for a community, a 'healer', how can such personal realizations of devotion prove accessible? That having been said, *Winterfold* remains Brown's most beautiful and achieved book of poetry to date, where traditional verse, devotional elements and modernist poetics rub shoulders wonderfully, reaching beyond words themselves.

In *Voyages* we find again the poet as witness to history, family and, for example, the first innkeepers in Stromness. The only poet actually commemorated in the volume is he who sings 'the ivory bird' of life – or rather, life as recorded by art, on his lute. The compression and brevity of human life is expressed in poem after poem and the collection ends with 'Countryman':

> Be silent, story, soon.
> You did not take long to tell

The final line, significantly, is unpunctuated, with no period-mark or limit, almost a unique example in this poet's writing.

The Wreck of the Archangel sees Brown assuming the personae of various bards in 'Poems to Kenna': the bard at Strathnaver gathers news of betrayal and survival after the flight of Bonny Prince Charlie and seeks 'salves for ancient pain' in the west. Section 3 seems a fairly autobiographical vision of a poet in Modern Orkney 'lost' between symbols. The word 'lost' recurs in these poems. In 'Interrogation', as part of a powerful self-confrontation, the 'man' is convicted of his own mortality. The community, 'Children', 'Love', 'Plough and fiddle', those he has sung and praised, are dust. The prospect of a future community forgetting him, of his land's indifference to his fate is mentioned:

> You are not a memory any
> more among you waters and cornfields and skies.
> What then?

The questioning voice reminds us of the tauntings of 'The Condemned Well'; it is at this point that Brown's poetic identity, firmly rooted and bound to a particular place and people, is challenged:

> You are lost, man, among the atoms and planets.

> I am content to be here beside a broken kirk
> where the poor have been fed.

Thus reaffirming his pledge to and identification with the poor of forty years ago and now.

The poem 'Greenpeace' shows the bard singing 'the goodness of the land' – he travels from Glasgow, to Barra and Iona and serves fishermen and warriors hungry for saga. The second section turns to a present of ecological devastation, the shoreline that can no longer be cleaned by 'The kind mother',

> A last bird at a tidemark
> Announces the death of the sea.

The 'songless one' is told to follow 'the harp' and find the sleeping pride in Atlantis.

Since *Winterfold*, the harp as a symbol for the poet's station, and a cipher of the link between song and poetry, has been central to the work. Like the folk poets of *penillion telyn*, ('harp verses') in Wales, this Orcadian has increasingly identified himself with the emblem of bardic traditions. In 'Four Poems for Edwin Muir', Brown returns his admired fellow-islander, as a lost child seeing a carved harp

> That rune will unlock
> Time's labyrinth, door after door,
> To the tree and the apple.

The boy of the poem dons his heraldic 'coat of creatures'; we are then given the song of one of Muir's forebears (perhaps an ancestral saint). Cormac's song encapsulates Muir's life as well – chronology is telescoped and folded together – for example, 'In middle Europe I woke from long sleep./ This harp stood at the wall' is probably a reference to Muir's reawakening as a creative artist in Dresden in 1921–2. Three poets – Cormac, Muir and Brown – are bound together in the final urgent 'Deo gratias'; so, again, we see a conception of artistic brotherhood in the Islands, which has helped shape Brown's vision. Muir himself has written that 'we receive . . . more than we can ever give . . . from the past, on which we draw with every breath'.[22]

The poems that close *The Wreck of the Archangel* involve voyages, some of them increasingly urgent ones, to old age, death, a moment of transfiguration or renewal. Tinkers, kings, a questing band of horsemen, the speaker who brings winter tribute – 'Travellers, rich and poor, are on the roads.' 'The Last Gate' which opens the door on these winter poems is perhaps the most searching of these and anticipates the way each ends with a vision in which the life of the poor and Christian images of redemption unite. Here, once the gatekeeper unlatches his door, the last blackness reveals a global cataclysm: 'the burnt ocean', 'vitrified cities', yet far in the distance the riders see a star or the guide to an inn.

7

A poet of an island community who, through his work, has been committed to identify himself with that community: to sing its past in these 'unpoetic' times, to resurrect its speech and stories and associate himself with its makars and poets. Indeed, to frame his work in the imaginative texture of Orcadian history: to make this medium and message. A poet who, despite writing of his ultimate responsibility to the Highest Mystery – silence – and his own aim of personal pleasure, has attempted to reveal the needful symbols for 'the health of that community'. Brown knows such commitments are suspect and unfashionable these days. Yet he is also a poet who realizes that he must strike out beyond community: to the non-human – to nature, to death, to existential lostness outside the 'doors' of town, village, family –

outside the confines of identity itself, to attend the 'pure essences'. It is in 'Water', a poem donated specifically for this volume, that Brown returns to his late poems of voyaging and doorkeeping. The 'intruder' here spurs the man to throw off social identities, slough away roles defined by successive communities; the roles he assumes and even that he is forced to assume, of an exiled criminal. The subject of the poem, like all Brown's poets, becomes a quester after the Word: 'seeks continually /The one syllable that might/ lock purity in the / ultimate crystal.' His final role, too, is that of doorkeeper confronted after all voyaging and affiliations by an image of transcendence in the ordinary.

Past, inside, outside, and *through* island community – it is ultimately this to which Brown splendidly bears witness:

Water

1

Find, said the intruder, *your*
    place of lustration,
I rose from my father's door.
(Birth binds breath to glebe
    and quern, till cess of hunger.)
A skipper enrolled me, vagrant.
Five winters yoked to oarlock
    in the ship 'Wolf',
Cold seas over the shipmen,
Was spindrift in the bread broken.
Put ashore, in Torshavn, again
    that stranger.
I showed silver wrung from my sea
    sweat.
Good water, he said, *the highway*
where men fish and trade, and
    consult charts.
Your place is otherwhere.

2

In Denmark, I dug a well.
I planted a tree beside the well.
I built a house
And I led Ingerth, a bride, to
    the door,

Was music in the long room
    that day.
I rode weekly to the ships and
    the market.
Water did not fail in our source.
Among waterfront merchants, the
    drift of faces,
Came the face like a star.
I mentioned wife and child, the
    cornfield, the well.
The space broke a core of
    sweetness,
My hands gloved in light
Raising the pitcher . . .
That is good water also (he said)
The well you are seeking is not
    here.

3

Surely I will tell the destroyer
    of peace
How I sat under an ice mountain
Set there, in exile, with others
    after knives and
    wounds in Trondheim.
Five, seeking assoilment
On the green tongue of a glacier,
Acquainted with wolf and
    walrus and arctic skua.
The rage
Burned down in me there, and
    down
Till was left a small ring of
    heart-wax.
Seven years I atoned for the
    killing at the sea-front,
I and the ness-gangers, the
    young careless ones, once
Falconer, broker, shipwright.
They left, one after other.
I waited, after the seven
    winters in Greenland,
    very far north

For scroll and pardon.
Seven winterlong burials of the sun,
Seven sun prowlings (all summer)
    through the sky,
A cold heart-eating lion.
Friends of salmon, caribou
    and walrus,
A drifting folk
Fed me at their fires, they taught
    me (smiling) secret by
    secret
The twenty-one intricate signs
    for 'snow' –
Breath and bread it was to
    them, the ice.
I sought continually
The one syllable that might
    lock purity in the
    ultimate crystal . . .
The guardian, then, in a blizzard
You have met the masks –
    snowflake, berg, glacier.
Element and essence are
    further on.

4

The convocation of old men. One
Had drained a marsh,
A Swedish lakeside, for ploughs
    and scythes and
    barns (twenty.)
One had stood where sea
    gargles in a river's throat
    with nets
And a scale for pearls and
    salmon.
One, under the sign of sheaves,
Enchanted the rain torrent
Into murmurous barrels, barley
    prisons
where merriment of ancients is set free.
I looked from my cup, heart-struck.
The friend stood at the tavern door,
    Not here, man. Not those.

5

Doorkeeper. They call this old
 man 'Brother Doorkeeper'.
Mornings, I stand at the door.
Out of today's dawn a child came,
 a ploughman, a woman
 with a shawl.
They dipped fingers in the
 hollow stone.
Thrice shaken, the shining inside the
 stone.

George Mackay Brown
Aberdeen/ Stromness
April 1990 – May 1992

Notes

1 G. M. Brown, *An Orkney Tapestry* (London, 1973), 16.
2 Ibid., 18.
3 Ibid., 19.
4 Loc. cit.
5 David Annwn, 'Correspondences', *Poetry Wales* Vol.27 No.2, 1991, 20.
6 *An Orkney Tapestry*, op. cit., 21.
7 G. M. Brown, Letter to David Annwn, 25 July 1992.
8 G. M. Brown, *Portrait of Orkney* (London, 1981), flyleaf note.
9 Ned Thomas, *Derek Walcott, Poet of the Islands* (Cardiff, 1980), 7.
10 Loc. cit.
11 Jeremy Hooker, 'Brut's Albion', in John Mathias (ed.) *David Jones, Eight Essays on his work as Writer and Artist* (Llandysul, 1976), 131.
12 'Correspondences', op. cit., 19.
13 *An Orkney Tapestry*, op. cit., 154.
14 Ibid., 183.
15 Ibid., 159.
16 G. M. Brown, *The Sun's Net* (London, 1976), 262–3.
17 Loc. cit.
18 Ibid., 268.
19 'Correspondences', op. cit., 21.
20 G. M. Brown, *The Sun's Net* (London, Hogarth,1976).
21 *Derek Walcott, Poet of the Islands*, op. cit., 1.
22 Edwin Muir, *An Autobiography* (London, 1968), 281.

Further reading

David Annwn, "Swatches from the Weave of Time' – The Work of
George Mackay Brown', in *Planet* 40 (Llandysul, 1977).
— *Inhabited Voices, The Poetry of Geoffrey Hill, Seamus Heaney and
G. M. Brown* (Somerset, 1984).
Alan Bold, *George Mackay Brown* (Edinburgh, 1978).
G. M. Brown, *Fishermen With Ploughs* (London, 1974).
— *Letters from Hamnavoe* (Edinburgh, 1975).
— *Loaves and Fishes* (London, 1959).
— *Poems, New and Selected* (London, 1971).
— *Voyages* (London, 1983).
— *The Year of the Whale* (London, 1965).
— *Winterfold* (London, 1976).
— *The Wreck of the Archangel* (London, 1989).
Various authors, George Mackay Brown edn. of *Chapman*, No.60,
Spring 1990, now out of print but possibly reprinting.

Broadcast notes:

BBC Scotland broadcast 'George Mackay Brown at 70', in Autumn
1991. This programme contained inserts from the 1976 programme
about the poet. There have also been Radio 3 and 4 interviews with G.
M. B. but one scheduled for 1993 was abandoned due to the poet's ill-
health.

See also: Maggie Parham, 'Master of an island universe', in *The Times*
Saturday Review, July 25 1992, 10–11.

Index